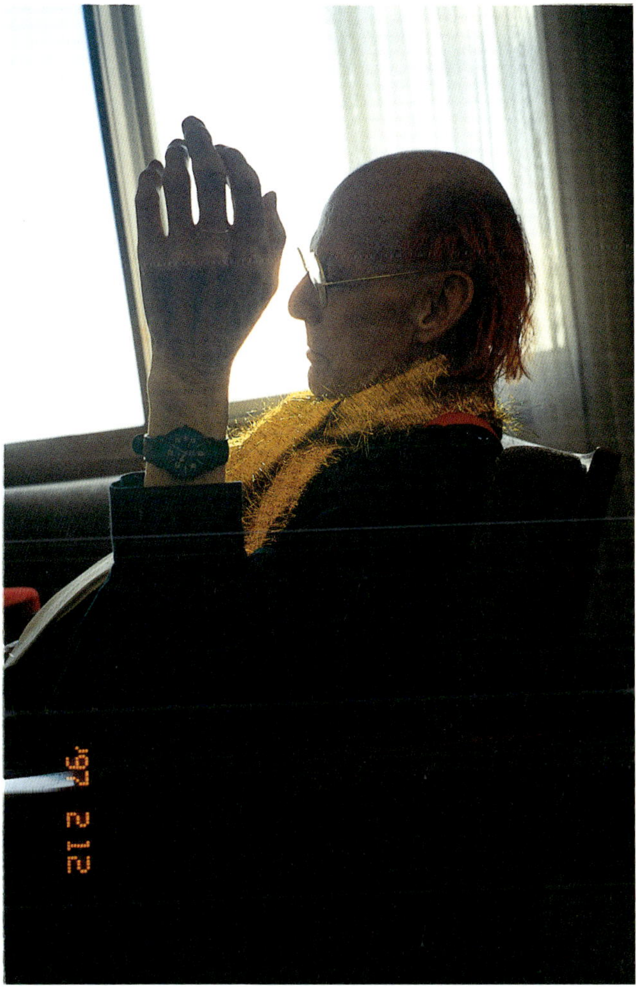
'97 2 12

"In Japan—my dreamland of the beautiful, which I first visited in 1958—I discovered the materials of my paintings, handmade linen papers and Chinese black ink. My technique is pure: I simply paint ink onto a sized or unsized Japanese paper, which is placed on the floor. Then it is stretched. I use the simple forms because they offer the most comprehensive interpretation; it may be an egg . . . it may be the abstracted perspective of time and space. The only prescribed idea is that one confront art for itself, as an experience."— James Lee Byars, 1961

"If I were not convinced he is a genius, I would think he is a madman."

Rand Castile
Founding Director of the Japan House Gallery, New York, and
Director Emeritus, Asian Art Museum of San Francisco

James Lee Byars
Days in Japan

Sakagami Shinobu

FLOATING WORLD
EDITIONS

Published by
Floating World Editions, Inc.
26 Jack Corner Road, Warren, CT 06777
www.FloatingWorldEditions.com

Floating World Editions are distributed in North America by:
ACC Distribution
1-800-252-5231
www.AntiqueCollectorsClub.com

Supported by Pola Art Foundation
公益財団法人
ポーラ美術振興財団
POLA ART FOUNDATION

This text is an expanded version of a series of 10 articles published under the title *James Lee Byars: Days in Kyoto* in the journal *Aida*, Issues 197 (October 20, 2012) to 209 (November 20, 2013).

ISBN: 978-1-891640-91-9

Translator: Alan Gleason
Editor: Meg Taylor
Designer: Oishi Kazuyoshi

Printed in Japan by Kowa Printing Co., Ltd.

Contents

Preface

Born in Detroit on April 10, 1932, the American artist James Lee Byars made his final home in Room 1204 at the Mena House, a hotel famous for its spectacular view of the Great Pyramid of Giza. He died in a Cairo hospital before dawn on May 23, 1997.

Byars spent much of his career shuttling between the United States and Europe, but he also spent a significant number of years in Japan when he was in his twenties and early thirties. It was a seminal experience that had a profound impact on his art and aesthetic philosophy, yet is virtually undocumented—until now.

Large-scale exhibitions of Byars's work have been held in various parts of the world, both before and since his death, accompanied by the publication of numerous catalogues and books. Oddly, however, these contain very few references to those early years or to his experiences in Japan. That oversight continues to the present day. Ample information can be found on his activities from 1967 on, when he first became well known in the United States. Yet there are only perfunctory references to what should be recognized as the prelude to those activities, the decade he spent in Japan from 1958 to 1967. Virtually nothing is written about how he lived his life there, whom he met, his influences, or his artistic pursuits. Nothing at all appears about his sojourn in Kurashiki before moving to Kyoto.

What accounts do appear in foreign publications are riddled with errors. Though various catalogues mention that he held three solo exhibitions at the Kyoto Municipal Museum of Art, the years of those events were recorded incorrectly early on and the erroneous dates passed down verbatim from one publication to the next. Even the venue is mistakenly listed as the National Museum of Modern Art, Kyoto, which did not even exist when Byars was there. (Launched as a branch of the Tokyo-based National Museum of Modern Art in 1964, it did not open as a separate museum until 1967.) This is just one example of information that could have been verified with a minimum of effort. Unfortunately many such errors appear in the existing literature on Byars.

I have done extensive research on the various periods of Byars's life in Japan: the decade from 1958 to 1967, when he lived there as a young man; his brief visit in late 1993; and the three months he spent in Japan from November 1996 to February 1997 before departing for Egypt. Initially I published the results of that research in a series of articles titled *James Lee Byars: Days in Kyoto*, which appeared in the Japanese-language monthly art journal *Aida* in issues 197 (October 20, 2012) through 209 (November 20, 2013). The English translation of those articles, with additions and corrections, forms the core of this book. I have also added an epilogue about Byars's final days in Egypt. The result is what I believe to be a thorough and accurate re-counting of Byars's life and art during those periods.

A one-day-only exhibition of Byars's work was held on January 14, 1967 at galerie 16 in Kyoto. When the gallery celebrated its fortieth anniversary in 2002, I was working there and was asked to prepare a record of its exhibitions over those four decades. That was how I first came to look into Byars's days in Kyoto. Learning that Byars spoke almost no Japanese and tended to cultivate friendships with other foreigners more than with Japanese people, I began by seeking out close acquaintances of Byars who had witnessed the events of his life, but made very little headway.

The key person to locate was, without question, Taki Sachiko, who had been Byars's lover at the time. Fortunately Inoue Michiko, the owner of galerie 16, found the address of Taki's family home in a fifty-year-old notebook. Using that address we were able to contact Taki and enlist her help. It turned out that she was living in Los Angeles and working as a psychologist. Thanks to Taki I was able to make further connections, pick up the trail of Byars's early years, and trace the outlines of his life in Japan.

I am also grateful to Abe Hiromu, who served as Byars's confidante and adviser for nearly ten years as curator at the Kyoto Municipal Museum of Art, and his wife, Noriko; Sengoku Sanae of galerie 16; friends and students of the late Lindley Williams Hubbell, the man who organized the one-day show in 1967, including Sato

Hiroaki, Yamamoto Shigeki, Ozaki Makoto, and Iida Yoko; friends of Byars from his Kyoto days, including Ban Fumio, Mas Kodani, Simon Blackall, Rand and Sondra Castile, Fuji Yoshiyuki, Kobayashi Tetsuo, and the antique art dealer Yanagi Takashi; friends and benefactors from Byars's time in Kurashiki, including Kawai Sumie, Makabe Tadahiko, Miyake Toshio, Ishigami Nobufusa, and Kaneshige Kosuke; the venerable Kyoto shops Saiundo, Kobaien, and Morita Washi, which Byars frequented; the art critic Hariu Ichiro, who is extremely knowledgeable about Byars's Kyoto career; and friends of Byars who became close to him during his final sojourn in Japan and cared for him in his cancer-ravaged state: Shiraishi Masami, Nishida Kosaku, Kojima Masamichi, Oyama Yoneko, Toyama Koichi, Namioka Fuyumi, Aoki Masahiro, and Stephan Kohler. Without their willingness to engage in voluminous correspondence and submit to repeated interviews, I could not have unearthed the true story of Byars's days in Japan. Still, these were memories of events that transpired, for the most part, over fifty years ago. Confirming, correlating, and when necessary resolving discrepancies among these recollections turned out to be an exhausting and time-consuming process.

In February 2014, Taki Sachiko and Inoue Michiko toasted the completion of the *Days in Kyoto* series in *Aida* with me at the elegant Kyoto restaurant Hyotei. Our conversation turned to Byars's circumstances in Egypt. Why had he chosen to live his final days in a room at a luxury hotel in Giza? Was he contemplating some sort of performance before the pyramids? Was he calling on his closest friends to join him there before he died? I decided that I should write something about his decision to go to Egypt, and his last days there, as an epilogue to this book. Subsequently I spent nearly two years researching Byars's time in Egypt, taking two trips there. That story, too, could not have been written without the generous cooperation of numerous witnesses to the last weeks of his life. They include Magdy Hafez, Byars's closest companion during his final three months; employees who worked at the Mena House while he was there; Hervé Chandes and François Quintin of the Fondation Cartier;

Vicente Todolí of the Serralves Foundation; photographer Rita Burmester, who documented Byars's burial; the Michael Werner Gallery, which supported Byars in Egypt; and Richard Byford and his wife, Ishihara Yukari, who worked with me on my on-site research.

Thanks to these individuals, I have been able to determine what really happened during Byars's final days. Ironically, however, I discovered that, much as with Byars's life in Japan, previous accounts of his time in Egypt had relied exclusively on a narrative constructed by a single individual—in this case the late American art critic Thomas McEvilley—ever since its first publication shortly after Byars's death in 1997. The research on which I have based the epilogue of this book repudiates much of that narrative.

Howard Carter, the archeologist who discovered the tomb of Tutankhamun, dug directly under what everyone else thought was a trash heap—a pile of debris that had accumulated over decades of excavations in the Valley of the Kings. Finally, he focused on what had been a blind spot of sorts: the remains of a workers' hut built during construction of the tomb of Ramses VI. There he dug, and made the discovery of the century, in a place overlooked by everyone else. The truth often lies buried in what at first glance appears to be refuse that has already been picked through. My research on Byars's days in Japan and Egypt made this painfully clear.

In this book I have tried as much as possible to eliminate subjectivity and limit myself to verifiable facts. However, thorough research alone is not sufficient to acquire a complete and accurate picture of someone's life and thought. I was able to obtain the cooperation of the people who speak in these pages because something in them responded to the enthusiasm and commitment with which I have pursued this project for more than fifteen years. I believe that such perseverance, however fruitless the quest may sometimes seem, is the strongest weapon a researcher can bring to her work.

Introduction

"If I were not convinced he is a genius, I would think he is a madman." So Rand Castile, the great curator of Japanese and Asian art, who knew Byars well, is said to have observed.

James Lee Byars suddenly appeared on the New York art scene in the late 1960s. He scattered sheets of paper bearing the satanic number 666, shouted nonsensical phrases from the roof of a church, and built a teahouse completely covered in gold foil. With their air of cult-like eeriness and apocalyptic tranquility, his performances established his reputation as an aesthetic heretic.

Byars did not conjure his aesthetic out of thin air. From 1958 to 1967, arguably his formative years as an artist, Byars spent most of his time in Japan. There is ample documentary evidence that he drew much of his artistic inspiration from diverse elements of Japanese culture, ranging from Zen Buddhism and Shintoism to Noh drama, the tea ceremony, and calligraphy. Yet there has been virtually no research conducted into these influences on his art, and little is known, even in Japanese art circles, about his life in Japan. What drew Byars to Japan? What sort of life did he live there, and how did the country's traditions come to affect him so profoundly? These are questions I have tried to answer in this book.

Byars was born in 1932 in Detroit, Michigan, where he grew up on Grayfield Street. It was a quiet neighborhood with beautiful rows of elm trees, where his family lived in a small house with a stream running through the back of the property. Nature, albeit in modest form, was there to be found. An only child, he was the son of Elliott Byars, a lawyer, and his wife, Ann. He was affectionately known by his middle name, Lee.

According to a memoir by Byars's first wife, Dolores Hart, he entered Wayne State University in September 1956, and it was there that he "found art." Byars, who boasted of having an IQ of 167, later told Taki Sachiko, with whom he became acquainted in Kyoto, that he had wanted to go to the University of Michigan but couldn't because his family was too poor.

Byars came to Japan as part of a study-abroad program at Wayne State. At first, it appears, he intended to stay in Japan only for the ten-month duration of the scholarship from the university. But he ended up living there for the better part of a decade, during which he traveled back and forth between the United States and Japan seven times.

1 Days in Kurashiki

Byars arrived in Japan for the first time in September or October 1958. He was twenty-six years old. In those days it was still common to travel between the two countries by ship; for students in particular that was the cheapest option. Byars most likely took a ship routed across the North Pacific, skirting the Aleutian Islands—a journey lasting a little more than two weeks.

In the 1950s, interest in Japanese culture was growing in the United States. D.T. Suzuki, who spent much of that decade in America lecturing on Buddhism, was instrumental in popularizing Zen in the West. Though it was a period that saw the rise of rock music and a new golden age for Hollywood, the late fifties was a time of cultural stagnation in the United States, owing in large part to the Cold War. Under the surface, however, a counterculture was brewing, and with it a wave of enthusiasm for things Japanese. Artists began visiting Japan one after another, among them Beat poets Gary Snyder and Philip Whalen. Byars was part of this wave.

Byars must have disembarked at the port of Yokohama, the gateway to Tokyo, since records show that he first stayed in the capital. There he met Yanagi Soetsu. Yanagi was a well-known philosopher and the foremost proponent of the Mingei folk art movement, which championed the beauty found in utilitarian objects—ceramics, dyed fabrics, lacquerware, woodwork, and so on—made by often anonymous artisans.

It is unknown how much knowledge of Mingei, or interest in it, Byars had before coming to Japan. However, records show that he visited the Japan Folk Crafts Museum (Mingeikan) after he arrived in Tokyo. According to a later newspaper account, he was "struck by the beauty of a woman's Bizen-ware necklace" he saw there. He subsequently traveled to the Bizen district by the Seto Inland Sea that winter and studied ceramic art under Kaneshige Toyo (1896–1967), who was later designated a Living National Treasure (Fig. 2). From the record one may surmise that Byars, inspired by the works he saw at the Mingeikan, sought a meeting with Yanagi, its director. Yanagi must have directed Byars to Kurashiki, which is close to Bizen, in order to research ceramic art and Japanese papermaking. Kurashiki is the home of Japan's second Mingei museum (after the Mingeikan in Tokyo), and the region is known for the high quality of its folk crafts. In any event, Kurashiki was the place Byars headed first, bearing a letter of introduction from Yanagi Soetsu. He ended up living there until his first trip back to the United States in the summer of 1959.

Kawai Sumie, an art journalist now based in Berlin, recalls a solo exhibition Byars mounted in Kurashiki:

> The first solo exhibition by James Lee that I saw was at the private home of Tonomura Kichinosuke, director of the Kurashiki Museum of Folkcraft. The house was on the corner of a row of storehouse-style buildings lined up across the river from the museum, and he was staying there at the time. When I opened the lattice door and crossed the broad earthen floor inside, I found him in a room with a gleaming black polished wooden floor, kneeling in the formal *seiza* posture in an indigo-dyed kimono on an indigo-dyed zabuton floor cushion. There were only two visitors, my mother and myself.
>
> Hanging in the tokonoma alcove was a single abstract painting, painted with squid ink on Japanese paper. I still cannot forget the beauty of the paper and the golden sheen of the ink. We viewed the painting, and that was the end of the exhibition. It was completely silent the whole time. I was overwhelmed by the tranquility of the atmosphere in that space. It was my first encounter with contemporary art and remains fresh in my memory.
>
> James Lee often came to my house. On rainy days he carried a traditional Japanese umbrella with a bull's-eye design, and he always brought a white lily. He listened to the chorus of frogs in the rice paddies and to the poetry of Kusano Shinpei that I read aloud, and murmured that it was like the music of John Cage. Then he would begin reciting Gertrude Stein's "Rose is a rose is a rose is a rose." At the end, he would ask me to sing the *Itsuki Lullaby* that he liked so much. That was over forty years ago. Meeting James Lee transformed my life. [Translated from Kawai Sumie, "Memories of James Lee," *Bijutsu techo* (July 2000): 162.]

The first time Kawai Sumie met Byars was in 1958, soon after he arrived in Japan. Later, Kawai studied at the University of California, Berkeley, from 1963 to 1967, then moved to Europe and made her home in Berlin. She says that Byars visited her often in Berkeley on his trips back to the United States.

Byars moved back to the States in 1967 and began traveling to Europe in 1969.

He truly came into the limelight on the continent in 1972 with his participation in *Documenta 5* in Kassel, Germany. It was Kawai who arranged for him to come to Berlin in 1974 on a one-year Artists in Berlin residency run by the German Academic Exchange Service. The relationship between Kawai and Byars—sometimes close, sometimes distant—continued until his death. The volume of letters exchanged between them is enormous. "His days, how he lived, that was his art," Kawai says.

Byars, who probably encountered squid ink for the first time in Japan, started using it often, both for his work and for writing letters. Although it is described as an ink, the blackness of the liquid is temporary. Initially it looks the same as regular ink, but pictures drawn with it fade over months or years, and in the end disappear altogether. It is said that in the past, the ninja wrote letters with squid ink to avoid leaving any permanent evidence. According to Ishigami Nobufusa, son of Tonomura Kichinosuke, Yanagi Soetsu used sepia ink, which inspired Tonomura to do the same. Ishigami conjectures that Byars witnessed this in Tokyo and Kurashiki. (The word *sepia* derives from the Latin for "squid," and natural sepia ink is made from squid ink.)

Time is a key concept in the solo exhibition Kawai described and in other activities by Byars—the passing of time and the changes in conditions that accompany it. There was a precedent for such art in Japan; in 1955, for example, Tanaka Atsuko, a member of the avant-garde Gutai Art Association, presented a work that used the sound of bells to make the audience conscious of time's passage.

The biggest difference between Tanaka's work and that of Byars is that the latter provided the audience with something akin to comfort, a serene ambience. One could experience in it the eternal flux of time and an encounter with the moment the beauty of an instant passing in the blink of an eye—under conditions that might seem bizarre, particularly to a Japanese participant. A foreigner in an indigo kimono kneeling Japanese-style on an indigo cushion on the wooden floor of a traditional Japanese house—this was a spectacle few would anticipate. The momentary shock engendered by the sight etched it into the memories of those who, like Kawai Sumie, had the opportunity to share that space.

According to chronologies of Byars's life found in several English-language catalogues,* Byars held a solo exhibition at a patron's house in 1958. One such publication, *The Palace of Perfect* (Serralves Foundation, 1997), describes it as follows: "In 1958, his Japanese patron holds an exhibition of Byars's ink drawings (all white with

* For Byars's exhibition *The Perfect Thought: Works by James Lee Byars*, held at the University of California, Berkeley, in 1990, a catalogue by that title was compiled from Byars's oral accounts by James Elliott, the curator. Since then there have been no other documents that cover his life as thoroughly as Elliott's work. Therefore, terms like "records" or "documents" in this book generally refer to *The Perfect Thought* or subsequent catalogues that heavily relied on it.

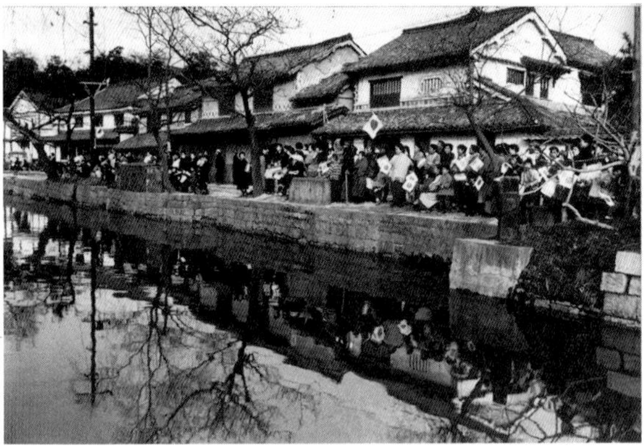

1 The visit of Julius Raab, Federal Chancellor of Austria, to Kurashiki in January 1959. The building on the far right is the Tonomura house. Photo by Nakamura Akio, from *Fukkoku zoho Kurashiki konjaku shashincho* (Photo album of Kurashiki now and then, new expanded edition), published by the Kurashiki Archaeological Museum, 2010

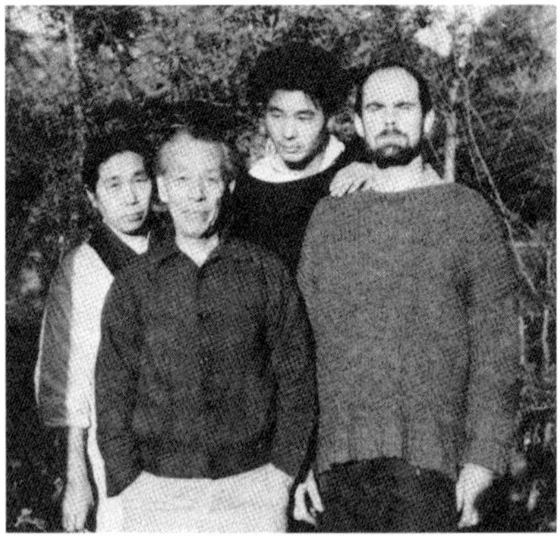

2 Byars, Kaneshige Toyo and his wife, and Toyo's son Kaneshige Michiaki, December 1958. From *Nihon no yakimono gendai no kyosho 10 Kaneshige Toyo* (Ceramics of Japan, contemporary masters 10: Kaneshige Toyo), published by Kodansha, 1978

solid black brush stroke in the middle) and paper boxes in his home. He invites friends and associates." Since the opening of the exhibition fell on a date traditionally associated with moon viewing, Byars invited his friends to a "moon-viewing party." However, instead of the customary rice dumplings, only a glass of water was served to the guests. The patron's house referred to here must have been the home of Tonomura Kichinosuke, director of the Kurashiki Museum of Folkcraft, where Byars was staying thanks to Yanagi Soetsu's referral.

Folk-art researcher Miyake Toshio lived in Kurashiki and recalls those days: "Although I do not remember the name Byars, I know that a young foreign man was staying at the house of the director, Tonomura, sometime during the Showa thirties (1955–1964). I also remember seeing the director mount a sumi-ink painting [the young man] did on a large panel." According to Miyake, the painting was "an abstract picture, not clearly of mountains or of clouds. The contour lines were drawn with great tenderness."

According to Tonomura's son Ishigami Nobufusa, a woman who was staying at Tonomura's house studying textiles at that time described Byars and his life in Kurashiki as follows:

> - Tonomura's house was a research center for textiles (currently the Kurashiki Dyeing, Spinning and Weaving Studio). Byars was commuting from somewhere else since young women were staying there.

- They had lunches together.
- He was dressed like a homeless man. His white skin and blue eyes were somehow unnerving.
- Mr. and Mrs. Tonomura treated him kindly.
- He was painting abstract pictures on large sheets of white paper.
- He was studying textiles but it looked like he was only playing at it.
- She doesn't remember anything about a solo exhibition or a moon-viewing party.
- He fell in love with a woman from Okinawa who was studying textiles there for a short time. When she returned home, he followed her. It seemed that he couldn't find her, and he came back with a forlorn air.

References to Byars can also be found in the Okayama Prefecture Folk Craft Association's journal *Sanyo mingei* (Sanyo folk craft), edited by Tonomura (quotations are translated from the Japanese):

- Byars was present on Saturday, February 28, 1959 for an hour-long event, *Suisu no fuzoku gento kai* (Swiss customs slide show), during which Sophia Raul of Switzerland presented slides depicting the natural beauty and life of her homeland at Tonomura's house in Mukaiba-cho, Kurashiki.
- "Ms. Raul visited Kamisuki-mura, Niimi-shi, with Mr. Byars the day after she stayed overnight in Kurashiki on February 28." From the *Kojin shosoku* (Personal news) column, issue 39, April 1959.
- "Lee Byars, Grayfield Street, Detroit, USA" from the *Shinnyu kaiin* (New members) list, issue 40, August 1959.
- "Mr. Lee Byars" from the *Showa 34 nendo kaihi ryoshu* (Annual membership fee receipts for 1959).
- "[Mr. Byars] left Japan for home at the end of July after an approximate ten-month stay on the mainland and Okinawa. A recent letter says that his life in America is dull and he is hoping to get back to Japan somehow." From the *Kojin shosoku* (Personal news) column, issue 41, November 1959.
- "Lee Byars, Detroit, USA" from the *Kaiin meibo* (Members list), issue 42, January 1960.
- "[Byars] took a position by invitation at a foreign language school in Kyoto." From the *Kojin shosoku* (Personal news) column, issue 43, May 1960.
- "Lee Byars, Okazaki, Kyoto" from the *Kaiin meibo* (Members list), issue 45, January 1961.

There were no subsequent references to Byars in the journal.

Ishigami Nobufusa recalls that "Tonomura left on a trip to research American and European folk art in October 1959 and stayed at Byars's house in suburban Detroit from October 23 to 26." According to the article *Kaigai tsushin Tonomura Kichinosuke* (Correspondence from Tonomura Kichinosuke abroad) in issue 42 of *Sanyo mingei* (January 1960), Tonomura "left Kurashiki the evening of October 8 with many people seeing him off, and departed from Haneda on the 12th." The trip consisted of three days each in Hawaii, San Francisco, Los Angeles, and Chicago, then five days in Detroit, three days each in Ann Arbor and Washington, D.C., two days in Philadelphia, and ten days in New York.

The October 6, 1959 edition of the *Kurashiki shinbun* newspaper mentions that "Museum Director Tonomura's visit to the United States was at the invitation of Mr. Byars of the University of Michigan, who had been studying Japanese life under the director's auspices." At the time it was difficult for Japanese citizens to obtain permission from their government to travel overseas; to do so required an invitation from the destination country. Byars may have sent the invitation to Tonomura as a way of repaying him for his help in Kurashiki. Thanks to Tonomura's trip, the Kurashiki Museum of Folkcraft was able to acquire a considerable number of items from abroad.

The December 16, 1958 edition of the *Sanyo shinbun* newspaper carried the following article under the headline "Young Byars Working on a Large Bizen-ware Piece":

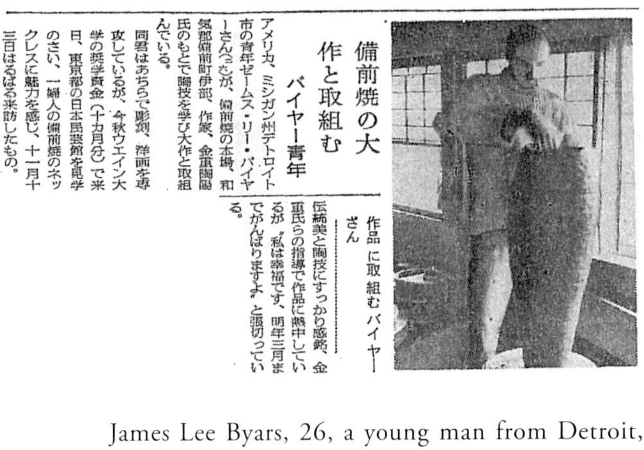

備前焼の大作と取組む
バイヤー青年

作品に取組むバイヤーさん

アメリカ、ミシガン州デトロイト市の青年ゼームス・リー・バイヤーさん(二六)が、備前焼の本場、和気郡備前町伊部、作家、金重陶陽氏のもとで陶技を学び大作と取組んでいる。

同君はあちらで彫刻、洋画を専攻しているが、今秋ウエイン大学の奨学資金(十カ月分)で来日、東京都の日本民芸館を見学のさい、一婦人の備前焼のネックレスに魅力を感じ、十一月十三日はるばる来訪したもの。

伝統美と陶技にすっかり感銘、金重氏らの指導で作品に熱中しているが"私は幸福です、明年三月までがんばりますよ"と張切っている。

3 Article in *Sanyo shinbun* titled "Young Byars Working on a Large Bizen-ware Piece"

James Lee Byars, 26, a young man from Detroit, Michigan, USA, is studying ceramic art and working on a large composition under the artist Kaneshige Toyo in Inbe, Bizen-cho, Waki-gun, the home of Bizen ware. He came to Japan this autumn on a ten-month scholarship from Wayne

> State University, where he was majoring in sculpture and painting. When he visited the Japan Folk Crafts Museum in Tokyo, he was struck by the beauty of a woman's Bizen-ware necklace, and made the journey all the way here, arriving on November 13. He is thoroughly enamored with traditional aesthetics and ceramic art and is absorbed in creating work under the tutelage of Kaneshige and others. He enthusiastically declares, "I'm happy. I'm going to work hard until March next year."

Below is a summary of an oral account provided by Makabe Tadahiko, who has been associated with the Kurashiki Archaeological Museum since 1950:

> Tonomura Kichinosuke was born in 1898, graduated from Kwansei Gakuin University, and became a pastor. A volunteer corps of female students from Okinawa, part of the student mobilization during World War II, was staying and working at Kurabo [Kurashiki Boseki, or Kurashiki Spinning Works] when Japan lost the war. Because the devastating Battle of Okinawa had left many of the girls without homes or families, they had no place to return to and remained in Kurashiki. Kurabo owner Ohara Soichiro, who advocated training girls in skills to provide them with a future, invited his acquaintance Tonomura, an expert on folk art, to Kurashiki. From 1948 Tonomura served as the first director of the Kurashiki Museum of Folkcraft, and in 1953 he began having the girls study fabric-dyeing while they lived at the Kurashiki Dyeing, Spinning and Weaving Studio.
>
> At that time, there was a lady named Takada (née Mori) Toshiko at Kurabo who was instrumental in bringing the girls from Okinawa to the company. There was also a woman from Okinawa among the members of the inaugural class of the studio—Taira Toshiko, who later became a Living National Treasure. I remember she was studying the Okinawan fabric known as *bashofu.* There were many women there from Okinawa.
>
> I recall that when the studio first opened, Tonomura was not living there but commuting from Sakazu, at the foot of the mountain on the north side of town. He may have gotten a house in Sakazu when he was first invited to Kurashiki. Because the Kurashiki plant of Kuraray [a synthetic rayon company launched by Kurabo] was first built in Sakazu, I assume it was a house he got with the help of Ohara. It's not clear to me where Byars had his room, but I don't think it would have been difficult for a foreigner to rent a room in the neighborhood where the studio was.

Kaneshige Toyo, under whom Byars studied Bizen ware, was a very easygoing person. His life got easier around the time his son Michiaki, who was about the same age as Byars, went to college, but until then he was living in reduced circumstances. Particularly because Bizen ware itself had been in decline since the beginning of the Meiji era [1868–1912], the years leading up to its revival were financially dire, regardless of how well recognized Kaneshige was as a key figure in the Bizen-ware revival.

In Kurashiki, neither Ohara Soichiro nor Tonomura Kichinosuke were paying attention to Bizen ware, so it must have been on Byars's own strong initiative that he developed an interest in Bizen ware and sought out Kaneshige.

The beautiful townscape of Kurashiki, with its black and white buildings, was no doubt attractive to Byars. Although the structures and ambience of that era are still preserved in Kurashiki's special historical district, back then there were almost no stores; it was just an ordinary neighborhood, unlike today. Then, it was called a "village," and the river running through the middle of it had been used as a canal for the transportation of goods to Osaka since ancient times. Before the Edo period [1603–1868], the entire area was a so-called "neutral zone," since the canal also served as the border between the Oda clan and the Mori clan.

After World War II, a Sanyo Line train station was built about ten minutes away by foot, and while the rest of the city was developed, this neighborhood was left behind, as a result of which the old structures survived.

In the postwar years it became more common to see foreigners in Kurashiki. The area had always been known for its many cultural figures. The Ohara Museum of Art, founded in 1930, played a major role in Kurashiki's development as a tourist destination. Soon after the war many exhibitions were held here, including exhibitions of French art traveling from Tokyo. People who missed those shows in Tokyo came to see them here, even making the trip all the way from Hokkaido. Kurashiki also became a popular film location because of its historical townscape. The area was designated a historical preservation district, and its yellowing stucco walls were repainted white and cleaned up. Maybe they even look a little too clean. But the black roofs are still the same as in times gone by. An ancient method is used to install these roofs with their antique-style *hongawara* tiles. During the Meiji era the canal was filled with commercial boats covered in straw mats, but after the war there were no more boats passing through, apart from some carrying oranges. Now the embankments have been restored and the waterway cleaned and dammed up, so it seems to be a river for tourists only. Just after the war you could sometimes see the mud on the bottom, but now the water level has been raised to make it more attractive for the tourists.

During the time Byars was here, though, it was still a rustic town with the lingering atmosphere of a village. Perhaps it was precisely this rustic ambience that attracted him to Kurashiki.

Photographs of the town around the time Byars lived there, as well as photos of nearby villages taken by Ohara Magosaburo during the Meiji era, can be found in *Fukkoku zoho Kurashiki konjaku shashincho* (Photo album of Kurashiki now and then, new expanded edition), edited by Makabe Tadahiko and published by the Kurashiki Archaeological Museum in 2010.

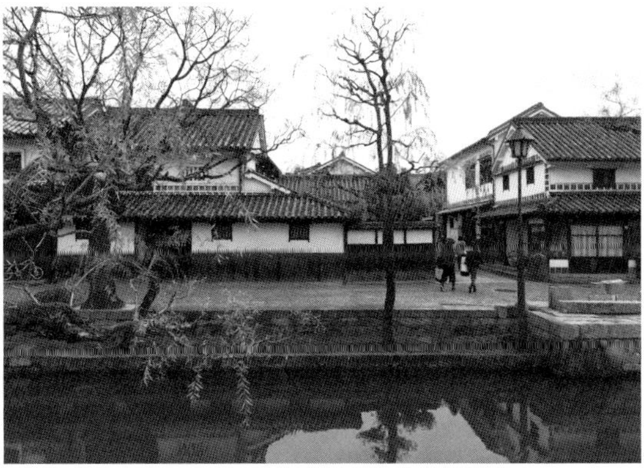

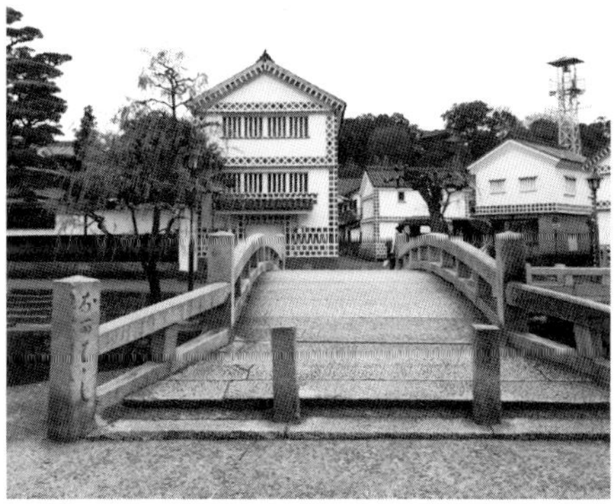

4, 5 The Tonomura Kichinosuke residence (left) and the Kurashiki Archaeological Museum (right) as they appeared in December 2015

The First Trip Home: Summer 1959 to Spring 1960

Byars returned to the United States in July 1959 and headed for New York with the works he had created in Japan. When he arrived there, he went directly to the Museum of Modern Art. Alicia Legg, who worked in MoMA's Department of Painting and Sculpture and later became a curator, recalls that despite showing up with no appointment, Byars harangued the receptionist until he was granted the opportunity to show his works to Legg. This led to his fortuitous encounter with a senior curator, Dorothy Miller. Known as "Mama MoMA," Miller had honed her curatorial skills under the museum's first director, Alfred Barr Jr. In 1959, the year Byars visited, she was working on the exhibition *Sixteen Americans,* which included Jasper Johns and Robert Rauschenberg. Evidently captivated by Byars's work, Miller gave him his first opportunity to exhibit at an American museum—and none other than MoMA at that. The exhibition was held in the emergency stairwell on the fifth floor of the museum, and it was up for only a few hours. Byars unrolled and displayed, in rapid succession, a series of scrolls with abstract paintings in sumi ink on paper. Among the buyers were Miller, Legg, and friends of the museum, including the architect and collector Philip Johnson.

Byars went on to write over a hundred letters to Miller, pestering her about matters ranging from grants and scholarships to exhibitions. Here is one of the earliest of these missives in full, with Byars's idiosyncratic punctuation reproduced intact. It is undated, but appears to be postmarked in late September, 1959 in Detroit:

> Dear Dorothy Miller,
> Again me, hoping, of you—
> Began in spring, April 10, 1932, Detroit Michigan
> Publicly schooled; precocious in drawing; teacher wrote father; No!; professional physician, I died his want.
> Nothing more in Art until senior University, Wayne, then I became me. Exhibited there and in my designed garden, one man both times. To Japan on private painting scholarship, white free, pure year, of experimentation with me. Painting is the ultimate finding, you, for everyone, in the beautiful self, universal, of Love.
> Semantics, elusive, cognitively the essence of Being, elusive, but we can live in its grace. Out of grace, beauty both, itself to itself, no touch with the temporary, all truth eventuating in One. Now, if I am blessed, my search for Being can go on in painting, here, is where, we first saw faces. My last exhibit was private, in the home of K. Tonomura, Curator, Museum of Folk Craft, Kurashiki City, sorry forget to include, above, most important too, sorry.
> Pray that you come soon, Pendle Hill begins October 1, I will have to reenter Wayne University, last choice, this coming week, unless, I hear from you.
> Have many designs, hopes, House of God, sculpture gardens, etc. Funds bind, Where can ideas go, happy I would be, to give them to those who could realize them, I am not so rich. Please help me find someone, interested, if you might.

> Beg that I may one day meet Mark Rothko, beautiful spirit, I love his sensitivity. Would you please tell me how I can, or where, to write to him? I prefer, not [Sidney] Janis.
> Mr. Noguchi, I would like to meet. Hope. Maybe.
> It would be an excitement, if I could teach painting to little children, could one like me, live in your City, from such, with time to paint for me? With much enthusiasm, and no degree; I wonder.
> Beg my questions cause you no discomfort, truly an answer I would appreciate. Forgive me and my not timid asking, informality, forgive
> Sincere James Byars.

The letter mentions an exhibition beginning on October 1, 1959, presumably in Michigan, where Byars was hoping Miller would visit him after his return home to re-enroll in Wayne State University. In a subsequent poem-like note dated February 24, 1960, he entreats Miller to come to another Michigan show:

> Please, come see
> Sculpture
> Past morning till the night
> March 11, 12, 13
> 38600 West 6 Mile Road
> Detroit, Michigan
> My Love
> James Byars

The MoMA Archives contain an undated newspaper clipping with a short, dismissive review of Byars's work in a show at "the Art Institute"—probably the Detroit Institute of Arts—during the same period:

> CRAFT ANNUAL: Edition 14 of the annual exhibition for Michigan Artist – Craftsmen is set for Wednesday night opening at the Art Institute. Winners will be announced at that time. Previewing the show in bits and snatches before it was assembled turned up the following vivid impressions of artists and their entries:
>
> James Byars – Tall, coiled jars with oddly personalized textures, strange faces. These are primitive sophistry.
>
> [. . .] The craftsmen's exhibit will be up through Feb. 21.

2 The Beginning of the Kyoto Years

In the spring of 1960, two years after he had first arrived in Japan, Byars moved to Kyoto from Kurashiki. Or rather, he came to live in Kyoto on returning to Japan after an absence of several months, having initially left Kurashiki for the U.S. in July 1959. One reason for relocating to Kyoto was that he had secured a position teaching English at the preparatory school of the Kyoto University of Foreign Studies.

In Kyoto, where he lived for most of the next seven years, Byars met many people and was involved in a number of dramatic events and happenings. The rich cultural ambience of the city clearly served as a source of inspiration for his artistic endeavors. It was here that he established a style that naturally incorporated elements of Buddhism and Shintoism as well as the refined qualities of traditional Japanese performing arts.

If we think of the Kurashiki years as a period of training during which Byars studied ceramics, painted with sumi ink on paper, and learned about textiles, then his days in Kyoto were a time of experimentation, of attempts to apply to "art" the techniques he had recently absorbed. It was also a time of contemplation that gave his wealth of artistic ideas a chance to take flight.

A Fateful Encounter

In Kyoto, where he was now living, Byars had a fateful encounter with a Japanese woman. Her name was Taki Sachiko. Twenty-two years old at the time, she was slender, with beautiful features, hair down to her waist, and a mysterious air. Anyone who met her had nothing but praise for her beauty and elegant manners. Taki lived in the city's Awataguchi neighborhood and met Byars on the campus of the preparatory school of the Kyoto University of Foreign Studies, which was less than ten minutes away by foot from her house.

Taki reminisces: "It was around the summer of 1960 that I met Jim. I was attending nursing school at the time. My younger sister was working for a bookstore,

Ohmsha, and they had a shop at the Kyoto University of Foreign Studies. Jim, who worked as an English instructor at the university, would visit the store and talk to her about random things. She said he always followed up her responses with some interesting comment. So my sister enjoyed talking to him.

"One day, I told my sister that I wanted to study English. She suggested Jim since we lived near each other; he was at Higashiyama-Nijo and my place was also in Higashiyama. It was just like that. So our first meeting was as English teacher and student."

Taki recalls thinking, "He might be fun to spend time with!" and she started to take an interest in Byars. She also demonstrated her understanding, in her own way, of what Byars called "art." Soon, she began to actively assist him with his work. Their relationship continued until Byars left Japan in 1967. Taki helped to prepare almost all of his exhibitions in Kyoto and Osaka. Moreover, she herself played an important role in Byars's performances as the physical embodiment of his aesthetic.

Byars was living on the second floor of a barracks-like building just past the gate of the Kyoto University of Foreign Studies prep school. Today the school (now known as the Kyoto Career College of Foreign Languages) is located only on the north side of Nijo Street, but back then the campus extended across to the south side. Byars's residence was next to the gate there and was apparently used to house teachers at the school.

Taki's story continues: "He often talked about Kurashiki. It seemed like he was an ardent admirer of the ceramic artist Kaneshige Toyo. I think he stayed in touch with him even after he moved to Kyoto. Kaneshige was a great master of Bizen ware and a Living National Treasure. Jim was easily influenced by the work of such people. He seemed very attracted to ceramic art, and he was especially fond of the natural changes produced by techniques like *hidasuki* [fire-streaking] and *kaiyu* [ash glaze]. The first thing he showed me when we met was a postcard printed by the Kurashiki Archaeological Museum. It was the one with the picture of a 'female figure of an earthenware pair, male and female, excavated in Chancay, Peru.' At that time he was making a lot of objects like that."

One of the works Byars made that was "like that," as Taki put it, is a doll, about 30 centimeters high, made of Kitayama *sugi* (Japanese red cedar from the northern part of Kyoto). It is carved very roughly, with conspicuous knife marks, and painted black with two holes for the eyes. Byars apparently placed the doll in a similarly black Mingei-style bag, with only the face sticking out and a hemp string tied around its neck. It was a small, simple, folk art-like object, one that exuded peace and warmth and might make viewers laugh in spite of themselves. People were always happy to receive one of them as a gift. Byars made many such objects and always had some on

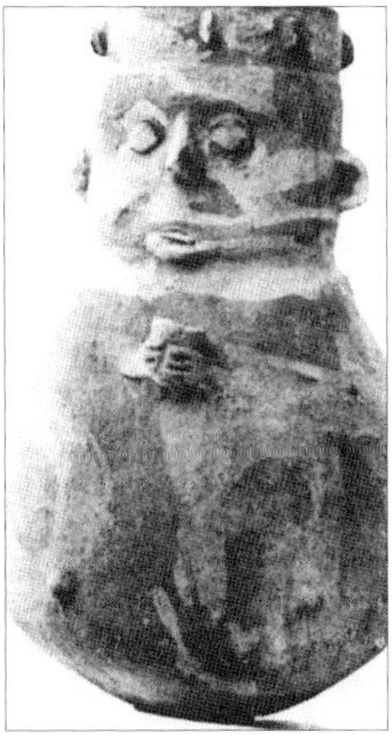

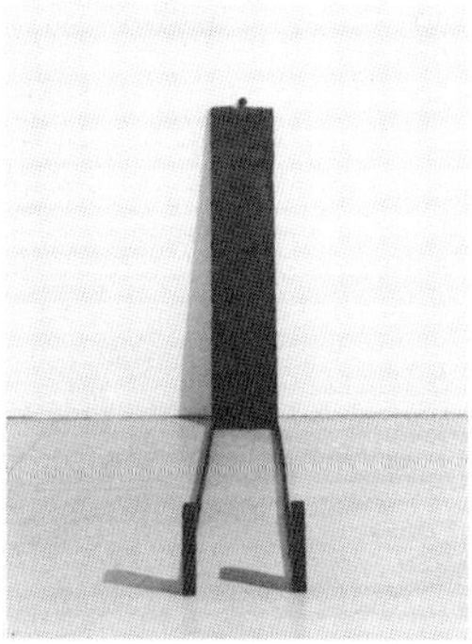

7 *The Black Figure*, c. 1959

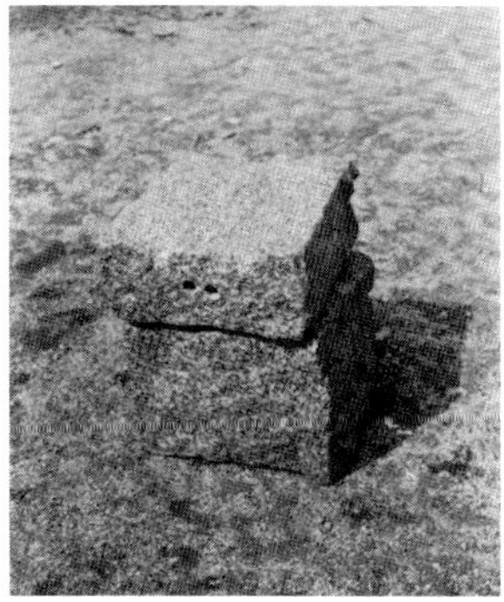

8 *Tantric Figure*, c. 1960 (photo found at Taki Sachiko's family home)

6 Postcard image showing the "female figure of an earthenware pair, male and female, excavated in Chancay, Peru" (published by the Kurashiki Archaeological Museum)

hand to give to visitors from overseas or when he traveled back to the United States.

Here I would like to introduce some of the early works that Byars is thought to have made around this time. *The Black Figure*, one of the oldest of his extant pieces, is believed to date to 1959. The wooden composition depicts a human figure abstracted in a treatment that Byars later referred to as "arbitrization."

Taki Sachiko recalls Byars telling her that he had been motivated to keep working on his art by the encouragement of a female art teacher at Wayne State University who had praised his work early on. *The Black Figure*, a human effigy made of pieces of wood painted black, may have been created as an experiment, harking back to the trial and error of those school years.

Around the same time, Byars also started constructing works from large sheets of paper or fabric, abandoning more robust and permanent materials like wood or stone. The new work was conceptually simpler as Byars shifted to expressions of ephemerality and transience, of gradual disappearance.

Tantric Figure is a work made of granite around 1960. A rectangular granite block lies atop another one, with two holes that resemble a pair of eyes drilled into the top block. The vertical arrangement of the blocks is somewhat reminiscent of Mark Rothko's paintings, which Byars admired. At the time, Byars had visited a quarry in Kitagishima, Okayama prefecture, and was researching various types of stone. A photograph of this work, taken on the grounds of the Kyoto University of Foreign Studies prep school, was found at Taki's family home. The work itself was kept for some time in the garden of the Taki home (see Fig. 8), but is no longer there.

Several other photos of what Taki describes as "small Mingei-like works," or extensions thereof, were also found at the Taki home (Figs. 9-11). Once again, the setting is the grounds of the Kyoto University of Foreign Studies prep school.

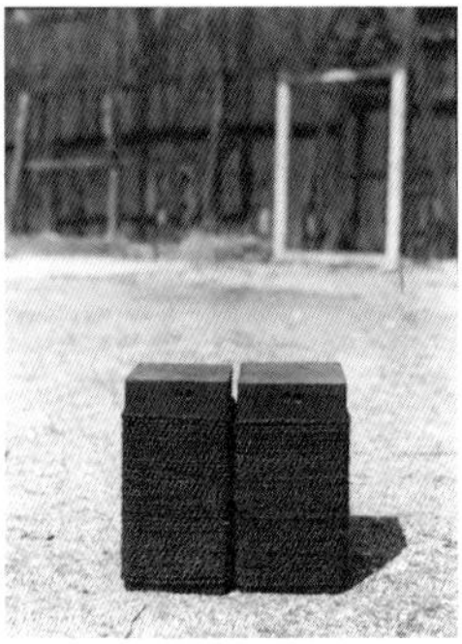
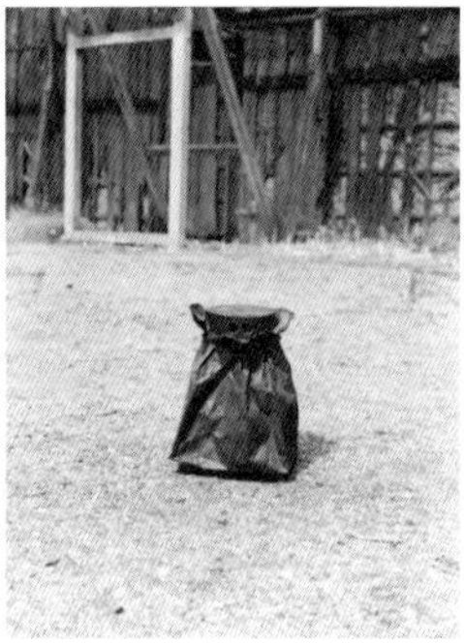
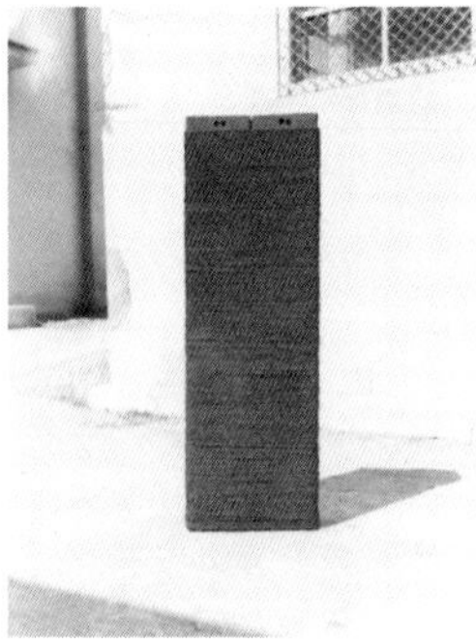

9, 10, 11 Other works created by Byars in Kyoto c. 1960 (photos found at Taki Sachiko's family home)

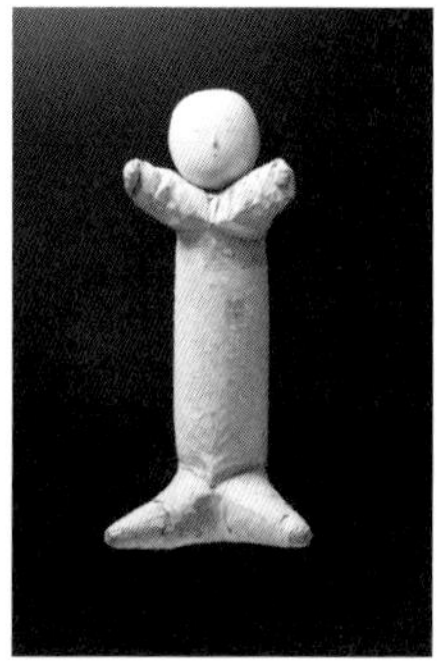

12 *Hina* doll purchased by Byars in Kyoto

Some years later, a doll (Fig. 12) purchased at Yanagi Takashi's antique art shop in the Higashiyama district was found at the house where Byars lived in Kyoto. A prominent art expert, Yanagi is legendary for his sharp eye, honed over years of appraising countless antique works. According to Yanagi, this was probably a *hina* doll from a period later than the *Kyoho-bina* dolls of the early eighteenth century. It is shaped like a *hoko,* a "crawling-baby" doll given on the occasion of the Doll Festival (Hinamatsuri), held on March 3. *Hoko* dolls often served as stuffed toys for infants. However, since the age of the dolls is usually determined from the kimono they wear, this one is difficult to date, Yanagi says. In any event the doll gives one an idea of Byars's taste.

Kyoto Companions

Byars made his living teaching English not only at the Kyoto University of Foreign Studies prep school, but also at the YMCA, Doshisha University, Heian Jogakuin (currently St. Agnes School), Matsushita Electronic Industrial Company, and Naniwa Junior College (currently Osaka University of Arts Junior College), as well as to a group of doctors who worked for companies based in Kyoto. He is remembered by those who knew him as teaching extremely orthodox English and having beautiful diction. An expatriate community had already formed in Kyoto, and foreigners who came to Japan could find jobs through connections with this community. Byars, too, relied on the good offices of fellow expats to pick up several side jobs as soon as he arrived in Kyoto.

Gary Snyder, who had been living in Kyoto since 1956, and Phillip Whalen, who arrived in Japan in 1966 and stayed for two years, were also members of this community. They often held parties at their homes where people could meet and exchange information. The parties hosted by Snyder were said to be the wildest of all, with sessions of drinking, reading poetry, and chatting late into the night in his garden. Snyder, who was undergoing religious training at a Zen temple, referred to sake by the priestly euphemism of *hannyato,* "water of wisdom."

Although Byars attended these parties, he did not develop a particularly intimate relationship with their hosts, perhaps because he was not much of a drinker. The center of the expat community was the Kyoto YMCA. Byars was very close to the secretary at the YMCA's English school, a man named Kuroda Yoshiyuki who often helped Byars and treated him generously.

The location of the YMCA at Sanjo and Yanagi-no-banba streets in the middle of town was convenient for Byars. He often took his YMCA students out walking around the neighborhoods of Kyoto.

Inoue Michiko, who had just opened galerie 16, a contemporary art gallery, at Teramachi and Sanjo—less than a five-minute walk from the YMCA—recalls, "He often brought his students to the gallery. . . . He would say things to them like 'Tell me in English what you think of this work.' One high point was when a student from his class of doctors answered, 'This shape looks like a liver!' Byars was a frequent visitor to the gallery."

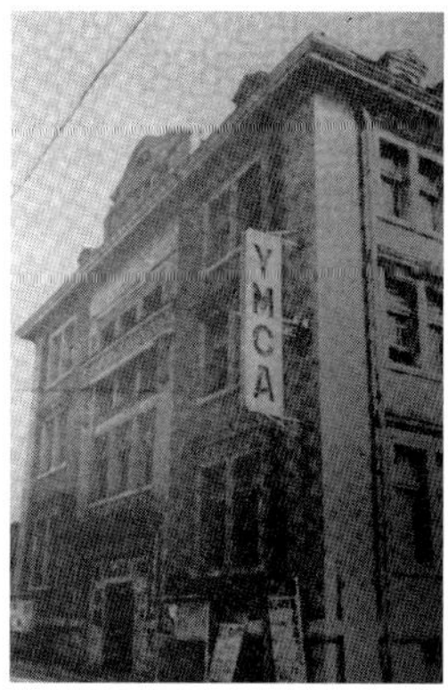

13 The Kyoto YMCA as it looked when Byars was there

After finishing their English lessons at the YMCA, Byars and his colleagues would go out for *oden* stew or to hang out at a coffee shop. Mas Kodani, a Japanese-American who taught English at the YMCA back then and was until recently the head minister of Senshin Buddhist Temple in Los Angeles, recalls: "One evening, we went to a coffee shop after work as usual. While we were talking about this and that, Jim suddenly said, as if he just came up with the idea, 'When we talk one on one, we listen focusing on the other person's voice. What would happen if there was another person talking? Let's all try speaking simultaneously and see if we can understand each other. We may or may not understand what each of us is saying. Let's try it!' Because he urged us on, we actually tried it in the coffee shop. There were three of us there—Jim, a lady, and me. I spoke, she spoke and Jim spoke, all together simultaneously. After trying it for a while, we discovered that the three of us, each speaking at the same time, understood everything the others said. It was surprising. Then Jim said, 'That was fun, wasn't it?' That's the kind of personality he had: bright, fun, charming. When I knew him he seemed to be thinking about things like that all the time. 'What about this? Let's try it.' He was always like that."

One time, Byars called his students up and made them meet in front of Higashi Honganji temple at five in the morning. Everyone who showed up followed his directions and placed straw mats around a lotus pond, sat down and waited for the sunrise. The reason for the gathering was that lotuses bloom at dawn, and it is said that the very first flowers to open make a popping sound. Byars told everyone that if this was true, they should be able to hear that sound. "If we're very quiet," he exclaimed, "we can hear it for sure!" His excitement was evidently contagious.

Byars always appeared excited and inspired by everything: colors, smells, sounds. Those around him loved him for that. That's why they came when he told them to meet at five in the morning, and happily participated in any happening that he devised. Even when he was simply teaching, he was always contemplating and creating. His students understood this and adored him all the more for it.

Itsuki Lullaby

Byars often played tapes of Okinawan folk songs for Taki. He must have discovered the music when he traveled to Okinawa during his time in Kurashiki. He also loved *Itsuki Lullaby*, a folk song from the Kumamoto region of Kyushu, and would frequently ask Taki to sing it to him. It seems that while in Kurashiki he often pestered Kawai Sumie to sing the song as well.

Odoma bongiri bongiri
bon kara sakya oranto
bon ga hayo kurya hayo modoru
ororon ororon ororonbai

Odoma kanjin kanjin
anhitotacha yoka shu
yoka shuya yoka obi yoka kimono
ororon ororon ororonbai

Odon ga uchinda chute

dare ga naichakuryuka
ura no matsuyamaya semi ga naku
ororon ororon ororonbai

Semi ja gozansen
imoto de gozaru
imoto nakunayo ki ni kakaru
ororon ororon ororonbai

This traditional lullaby recounts the feelings of a poor farmer's daughter while she endures a hard life far from home; her family is unable to feed her and has sent her off to work as a domestic servant.

As soon as Bon* comes I will leave.
The sooner Bon comes, the sooner I will go home.
I am no better than a beggar.
These are rich people, with nice kimonos and sashes.
Who will cry for me when I die?
Only the cicadas on the mountain.
It's not cicadas I hear. It's my little sister.
Don't cry, little sister, you'll worry me.

* Bon: the midsummer Buddhist holiday when Japanese return to their hometowns to pray for their ancestors.

So it appears that Byars asked women of his acquaintance to sing this song to him both in Kurashiki and Kyoto. As he listened he would writhe around as if he were trying to dance; it seemed that the melody truly touched his soul, Taki recalls.

Dealings with Artisans

Although he was teaching English at several schools, Byars spent nearly all of the money he earned on expensive Japanese paper (*washi*) made of hemp. This was a strong, durable handmade paper used mainly for Japanese-style painting. The sheets of hemp paper he used for his works were all quite large, and he always bought them from the Morita Washi shop at Higashinotoin and Bukkoji. Sheets that were too big for the store to carry—as large as 7 x 13 *shaku* (212 x 394 centimeters)—were specially ordered through the store from papermakers. Each of these sheets cost around ¥100,000 (equivalent to about $4,000 today). Byars somehow managed to

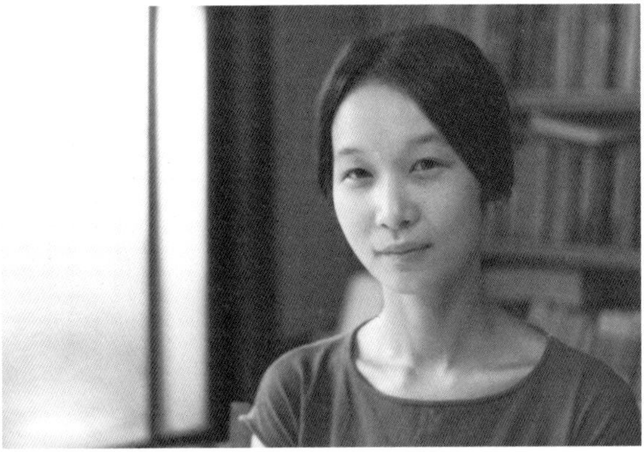

14 Taki Sachiko in the early 1960s

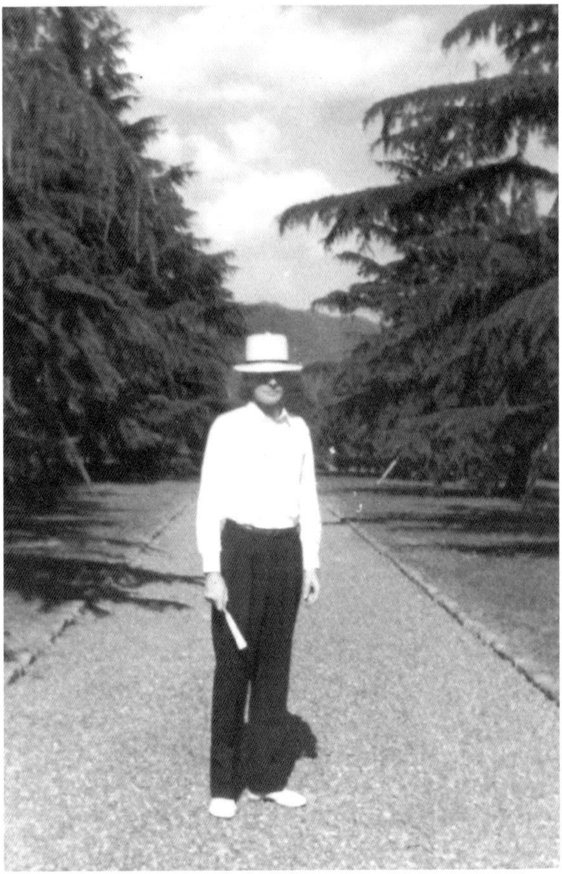

15 Byars in the Kyoto Botanical Garden, in the early 1960s

cover these expenditures with his limited salary. Then he would paint his favorite circles and lines with sumi ink on the paper, one after another. As soon as a piece was finished, he would take it to Nakamura Enshindo, located at Higashiyama and Niomon, for mounting.

"It must not be even one millimeter off!" Byars would nervously insist to Nakamura, the proprietor. A patient man with the temperament of a seasoned artisan, Nakamura dealt with difficult and unusual orders with composure. Because it was handmade, however, the hemp paper was never perfectly straight. No matter how much skill and precision went into the mounting, some deviation inevitably occurred. When that happened, Byars got upset.

"Such a precious work, and now it's ruined!"

Since he was spending most of his salary on these expenses, anger and despair overwhelmed him at such times, and the task of calming him down fell to Taki.

Of the works Byars completed during this period, some were mounted on plywood panel, some were made into scrolls, and others were made of wood or stone. Surprisingly, Byars shipped these large pieces to the U.S. by the cheapest freight available. Bound for New York, the works were meant to be shown in museums and to rich collectors who might be interested in purchasing them.

For painting his lines and circles, Byars bought sumi powder at Kobaien (at Teramachi and Nijo) and brushes, paints, and other materials at Saiundo (at Aneyakoji and Fuyacho). For printing special texts he relied on Benrido. He always chose to buy his art supplies at established, reputable shops that appealed to his weakness for wealth and status. He loved brand names and was a shopaholic. Yet it was not just the prestige of the names that attracted him; he respected the tradition-based formality and high-class sensibilities of such businesses. Moreover, these old Kyoto shops did not function merely as sellers of art materials. They were also authorities on how to use the myriad types of paints and brushes available, and they worked with their artist clients in the development of new products. Thus they served as consultants to artists, contributing to their efforts to improve their painting. The shops also introduced novice painters to art instructors.

Byars was said to be particularly fond of the wife of the Saiundo proprietor. According to Taki, she was a beautiful woman with a face like a Noh mask; her expression, even the way she smiled, resembled a mask. Byars constantly sang her praises, calling her the Lady of Saiundo, and bringing her a single poppy flower whenever he visited the store. The proprietress reciprocated by giving Byars advice, introducing him to specialists, and generally doting on him. He acted the same way toward the similarly lovely and gentle proprietress at Kobaien. Byars was always extremely solicitous of those to whom he took a liking.

Nakamura Enshindo, where Byars had his work mounted, was also a first-class shop, needless to say. Indeed, Nakamura was the artisan Byars most frequently turned to for assistance during his sojourn in Kyoto. After Byars left for the United States in 1967, Enshindo, through which nearly all of his works had passed, retained many of them. But today there are no traces of Byars to be found at the store, which is no longer in business, and the whereabouts of the works he left behind are unknown.

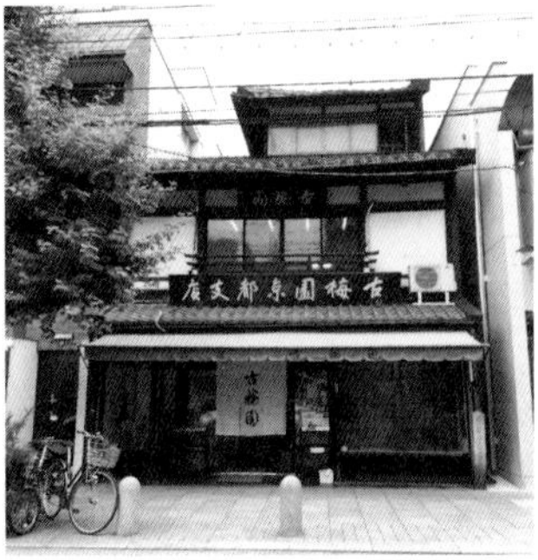

16 Kobaien, where Byars bought sumi powder in the 1960s, July 2015

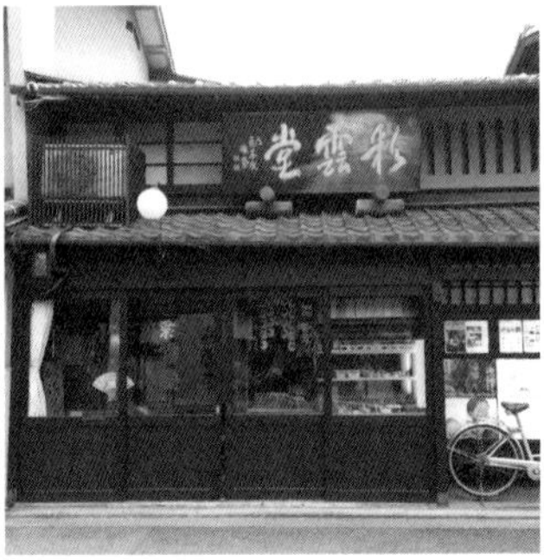

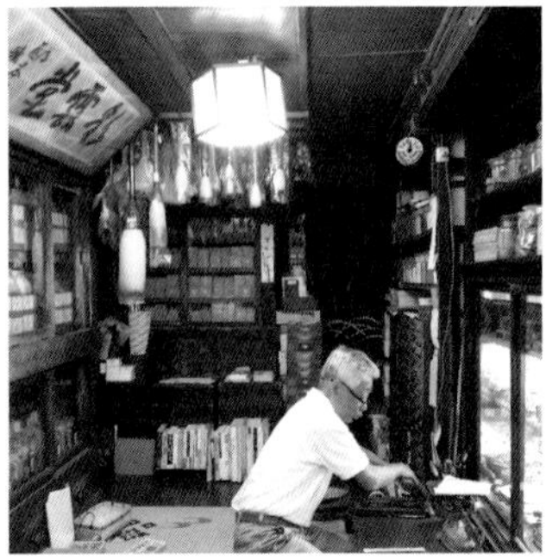

17, 18 Saiundo, where Byars bought art supplies in the 1960s, July 2015

Here is a letter Byars wrote to Dorothy Miller around this time, postmarked November 5, 1960 in Kyoto:

> Dear Dorothy Miller
> The "MA" in Noh Drama is the interval between words, a sacred absence, giving the sound, its chance to become. Beautiful quiets, full of everything, isolated pure sounds, high clear, full of sorrow and joy. My new world, again;
> Have checked with paper authorities in Kyoto, nothing can be done to successfully clean the paper without harming the work or the soft texture. Only, can we allow a natural patina, to be, which I love very much. When something of love is born, even as it deteriorates, beauty never leaves, only shows a wider face, For example, the ancient oriental house or barn; With my work, I wish whatever the air wishes. The Kozo paper lasts up to 600 years, exposed, naked. My paintings, like all of us, must take their chances, I am happy with them, like life, that way.
> As to mounting, the best is to line the paper with linen, oversized and stretch on a good frame with control corners.

Handling remains, difficult, nothing but a white sheet, a white glove, can be used — I will just have to trust that we are all sensitive and careful with something we love. Am sorry, that no better solutions are available for my work, yet I cannot change material!
Have made, now, giant beautiful, beautiful paper 9 x 7 feet. Mounting is too expensive for my teacher's salary.
Am busy with stone people, big, simple, squares, rounds in balance, and painting on these unbelievable papers.
Please I need the grant to do much work, if I qualify; I beg you, to send what they need at Tiffany and later Gugg. I am very sorry to ask of you, so busy, so kind; forgive me.
My love
James Byars
Please, my regards, to All there

First Solo Exhibition: Yamada Gallery

Byars's first exhibition in Kyoto was a solo show at Yamada Gallery, held from October 16 to 22, 1960. The gallery is on a corner on Shinmonzen Street in Higashiyama, a neighborhood full of antique shops. Its founder, Yamada Tetsuo, who hailed from Shingu, Hyogo prefecture, worked for the Allied Occupation after World War II and spoke fluent English. He opened the gallery on Shinmonzen in 1954. At that time the dollar was strong, and the district was popular with American tourists, who bought up a lot of Japanese antiques. Photographs from the period show that most of the antique shops there had signs in English. It is safe to say that tourists bought pretty much anything the stores carried—not only antiques, but hanging scrolls, tea utensils, and so on. Yamada Gallery boasted such customers of note as Avery Brundage, the fifth president of the International Olympic Committee, and publisher Harry N. Abrams.

In those days the gallery was dealing in woodblock prints, and Yamada Tetsuo also carved woodblocks himself. The prints he so casually turned out sold so quickly that he couldn't keep up with demand, so he decided to carry other people's work in addition to his own. Thus while the first floor served as a shop, the second floor became a gallery space. Among its exhibitors were Yagi Kazuo of Sodeisha, an avant-garde ceramic art group based in Kyoto, and artists of the Pan-real Art Association of Japanese-style painting. There is evidence that Byars interacted closely with Yagi while he was in Kyoto, and it seems likely they met at Yamada Gallery. At the time there were few other galleries in the city where artists could exhibit their work. Moreover, Yamada's English skills drew many foreign artists living in Kyoto to his shop. Taki recalls that Byars always carried several small works with him, such as the dolls he carved out of Kitayama *sugi*, to hand out as gifts to foreigners visiting the gallery.

Eventually, Byars got to hold his own exhibition there. He displayed twenty pieces, both large and small, many of them featuring black circles painted with sumi ink on white paper.

One work had a black circle of sumi ink in the middle of an approximately 120 x 150 centimeter sheet of hemp paper, with a tiny white circle left like an aperture at the bottom of the black circle. In another, a black oval shape filling a large hemp-paper sheet had a white circle left in the middle. A postcard-sized sheet contained twin black circles touching each other at the edges; at the center of each circle was a pair of tiny white circles, barely visible without a magnifying glass.

It was the first exhibition in a gallery for the twenty-eight-year-old Byars. Taki says in retrospect, "Even though he was normally very secretive, I'm sure he would have proudly told me about any works he sold." The fact that he did not suggests that sales did not go well.

Local newspapers carried these reviews of the show:

> An English instructor at the Kyoto University of Foreign Studies, inspired by washi and sumi paintings, is exhibiting twenty works from the 17th to the 23rd at Yamada Gallery on Shinmonzen. James Byars, an American born in Michigan in 1932, created a stone sculpture in 1958 in the garden of a place called Crane Brock [*sic*], and this was discovered and purchased by the Museum of Modern Art, New York. Receiving a scholarship that same year, he came to Japan and studied under the director of the Museum of Folkcraft in Kurashiki. Though there are other artists who work in black and white, this show achieves a singularly Oriental tone that reflects an adroit grasp of the attributes of handmade washi and the blackness of sumi. [Translated from *Yukan Kyoto,* October 17, 1960]

> James Byars Solo Exhibition. An American artist who studied painting and sculpture at an art school in Detroit, he arrived in Japan in May this year. While teaching at the Kyoto University of Foreign Studies he grew interested in washi and sumi, which he utilizes in the twenty abstract paintings presented here. Until the 22nd at Yamada Gallery, Shinmonzen. [Translated from *Kyoto shinbun*, October 20, 1960]

The "Crane Brock" mentioned in the first article is presumably the Cranbrook

Academy of Art near Detroit. As for the private purchases of his work in 1959 by MoMA's Dorothy Miller and others, and the reference to his scholarship from Wayne State University, it is hard to tell whether this information was garbled by a Japanese reporter with limited English comprehension or whether Byars was simply embellishing his résumé. Some exaggeration notwithstanding, the reports do convey Byars's interest in washi and sumi, and the inspiration he found for his works in Japanese culture.

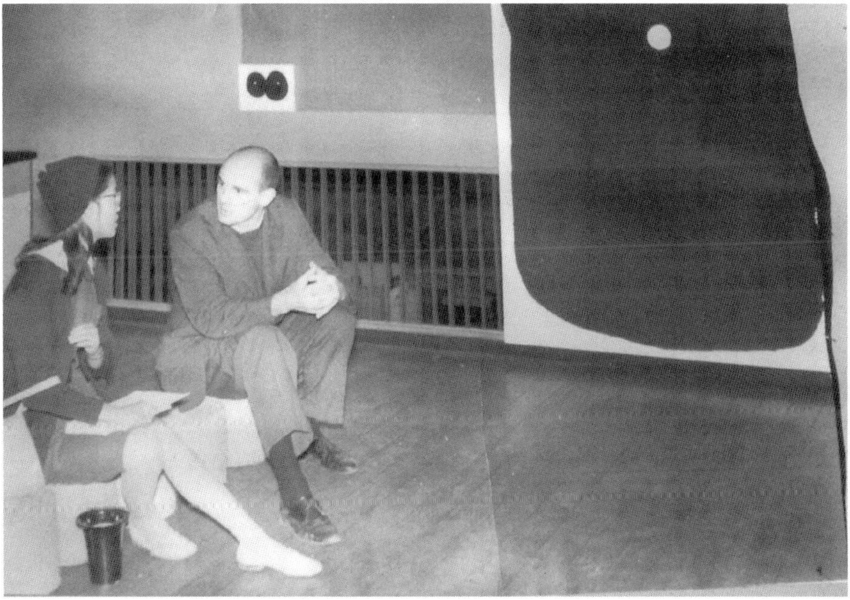

19 Kawai Sumie and Byars at Yamada Gallery, October 22, 1960

20 Photo of a work included in the Yamada Gallery show, used in a mailing by Byars

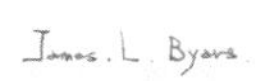

21 Byars signed the photo on the back; several copies were found at the Taki home

A photograph (Fig. 19) of Kawai Sumie, whom Byars met in Kurashiki, shows her sitting with Byars at the gallery, taken when she traveled from Kurashiki to see the exhibition. In the picture Byars looks like a handsome, clean-cut young man, though the hair on the top of his head is already starting to thin. He is dressed in a jacket and trousers—no cloak, top hat or white suit, the costume that would later become his trademark, or what could be called an eccentric affectation. The Byars of that time evidently didn't dress to get attention. Taki remembers Kawai visiting Byars's house at Higashiyama-Nijo once; if so, it was probably at the time of this exhibition.

First Group: Action

Byars formed a performance ensemble, which he named Action, with a large group of people under his direction. According to published sources, in 1960 he had 100 students stand in a circle at the Yukawa Institute for Theoretical Physics, Kyoto University, and recite 100 lines from the poems of Gertrude Stein, including "If I told him would he like it. Would he like it if I told him," from "If I Told Him: A Completed Portrait of Picasso." However, except for this bit of information, which appears in catalogues published outside Japan, no trace remains of the event, such as written invitations or recollections by any of the participants.

Kyoto Indépendant

(March 7–13, 1961, Kyoto Municipal Museum of Art)

Kyoto Indépendant was an annual exhibition organized in 1955 by a private group of artists, the Kyoto Seinen Bijutsu Sakka Shudan (Kyoto Young Artists Group), commonly abbreviated as Seibi. It was a non-juried show at which anyone who wanted to could freely present their work.

An exhibition titled *Nihon Indépendant,* hosted by the Japan Communist Party–affiliated Japan Art Association, had been launched earlier, in 1947, and another *Nihon Indépendant* (which changed its name to *Yomiuri Indépendant* in 1957), hosted by the *Yomiuri shinbun* newspaper, opened in 1949. But the *Kyoto Indépendant* was probably the very first truly "independent" exhibition organized in Japan by individual artists.

At the beginning of 1961 Byars, along with Taki Sachiko, showed up unannounced at the office of the Kyoto Municipal Museum of Art. Abe Hiromu, the museum curator who was in charge of the *Indépendant* exhibition, met with them. "What is the purpose of your visit?" he asked.

Byars responded, "I'd like to participate in the *Indépendant.*" Anyone could do so, regardless of nationality or race, as long as they paid the application fee, so Abe initiated the usual registration procedure. He handed over an application form and inquired where Byars lived. "What is your address?" Abe asked, several times over. Suddenly Byars lost his temper and shouted in a high-pitched voice, "*Dokodemo ii!* (Anywhere is fine!)" Although Byars had Taki translate most of the conversation, he certainly would have understood some of Abe's Japanese. "No, no. You misunderstand. I'm just asking in case we have to contact you if you present your work in the show." The address Abe managed to extract from Byars was that of the teachers' housing at the Kyoto University of Foreign Studies in Higashiyama-Nijo:

J. L. Byars
c/o Kyoto Preparatory School
5 Tokusei-cho, Okazaki Higashiyama-Nijo, Sakyo-ku, Kyoto-shi

The works Byars presented were similar to the ones he had shown at Yamada Gallery. The exhibition record lists them as follows:

Room 1 (Paintings)

Untitled	James L. Byars
Untitled	James L. Byars
Untitled	James L. Byars
Untitled	James L. Byars

4 works exhibited

A round-table talk by the artists participating in that year's *Indépendant* is summarized in issue 37 (March 30, 1961) of *Kyoto-shi Bijutsukan nyusu* (Kyoto Municipal Museum of Art news). Included is a paraphrase of Byars's remarks: "The works in this show seem to have been installed in the order in which the participants paid their fees. This automatic approach to display, without any consideration of the character of each work, is no good." To cite the worst example, this particular *Indépendant* exhibition had an abstract work displayed right next to a landscape in a shiny golden frame. This infuriated Byars, who demanded that changes be made.

With this connection as an "in," Byars started calling the Kyoto Municipal Museum of Art over all kinds of matters. It was always Abe, the curator, who answered his calls. "I'm doing a solo show. Can you come?" "I want to hold an exhibition at such and such. What do I need to do to make that happen?" "I want to meet so and so . . ." Byars called about every conceivable topic, not only those related to art but random personal concerns as well.

In hindsight Taki says, "He must have been a real headache for Mr. Abe, asking questions and bothering him about all sorts of things."

Abe says, "Well, it wasn't easy, but I didn't think it was all that much trouble."

Taki and Byars, always together, often met Abe at Arena, a coffee shop now located on the north side of the Kyoto Municipal Museum of Art. Back then it was across the street in front of the museum, on the west side, where the National Museum of Modern Art, Kyoto, currently stands. Abe went there, he says, to sit face to face with Byars and listen while he held forth on various subjects.

The Kyoto Municipal Museum of Art, which played such an important role in introducing Byars's work during his Japan sojourn, was built to commemorate the enthronement of the Showa Emperor, held in Kyoto in 1928. Opening five years later, in 1933, it was Japan's second major public art museum, after the Tokyo Prefectural (now Metropolitan) Art Museum. It continued to hold regular exhibitions even during World War II; the war ended while its *9th Exhibition from the Permanent Collection of Local Artists* (August 1–23, 1945) was in progress. From 1946 to 1952 the building was requisitioned by U.S. Occupation forces and used as a hospital and ammunition depot; American troops played basketball in the galleries, and rows of latrines were installed in the beautiful marble and tile foyer. A dart board was drawn on a gallery wall, in which darts remained stuck for some time after the building's return. Traces of this postwar era were still visible when Byars arrived in Kyoto in 1960. A plaque in English describing the museum's history under the Occupation hung on a wall in the foyer, and Abe recalls reading it with Byars. He says that Byars told him then that he had served in the U.S. Navy. The same plaque was still hanging there in 2015, but for the past several decades it has been used as a notice board and covered with posters; the historical text underneath is usually not visible.

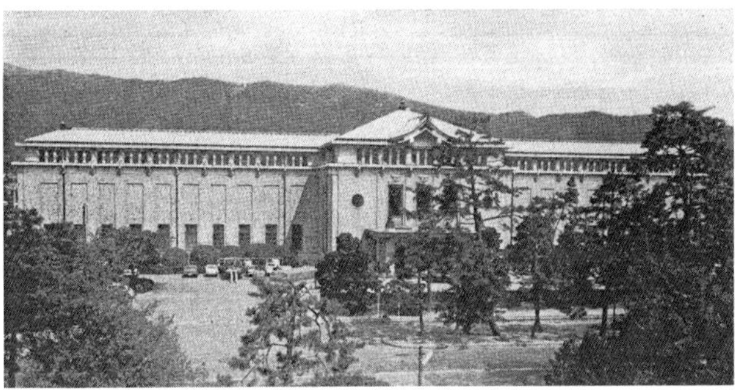

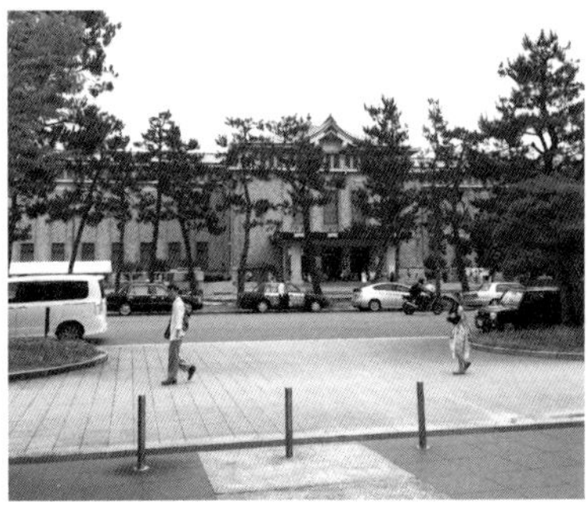

22, 23 The main building of the Kyoto Municipal Museum of Art as it appeared in 1974 (left) and 2015 (right)

With his participation in the *Indépendant* paving the way, Byars was able to present his work in *Adventure in Today's Art of Japan* (titled *Gendai bijutsu no jikken*, literally "experiment in contemporary art," in Japanese), an exhibition at the National Museum of Modern Art, Tokyo, in April that same year.

Adventure in Today's Art of Japan (*Gendai bijutsu no jikken*)
(April 12–30, 1961, National Museum of Modern Art, Tokyo)

The National Museum of Modern Art, Tokyo planned a revolutionary, unprecedented exhibition which, as the title suggests, would introduce young, cutting-edge, avant-garde artists who were garnering attention in shows like the *Indépendant*. Historically, *Adventure in Today's Art of Japan* proved to be one of the most significant art exhibitions of Japan's postwar era. At the time, however, it received generally unfavorable reviews and few visitors.

There were sixteen participating artists: Arakawa Shusaku, Indo Hisashi, Ochi Osamu, Kikuhata Mokuma, Kudo Tetsumi, Kuno Shin, Kobatake Hiroshi, Shiraga Kazuo, Tanaka Atsuko, Tanaka Eisaku, Nakanishi Natsuyuki, Higuchi Shin, Matsuzawa Yutaka, Motonaga Sadamasa, Yoshinaka Taizo, and James Lee Byars.

Kikuhata Mokuma's eerily visceral, ritualistic *Dorei keizu* (*Slave Genealogy*), archived in the Museum of Contemporary Art, Tokyo, boasted two thick telephone poles—one with a phallic protuberance and the other with something resembling female genitalia—which lay obliquely in parallel, covered in five yen coins (adding up to tens of thousands of yen) and hairlike tangles of black cloth cords, with more five-yen coins scattered around them. Nakanishi Natsuyuki submitted a grotesque object that resembled a clump of solidified lava with numerous spoons and forks covering

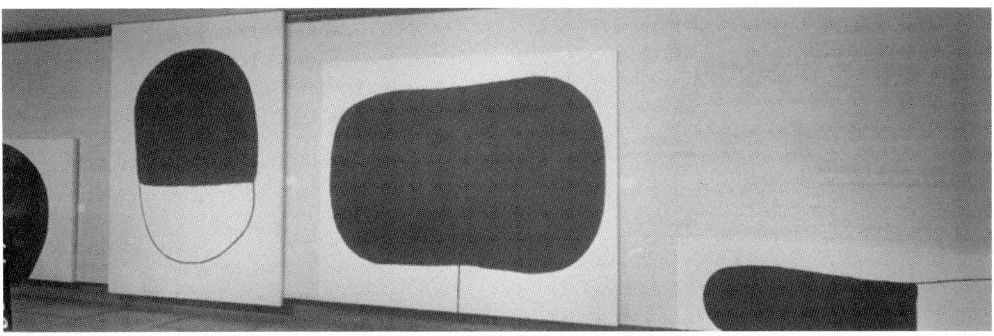

24 Exhibition view, *Adventure in Today's Art of Japan*, 1961

its surface like fish scales. Most of the works on display must have emitted a similarly bizarre aura.

In the midst of this, Byars exhibited the same four pieces he had shown at the *Indépendant* in March. They included a sumi-ink painting of a large black circle on a large white sheet of paper, and a more geometrical composition with a black half-circle sitting atop a white one, looking a bit like a human head with a page-boy haircut. This latter piece was featured on the cover of the National Museum of Modern Art's May 1961 newsletter *Gendai no me* (Contemporary eye).

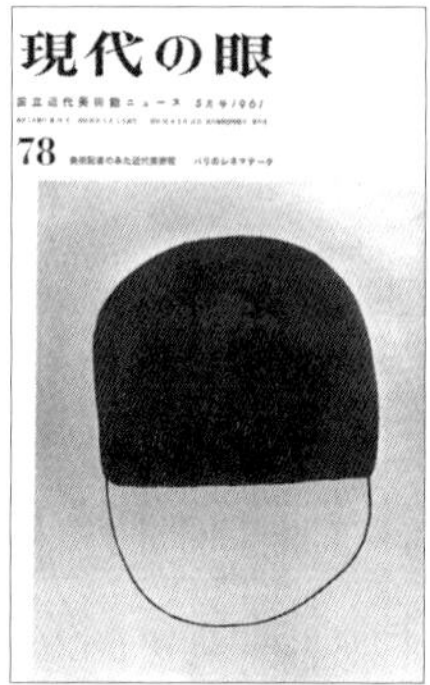

25 Cover of *Gendai no me*, May 1961

Fifteen of the artists—all except Byars—were already known to some extent, their youth notwithstanding. In comparison, Byars was a virtually unknown foreign artist who had just had his first solo show the previous autumn in Kyoto. Why was he selected for this historic exhibition? It was actually on the recommendation of Imaizumi Atsuo, then assistant director of the National Museum of Modern Art, Tokyo. Imaizumi, who was on the board of the *Indépendant*, took notice of Byars's work there in March and promptly arranged for him to exhibit at *Adventure in Today's Art of Japan*. "Imaizumi was an amazing person," says Abe. "There were several hundred artworks on display in this large space, but he remembered everything—what kind of works they were, the names of the artists—just by going around the gallery once. Then he even managed to review them." The role of *Indépendant* board members at the time was to support the exhibition as well as critique the works at a joint review held on-site.

The aforementioned May 1961 issue of *Gendai no me* also published a statement by Byars. Unfortunately his original English text cannot be found; the following is a translation from the Japanese:

> My Statement
> James Lee Byars
> Painting today gives a more direct impression of having a free, independent life of its own. That spirit transcends the limitations of name and narrative, speaking of the significance of life through abstraction. By doing so it lets the viewer experience infinite encounters. If it is something that serves to exalt life, then you may feel life of some sort, perhaps your own, by viewing a single line. And after that experience, you may respond freely and gently to lines wherever you see them. The line can open up powers of recognition, of perception, within your consciousness. This is how any ele-

> ment of a painting is discovered. The more someone approaches life with this freedom, the more that person's existence will be filled with beauty. With each discovery, our personal limits are conceptually expanded, and will extend as far as our senses allow. In this way paintings demand to live and to share their life with everyone, to belong to a pure concept of existence. Even if they evoke only a hazy, unclear response, that quiet moment may be the beginning of discovery. At the least it is the pause before a question arises. And the question is simple: how does one find truth, beauty, and life in a painting?

The exhibition leaflet included the following profile of Byars in Japanese and listed the works he exhibited in English:

> James Byars (1932–)
> Born in Detroit, USA. After graduating from Wayne State University, arrived in Japan in 1958 to study contemporary painting. Returned home recently after producing work in Kyoto and Tokyo. Had a solo exhibition at Yamada Gallery in Kyoto in 1960.
>
> Work 1 1960
> Work 2 1960
> Work 3 1960
> Work 4 1960

The June 1961 issue of the art journal *Bijutsu techo* (Art notes) featured *Adventure in Today's Art of Japan*, publishing an article titled "*Jikken-ten to iu na no jikken*" (An experiment named "experiment") by the critic Hariu Ichiro, along with photographs of each participating artist's work. However, Byars was not mentioned at all. I asked Hariu why he did not say anything about Byars, and he replied as follows:

> The reason I did not mention Byars was because Imaizumi Atsuo, who was [later] the director of the National Museum of Modern Art, Kyoto, had recommended him. There were many instances when the line got blurred between his personal relationships and his public function as a critic. For example, around that time, he casually promoted one artist whom he had learned was from his home prefecture [Yamagata] after the final selection stage for the Yasui Award. He also tried, very arbitrarily, to push Furuta An, head of the Kansai-area Chinese restaurant chain Minmin and a

> member of the Dokuritsukai [Association of Independent Artists], as an international artist [for selection as a guest artist at the *Mainichi gendai* exhibition]. That was one of my motivations to write about who promoted whom in which screenings, and what they said, with everyone's actual names, in a series of pieces I called "insider criticism" that appeared mainly in *Geijutsu shincho* [Art news] in 1961 and 1962. I then compiled them into *Gendai bijutsu no karute* [Clinical chart for contemporary art, a book published by Gendai Shobo]. I believe *Bijutsu techo* also omitted mention [of Byars] because Imaizumi had promoted him. [Translated from a letter sent to the author in 2005]

Adventure in Today's Art of Japan was covered in several other Japanese-language magazines and newspapers, but none mentioned Byars. However, in the *Japan Times*, a Tokyo-based English-language daily, art columnist Elise Grilli reviewed the show and made this comment about Byars:

> The lone American, James Byars, who has strayed into this meeting, performs very precise balancing acts in black and white that outdo the Japanese at their ancient feats, but I'm not clear as to the reason for the huge scale of these exercises. [Elise Grilli, "Art, East and West: Arts in an Age of Anxiety," *Japan Times*, April 29, 1961]

Ogura Tadao, who was working at that time in the planning office for the National Museum of Modern Art, Kyoto (which would open in 1963), asked Abe where to return Byars's artworks when the exhibition closed. Since Byars's quarters at Higashiyama-Nijo were close by the office as well as being near the Kyoto Municipal Museum of Art, Abe says he accompanied Ogura to Byars's room at the Kyoto University of Foreign Studies prep school to deliver his work.

The Second Trip Home: Spring to Late December 1961*

The Palace of Perfect (Serralves Foundation, 1997) contains this passage describing events during Byars's second trip back to the United States. The Willard Gallery exhibition it mentions took place from October 3 to 28, 1961.

---

* The approximate dates and durations of Byars's second and subsequent trips to the U.S. were determined from the diary of Abe Hiromu, then curator at the Kyoto Municipal Museum of Art, and from the postmarks on letters Byars sent to Abe from the States.

> Dorothy Miller encourages dealers to take an interest in Byars's work. Exhibition at Marion Willard Gallery where he shows ink drawings and sculptures consisting of two or three round black stones arranged on white grounds.

Byars wrote the following letter to Miller, postmarked May 29, 1961 in Detroit. It's a revealing document that merits verbatim and unabridged reproduction here:

> Dear Miss Miller, would it not be fine, to see life as a total, allowing each its uniqueness, and freedom to grow each his way, doesn't the lovely life of painting belong in the everyday life of us, to enter freely the experience of concern in present consciousness of painting, given now, anonymously to all life to discovery if it should wish and with every availed effort to interpret the truth in terms intelligible to any seeking, it is inherent in discovery to wish it shared for the total development of life, such concern must it seems become available if we are to create beliefs meaningful to the rapidly growing consciousness, some fine day in my fantasy the leaders will awarely sense the need of the total people to enjoy beauty in its time of discovery by helping to grant support given by the people to the painters, poets, writers, for the immediate scene does it seem unreal to now give away towards that dream, can we not interpret? is true concern absence? I cannot be convinced of this, and I hope, this is one reason For my return to seek the authority where ever it can be found to attempt the dreams accomplishment, to make the no name gift given in hope to the potential of spiritual awareness, inherent awaiting in people, I have written to the United Nations, can we not give our concepts of the present in our reality to the other peoples, would it not be encouraging to share the significance of discovery, is all activity not eventually directed towards the enlargement of consciousness, and would it not be fair to see it oriented towards truthful total concern. in last and high analysis do we own anything? how right it seems to give life to life for each who wishes the experience, everyones, yet not possessed, unowned, free to be felt for itself, little can be done without trust, I appreciate your pure concern, the idea has been somewhat accomplished in Japan, the National Modern has agreed to the quiet presentation of the large cube, given anonymously, to the people's spirit, yet I wish it more free in the unexpected and more free public structure for the experience devoid of unnecessary attentions, I hope this interests you and perhaps you would help to find concern in this direction, you do the high

real things and I would like to help.

I asked your secretary and she said you often stay in the evening quiet to read and that letters from me may be all right, there are many things now that my work has taught me, that I can articulate and would like to with you, if it does not bother you and interests you, but please tell me frankly, for I am direct and I don't know of life there very well, As to my existence, first I must provide enough to survive and then to work, my needs are small except materials for painting, I will go to any country where my ideas make sense, I have hope in America for it is my home. Miss Willard is fair and young to show my departure in October, I love her concern, and Mr Messer came with hope, Mr Lippman from "art in america" is also trying to help, I am very fortunate and thankful my work with you I don't know what to do about in my indefinite summer, I am trying to get to NY with my show may I then make some move or whatever you wish to do with it before then I will take a job but no one will hear my not packaged ideas in Art disciplines but I can do some work to get by, may I please in the fall try to pay you the expenses of the Guggenheim, etc, my Willard selling only paid my expenses there, please sometime a word

JB

The works Byars displayed in October at the Willard Gallery appear to have met with a favorable reception, as Dorothy Miller indicates in her letter dated October 25:

Dear James:

Thank you for your letters. Please stop worrying about things. My only concern is to have all of your pictures which are now here in the Museum join those in the gallery after the exhibition is over since it is impossible for me to store them any longer here, but you already know this.

I thought the exhibition really looked beautiful and was sorry not to see you there. I think the new paintings are more interesting than the previous ones and the arrangement is splendid. I also liked the sculpture very much indeed.

I loved the little cones you left here. I did not know what they were un-till Miss Mazo explained to me.

I will certainly recommend you to the Tiffany Foundation and I am finding out whether they simply want a letter or if there is a form which they should send me.

Best regards,

Sincerely,
Dorothy C. Miller
Curator of the Museum Collections

At the bottom of the MoMA copy of the letter is this handwritten note:

10-27-61 he took all the rest of his work away from the Museum.

3 Meeting Hayashi Shuseki

An American Scholar Who Became a Japanese Citizen

Lindley Williams Hubbell, whose Japanese name was Hayashi Shuseki, had a profound influence on Byars's art. A professor of English literature at Doshisha University, Hubbell was a naturalized Japanese citizen born in the United States. A "Japanese" who didn't speak Japanese at all, he was nonetheless extremely knowledgeable about Japanese culture; he had even translated Zeami's famous treatise on Noh, *Kadensho,* into English. A conversationalist with a wit informed by his extensive knowledge, sophisticated artistic views, and a deep understanding of Japanese traditions, Hubbell proved an indispensable font of learning for Byars. No doubt Byars also admired him for his close friendship with Gertrude Stein. The letters exchanged between Stein and Hubbell are currently archived and published by the Stein Collection at Yale University.

According to Yamamoto Shigeki, one of his students, Hubbell was particularly devoted to Donald Richie, a younger American expatriate writer who essentially introduced Japanese films to the Western world. Hubbell was interested in young talent, loved art, hated poseurs, and demanded authenticity. In Byars he found a new talent and generously encouraged and inspired him.

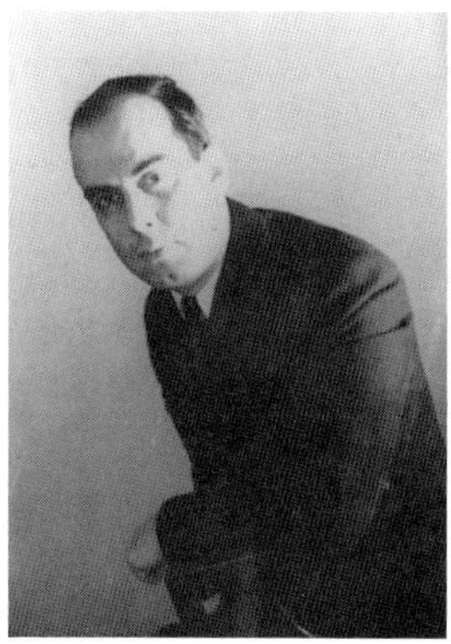

26 Hayashi Shuseki (Lindley Williams Hubbell); photo provided by Yamamoto Shigeki

> Hayashi Shuseki (Lindley Williams Hubbell) was born in Connecticut, USA, on June 3, 1901. He became familiar with the *Complete Works of William Shakespeare* at the age of eight, and kept the tome close throughout the rest of his life. In 1927, he received the Yale Young Poets Award. He arrived in Japan on October 6, 1953. After that

date he never once left Japan and in 1960 he became a naturalized citizen. He taught at Doshisha University and Mukogawa Women's University. He wrote seventeen books of poetry, eight collections of essays, and numerous articles, as well as translating four books. He loved Noh, classical music, opera, popular songs, painting, sculpture, and film. He died in Kyoto on October 2, 1994. [Translated from a description by Yamamoto Shigeki of a memorial stone for Hayashi Shuseki inscribed with one of his poems, installed at Yamazaki Kannonji temple in Kyoto]

An Exhibition "on the Theme of Question"
(Doshisha University, c. 1961)

Byars held an exhibition titled *Ten Philosophical Sentences, or The Exhibition of What Do You Know Mister*, the only extant references to which are found in English-language catalogues published overseas and nowhere else. Though these sources describe it as being "on the theme of Question," it is impossible to identify the contents of the exhibition, to ascertain that the year was in fact 1961, or to determine exactly when it occurred. Moreover, all of the English sources give the location of the exhibition as the nonexistent "Jisha" University, though it is easy to recognize this as a misspelling of Doshisha.

According to these records, the exhibition was based on ten philosophical sentences from Act 3, Scene 3 of Shakespeare's *Romeo and Juliet*, one of which was "Hang up philosophy!" However, these sources do not reveal any details, such as whether this was a performance piece based on the questions found in the play, or if the text was printed and distributed or otherwise displayed. Still, it can be surmised that Byars was inspired by Hubbell's lectures to his Shakespeare class at Doshisha University, which he often attended.

According to Taki Sachiko, Byars was always writing letters that posed questions. He was not expecting answers from anyone, but simply voicing rhetorical questions in a fashion that reminded Taki of Zen *mondo* (dialogues). Much later, in a 1996 performance at the Nara Hotel near the end of his life, Byars asked the question "Is is?" Byars never demanded answers, but simply tossed questions in the air. From his early days until his death, this constant questioning was a defining element of his style. The Doshisha exhibition "on the theme of Question" must have been one of his first performances in the "question" mode—possibly the first he ever held in public.

"Questions" Answered by Hubbell

"I had three mysterious postcards from the USA, so I thought that they, and my answers, might amuse you."

Postmarked April 17, 1968, the year after Byars returned to the United States for good, Hubbell sent a curious letter to the English-language poet Yoko Danno. The letter reproduced several "requests" from the writer Howard Junker, a U.S. resident, and Hubbell's answers to them. These anecdotes reveal how Hubbell and Byars stimulated each other's intellectual curiosity and enjoyed the interplay of their relationship.

Three postcards from America

1

Please send me three joyful anecdotes concerning James Lee Byars. Yours,

Howard Junker
400 West End Ave.
New York, NY 10024

2

Please relate 6 (six) meaningful incidents from the life of James Lee Byars. Thank you

Howard Junker
400 West End Ave
New York, NY 10024

3

Junker
400 West End
New York, 10024

Please send me 2 (two) vexing polarities to be found in J. L. B. Thank you.

---

1 (joyful)

Years ago, before I knew Jim very well, I met him one day when I was walking through Maruyama Park. After we had exchanged greetings he said, You might be interested to know that three of my works are going to be exhibited simultaneously in three different parts of Kyoto.

That's very interesting, I said, When does it happen?

Oh, nobody knows that, he said.

2 (joyful)

Some years later he sent me an invitation to one of his presentations which was to take place in the grounds of the Imperial Palace at 5 a.m.

I replied that I wouldn't get up that early to see all three members of the Trinity.

Afterwards he wrote me about it and said, It was witnessed by a dog and a crow.

3 (joyful)

The first time that Jim called on me was in winter and Japanese houses are not heated and right in the middle of my little living room there was a big ugly beat up old iron stove with a pipe going up to the ceiling, along the ceiling, and out through a hole in the wall. I'm not a particularly conventional person but I was really conscious of the fact that an artist was calling on me for the first time and I thought boy wait till he sees this stove.

He arrived, sat down, looked around the room, and his first words were, What a beautiful stove!

4 (meaningful)

One night exactly at midnight

I know it was midnight because I always turn on my radio at twelve to set my watch and hear the National Anthem which they play when they go off the air and I had just turned off the dial when

I heard a knock on my window. I went to the front door and opened it. There stood Miss Taki, a friend of Jim's, completely covered with white feathers. She was wearing a sort of robe which went all the way to the ground and was made of white feathers and on her head was some sort of headdress of white feathers and she stood there all shimmering white in the half light of my garden at midnight.

Without a word she handed me something. I took it, bowed, and she disappeared without a word.

I went back in the house and looked at it. It was a small white disk of celluloid, or something like celluloid, about the size of a dime, and on it was printed in tiny black letters the word PEACE.

5 (vexing)

Ever since I was a little boy I have known hundreds and hundreds of lines of Shakespeare by heart and in my Shakespeare classes I never have to use a book when I read it with them.

Jim used to attend my Shakespeare course and when I would say Shakespeare he would stare at me so intensely that it was very disconcerting. Finally one day he stared at me so wildly that I completely forgot what I was saying. It was the first time in my life I ever forgot a word of Shakespeare.

After the class Haru-chan said, I never thought I'd see you forget Shakespeare.

It was that son of a bitch Jim Byars, I said.

4 Cultural Encounters in Kyoto

Finding Beauty in Paper

Sometime around 1962, four years after his arrival in Japan, Byars began creating works in a format that resembled Buddhist sutra books: large, long sheets of washi paper linked edge to edge to form an accordion-folded hand scroll. Such works would be displayed folded, but in exhibition performances they were opened, gradually extended, then gradually closed again in a process that could take hours. These movements evoked those of the Noh theater: slow, stately, with the utmost care given to the slightest motions, the performer's attention never wavering for an instant. Byars called works of this sort "performable paper"—that is, "paper that performs." He must have gotten the idea from watching the ritual expanding, little by little, of accordion-folded texts during the chanting of sutras at Buddhist memorial services. Perhaps he sensed a spiritual quality, transcending materiality, in the way a simple sheet of paper accommodates layering and folding many times over.

Byars took notice of the Japanese predilection for wrapping things. Every time he saw paper wrapping, he got a twinkle of excitement in his eye and said, "Look! Paper!" He was especially enthusiastic about making paper invitations for exhibitions. For one such project he took a square sheet of very thin white paper, with tiny, beautifully typed letters telling the time and location of the show, and inserted it into a square crimson envelope. Another time, he used a large sheet of thin paper with very small typewritten letters on it, rolled it up, and tied a thread around the middle.

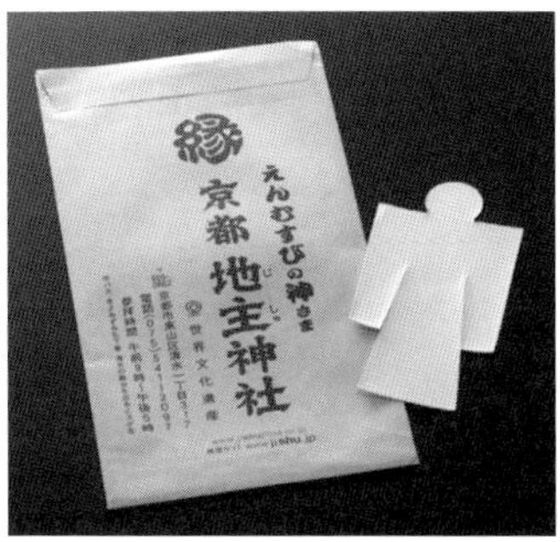

27 *Hitogata* paper doll from Jishu Shrine, Kyoto

Every invitation was stylish. Like gift wrapping and giving, Byars saw exhibitions as an opportunity not just to create and display artwork but also to prepare invitations and present them to people.

His close friend Hubbell customarily went to see performances of the Shinto theatrical dance known as Kagura at Ota Shrine, in the Kamo marshlands of northern Kyoto, on the tenth of every month. Byars often visited the shrine with Hubbell and asked many questions of the Shinto priest every time he went. The shrine had numerous paper fortunes, charms, and doll-like figures (*hitogata*) tied to trees. People would write their names on these figures, blow on them, and place them on trees inside the shrine precincts to ward off evil.

The shape of these paper effigies subsequently became one of Byars's recurring motifs. One famous example was a performance he held in 1967 after he returned to the United States, when he covered a New York City street with a huge human figure made of a type of paper that dissolved completely in water. In 1975 he spread another gigantic figure, nearly 100 meters long, over the Piazza San Marco in Venice. He also frequently wrote letters to his closest acquaintances on paper shaped like human figures.

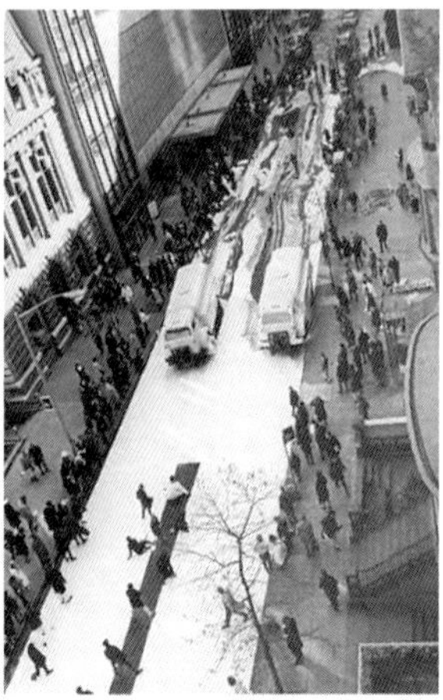

28 *The Giant Soluble Man*, New York, 1967

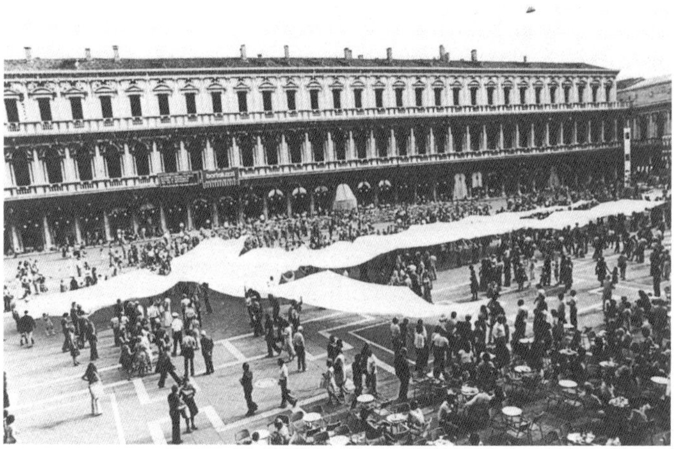

29 *The Holy Ghost*, Piazza San Marco, Venice, 1975

Interests in Noh and Gagaku Music

In addition to attending Kagura performances at Ota Shrine, Byars went to Heian Shrine at every opportunity to see Takigi Noh, which is performed at night on a torchlit outdoor stage. He also attended Noh plays at the Kongo Noh Theatre in Muromachi. In those days box seats with tatami mats had not yet given way to Western seating. Byars enjoyed watching Noh from the box seats and often went there with Taki.

Byars's interest in Noh inspired him to take lessons from a Noh flute player of the Morita School, Sugi Ichitaro, for a period of time. It appears, however, that it was Sugi's performances that attracted Byars, and he was not actually interested in performing himself. In any event he was not a particularly good student. He also cajoled his girlfriend Taki into studying the *sho*, a reed instrument used in the ancient imperial court music known as Gagaku, which she did with Yamada Sentaro, a maker of Gagaku instruments.

Byars also learned how to make gold leaf and apply it. Many of his works used gold leaf applied to paper, and he was fairly knowledgeable about its uses in Buddhist architecture. Mas Kodani, the aforementioned member of Kyoto's expat community, was a student then at Ryukoku University, a Buddhist institution, and recalls that Byars often talked to him about gold leaf.

5 Frequent Moves and an Expanding Network

Second Participation in *Kyoto Indépendant*
(January 11–15, 1962, Kyoto Municipal Museum of Art)

> "A Lineup of Strong New Works: The *Indépendant* Opens to Big Crowds"
> The 1962 *Indépendant* exhibition, hosted by the city of Kyoto, opened at the Kyoto Municipal Museum of Art in Okazaki on the 11th. An unusual exhibition that provides wall space to all comers without any review process, it features many ambitious works by young artists. Participants hail mainly from Kyoto and environs but also from Shiga, Osaka, Hyogo, Nara and Wakayama. This time there are 390 works of painting and sculpture, 60 more than last year. The artists represent the whole gamut of groups and associations, among them Tekkei-kai, Kera Bijutsu Kyokai, Seinen Bijutsu, Dokuritsu, Kodo, Kofu-kai, Femina, and Jiyu Bijutsu. One artist, James Byars, is exhibiting several works titled "No NAME," which are box-like three-meter-high black and white objects with patterns drawn on them in chalk and sumi ink. These are hard to categorize as either painting or sculpture, which is just what one would expect of the *Indépendant.* Most of the paintings here are abstract but not anti-painterly, and many evince an improvement in technique. The exhibition closes on the 15th. [Translated from *Kyoto shinbun*, evening edition, January 11, 1962]

The above article in a local newspaper suggests that Byars was gaining some recognition in the Kyoto art world. The works he exhibited this time were listed as follows (with titles in English):

> Room 8 (Paintings)
> No NAME James L. Byars

No NAME James L. Byars
NOTHING James L. Byars

One other difference was that the address for Byars provided on the exhibition leaflet was no longer the faculty housing of the Kyoto University of Foreign Studies in Higashiyama-Nijo:

JAMES BYARS
c/o Kitamura Katsusaburo
73 Kita-Shirakawa Higashi Kubota-cho, Sakyo-ku, Kyoto-shi

From Faculty Housing to the Abe House in Okazaki

In the year between the previous *Indépendant* in 1961 and this one, Byars changed his residence twice. His first move was from the faculty housing in Higashiyama-Nijo to the home of a literary scholar named Abe, located in Okazaki. The address of the Abe house is unknown, but it appears to have belonged to relatives of Abe Hiromu, the Kyoto Municipal Museum of Art curator who was so helpful to Byars. Above all, Byars wanted a larger, quieter space than the cramped faculty housing, somewhere he could work at leisure. He frequently asked Abe Hiromu if he knew of any "good places to live." Each time Abe would write him a letter of introduction providing the potential landlord with details about Byars, sign it, and stamp it with a red seal. Byars appeared to thoroughly enjoy this process, and the letters of introduction of course proved useful.

At the Abe residence in Okazaki, there was a tall zinc-roofed storage shed beside the main house, and this is what Byars rented. He painted it silver inside and out. Though the shed was in back of the house and Byars's paint job couldn't be seen from the street, the lady of the house evidently hated it. After a while, Byars had to move out.

From Okazaki to Kita-Shirakawa

Next Byars moved to the house of Kitamura Katsusaburo in Kita-Shirakawa. This became his favorite residence, and he remained there until around 1965. A typical Japanese-style mansion, it could be seen on a corner of the street that buses take from Higashioji east toward Ginkakuji temple. Katsusaburo's older brother was the businessman and tea ceremony expert Kitamura Kinjiro, who founded the Kitamura Museum, which specializes in antique art and tea utensils. Their father, Kitamura

Matazaemon, was known as "Japan's forestry king."

After World War II, U.S. Occupation troops had requisitioned this large residence. Its tatami flooring had been especially beautiful, but the Americans replaced all the tatami with wood floors and even painted the tokonoma alcoves. Byars was very upset about that. Nonetheless, the long, spacious wood floor on the second story was eminently suitable for producing large paper works or long accordion-folded pieces.

Byars also made a close friend in the neighborhood, a British lady of about seventy named Katharine Ormiston. Her husband was the president of Cathay Bank's Japan branch, and they had moved to Japan after living in Hong Kong. Katharine, an artist, was a frail woman with a slender figure like a Giacometti sculpture, a look that she apparently favored. Her work, too, had a nervous quality. "She would draw a human face inside an oval like an acorn, with vertical lines between the eyes—pictures like that," Taki recalled.

When Byars and Taki visited the couple's house, they were always served *oyako donburi*—bowls of chicken and egg on rice. The couple adhered to this very plain diet, and "walked very quietly, sort of creeping along"—rather plant-like, a rare trait in Westerners. Evidently Byars was quite fond of their delicate attributes.

Parties and Banquets

Abe Hiromu, the former curator at the Kyoto Municipal Museum of Art, remembers a time when he was invited to dinner with Byars at the Kitamura house: "We sat facing each other at a cardboard box table on a wooden floor. The meal was just bread, boiled eggs, and wine, which was poured into plain, undecorated glasses."

Byars was very fond of the Kitamura house, and would often invite his friends there. He also hosted a variety of parties. For instance, there was the "white party," for which he wrote the invitations on white paper with white ink. Though one could tell that something was written there, the text was completely illegible. When asked about it, Byars would say, "I'm hosting a white party. Please come dressed all in white. If you only have black shoes, bring white socks or tabi socks."

When the guests arrived, they entered a room covered in white paper. Everything was white. One could only see the other guests from the neck up. The meal that was served consisted of tofu on white plates, milk in white cups, and white rice. It seems that Byars, who adored the diverse styles and shapes of Japanese dishes, had searched high and low for simple, unadorned white tableware for the occasion, and finally found some at the Noritake shop.

Kodani and Taki both recall that on another occasion he held a "black party." At one such gathering, Taki, clad in a long black dress, welcomed guests and led them into a room where they sat and waited. Taki brought out a large plain silver tray with a single strawberry placed in the middle, which she offered to the guests. Another time, oranges were served, cut evenly and placed neatly on a white plate. On other occasions, only glasses of water were served.

These were not so much performances as vignettes from Byars's daily life. All the guests who visited his house would head home feeling a bit stunned and wondering if they'd been tricked, saying, "That was a strange experience. What was that all about?"

For his part, Byars demanded that his guests adhere to his aesthetic standards. "I don't like how that guest disposed of the skin after he ate the orange," he might complain.

Byars followed his own peculiar muse not only at home but when he went out. Whenever he visited Taki's house he would arrive bearing a single garden poppy. When he visited Abe, from whom he received a lot of assistance, he would always present a red rose to Abe's wife. Every time he went to the Nishiki Market, which was filled with rare food products and the best place to find unusual items, he would purchase exactly one interesting thing and take it home.

Byars's days, from morning to evening, were his art. Every fragment of daily life was a creative work to him. However, his usual artistic method involved re-enacting or reconstructing vignettes he found memorable, rather than using them as fodder for performances or staged events.

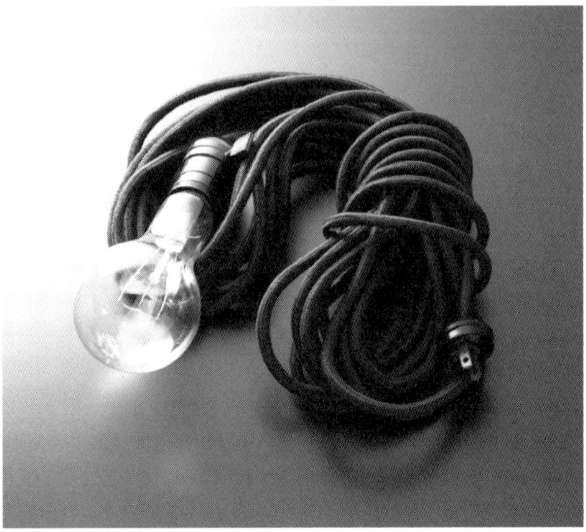

30 A light bulb left behind in Byars's room. He spent considerable time searching for and selecting even the most everyday furnishings

6 Proliferating Exhibitions

Excellence in Contemporary Art Exhibition, Kyoto
(*Gendai bijutsu Kyoto shusaku ten*)
(April 6–19, 1962, Kyoto Municipal Museum of Art)

In 1962 the first *Excellence in Contemporary Art Exhibition, Kyoto (Gendai bijutsu Kyoto shusaku ten)* presented some 160 of the best works in such genres as Nihonga, Western-style painting, sculpture, and crafts by artists from Kyoto (as well as neighboring Shiga prefecture) that had appeared in exhibitions throughout the region in 1961. Held amid much fanfare, it purported to offer a digest of "Kyoto art today." Its sponsor, the *Kyoto shinbun* newspaper, devoted considerable page space to daily reports on the show's success.

> Sponsored by *Kyoto shinbun* with the aim of contributing to the development of the Kyoto art scene, the first *Excellence in Contemporary Art Exhibition* opened today at the Kyoto Municipal Museum of Art in Okazaki. [. . .] With the recent flourishing of art education, the show has enjoyed attendance by a great many elementary, junior high, and high school students, and young people interested in art have come not only from Kyoto city but from outlying parts of the prefecture and Shiga as well. Intriguingly, they seem attracted to abstract paintings, making such comments as "There are no representational forms here, but the colors are superb." Exhibiting artists have also made an appearance; this morning the Western-style artists Yamaoka Koji, Ito Kazunobu, and Zames Bakyars [*sic*] were intently studying other works and comparing them with their own. [Translated from *Kyoto shinbun*, evening edition, April 6, 1962]

Although this exhibition was held annually in April five times through 1967, there are no records of participation by Byars after this first year.

Solo Exhibition

(May 20–28, 1962, Kyoto Municipal Museum of Art)

This was the first of three solo exhibitions by Byars at the Kyoto Municipal Museum of Art. When the museum rented out its galleries it was nearly always to artist groups or organizations hosting open-call exhibitions. Only rarely was space rented to an individual.

> James Byars (29), who is having a solo show at the Kyoto Municipal Museum of Art from May 20 to 28, is a young painter from Detroit, United States. An unusual artist who paints circles and lines with sumi ink on white washi, he came to Kyoto two years ago. Besides studying painting, he currently teaches English conversation at Doshisha University. His first solo exhibition was at Y [Yamada] Gallery in Kyoto in September the year before last. He was also recommended for inclusion in the *Excellence in Contemporary Art Exhibition* hosted by the *Kyoto shinbun.*

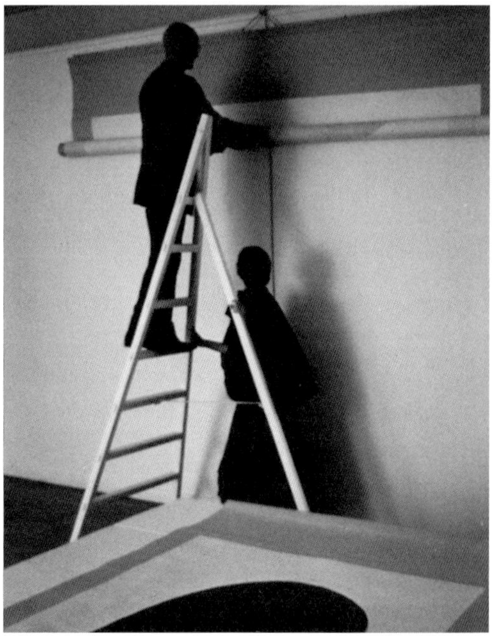

31 Byars and Taki Sachiko hanging a work at his solo exhibition, 1962. Gelatin silver print, $9\frac{15}{16}$ x 8". James Lee Byars Correspondence, I.5, The Museum of Modern Art Archives, New York, cat. no. MA1962, © 2016. Digital image, The Museum of Modern Art, New York/Scala, Florence

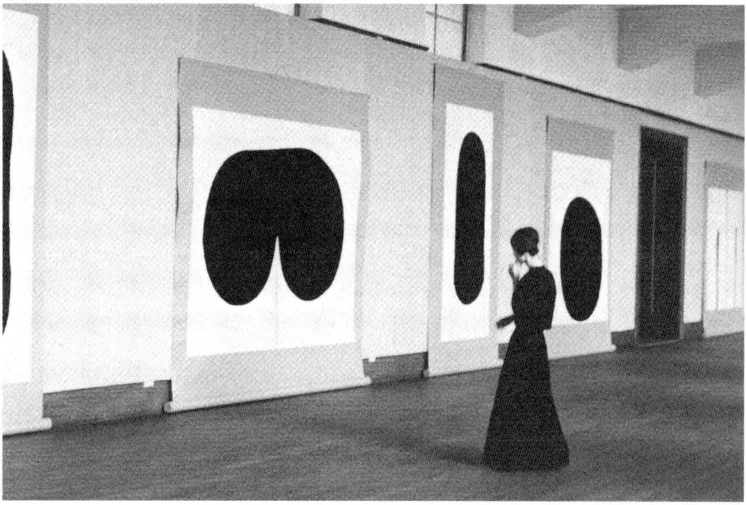

32 Taki Sachiko, wearing a Pierre Cardin dress, at Byars's solo exhibition, 1962

On display are approximately twenty paintings of avant-garde calligraphic art that highlight delicate contrasts between circles and lines. Eight of the works are mounted on pale orange hanging scrolls. A "music box" placed in the center of the gallery plays modern music like that of the American contemporary composer John Cage. Some of Byars's English students from Heian Jogakuin Junior High School show up on occasion to recite the poetry of Gertrude Stein in English. The idea is to have each visitor enjoy the art while sitting in a chair placed in front of the pictures and listening to the music or poetry. Byars casually chats with visitors and explains, "If you view them with a liberated feeling, that's good enough." [Translated from *Kyoto shinbun,* May 22, 1962; reporter: Fuji Yoshiyuki]

"With Music and Poetry: An American's Offbeat Art Show"

Amid a variety of art exhibitions this spring, one conspicuously eccentric solo show opened on the 20th at the [Kyoto Municipal] Museum of Art. Described as an event "with music and poetry," American James Byars's solo exhibition offered 17 or 18 paintings consisting entirely of monochromatic sumi-ink circles and dots on white washi paper, and around five box-shaped objects on which similar paintings had been mounted. Initially he planned to hire a *komuso* Zen priest to play the shakuhachi in the gallery, but gave up because it would "cost too much"

and instead recruited some school girls to recite poetry. Byars (29) (c/o Kitamura Katsusaburo, Kita-Shirakawa Kubota-cho, Sakyo-ku), is from Detroit, USA, where he graduated from Wayne [*sic*] University. He came to Japan two autumns ago. While teaching English at Doshisha and elsewhere, he paints utterly non-figurative works in black and white, imbued with an East Asian sensibility influenced by his background in philosophy, psychology, and Zen. Until the 28th.
[Translated from *Yukan Kyoto*, May 21, 1962]

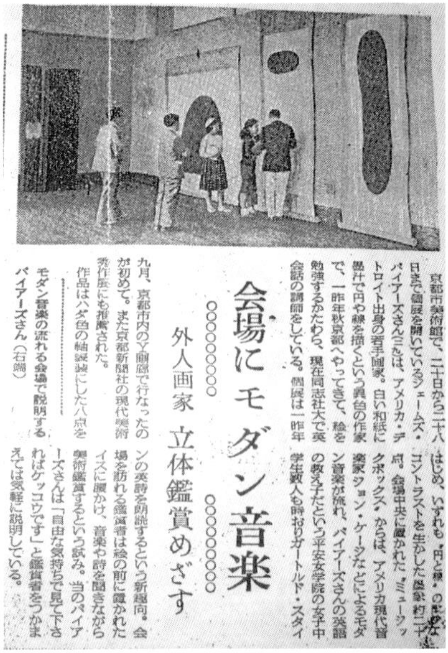

会場にモダン音楽

外人画家 立体鑑賞めざす

京都市美術館で、二十日から二十八日まで個展を開いているジェームズ・バイアーズさん(二九)は、アメリカ・デトロイト出身の若手画家。白い和紙に墨汁で円や線を描くという異色の作家で、一昨年秋京都へやってきて、絵を勉強するかたわら、現在同志社大で英会話の講師をしている。個展は一昨年九月、京都市内の画廊で行なったのが初めて。また京都新聞社の現代美術秀作展にも推薦された。作品はハダ色の軸装にした八点をはじめ、いずれも"円と線"の[illegible]コントラストを生かした墨象約二十点。会場中央に置かれた"ミュージックボックス"からは、アメリカ現代音楽家ジョン・ケージなどによるモダン音楽が流れ、バイアーズさんの英語の教え子だという平安女学院の女子中学生数人も時おりガートルド・スタインの英詩を朗読するという新趣向。会場を訪れる鑑賞者は絵の前に置かれたイスに腰かけ、音楽や詩を聞きながら美術鑑賞するという試み。当のバイアーズさんは「自由な気持ちで見て下さればケッコウです」と鑑賞者をつかまえては気軽に説明している。

モダン音楽の流れる会場で説明するバイアーズさん(右端)

33 *Kyoto shinbun* article on Byars's solo show at the Kyoto Municipal Museum of Art, May 22, 1962

Below is the rental gallery record of the exhibition as archived by the Kyoto Municipal Museum of Art:

May 20–28, 1962
Byars Solo Exhibition
Rooms 101 and 102
Organizer: Taki Sachiko

Rooms 101 and 102 were the first and second galleries on the north side of the first floor. All of Byars's solo shows at the museum were registered under Taki's name.

A sumi-ink painting of an ellipse extending down a long vertical sheet of white paper, visible on the far right in the newspaper photo (Fig. 33), was mounted on the wall as a hanging scroll. To the left of that hung another long scroll of white paper with a horizontal sumi-ink ellipse at the very top. Further to the left was a circle with its top half filled in with sumi ink in the center of a 2 x 2 meter square sheet.

The scroll backings were a muted orange. In the back of the room were two tall boxlike objects, a little over 2 meters high, which looked like stout black columns. Two white ellipses touching each other had been painted in the middle of the left-hand box. Apparently there was another box with a circle painted at the top, from which a long line drawn in crayon extended straight down. These lines and circles were painted only on the front of the boxes, but visitors could walk around and see the other sides.

In the newspaper photo, the man looking on with his arms folded is Abe Hiromu. Behind him stands Fuji Yoshiyuki, the art reporter for the *Kyoto shinbun*. Byars, with his back to the camera, appears to be explaining something to a female visitor.

The work that appeared on the cover of *Gendai no me* (Fig. 25), when Byars participated in *Adventure in Today's Art of Japan* at the National Museum of Modern Art in 1961, was exhibited in the other room. Taki recalls that the white pictures seen in Fig. 34 were each titled *Bird* and that each consisted of a single curved line in pencil.

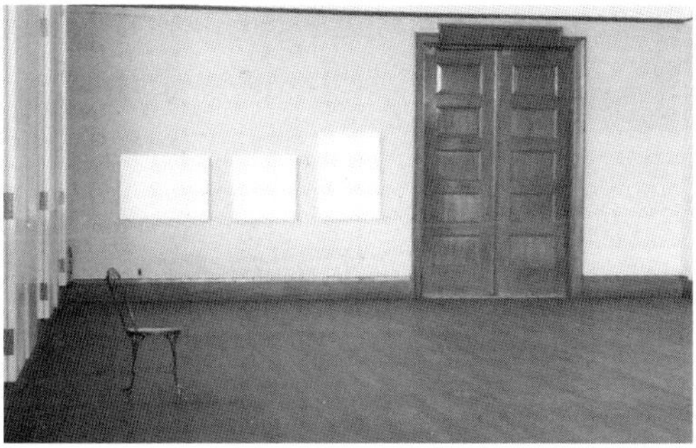

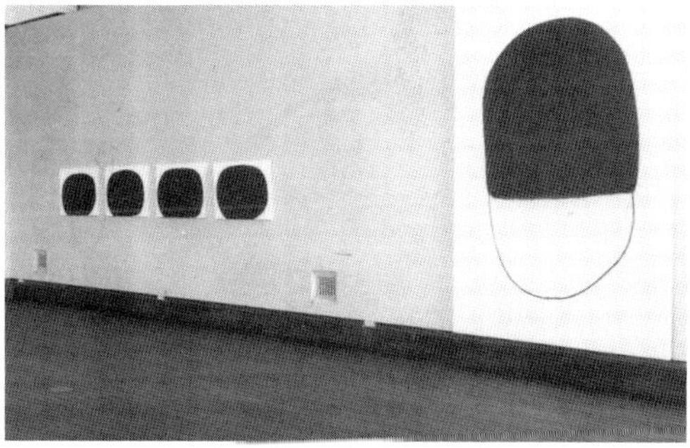

34, 35 Installation views; photos by Abe Hiromu

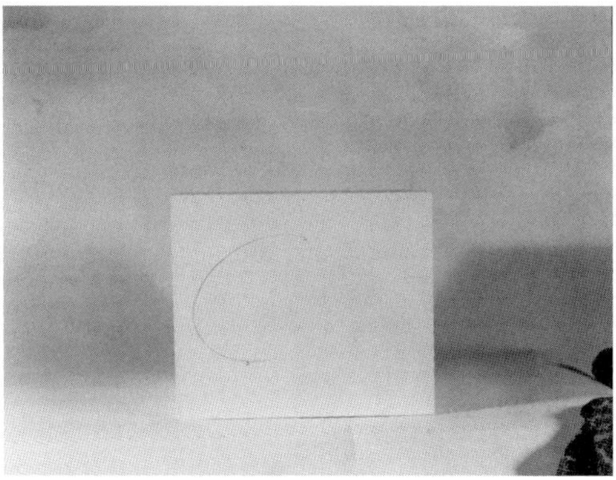

36 *Tori* (Bird), shown in one of the photos of Byars's artwork found at Taki's family home

It is unclear if Gertrude Stein's poems were actually recited at the exhibition. But if so, they probably included the line "Rose is a rose is a rose is a rose." As Kawai Sumie mentioned in her reminiscences ("Memories of James Lee," published in the July 2000 issue of *Bijutsu techo*), Byars often murmured the poem to himself during his Kurashiki days. Taki, too, believes that if anything of Gertrude Stein's was read aloud, it must have been "Rose is a rose is a rose is a rose," although she can't say for certain.

Around this time Byars was always reading a thin book, possibly a first edition, by Gertrude Stein. As previously mentioned, Hubbell, through whose good offices Byars probably got his teaching position at Doshisha University, was close to Stein and was one of the first people to recognize her talent as a poet. Although Stein's poems are in English, when read aloud they could be said to sound somewhat like Buddhist chanting. Besides Stein, Byars was also enamored of the works of Kusano Shinpei and Lafcadio Hearn, both of whom made innovative use of onomatopoeia. For example, Kusano's use of the single character *ru* in the mystical expression "rurururururu rurururururururururururururururu" resonates like a kind of minimal poetic music, one that transcends national and cultural distinctions. Perhaps Byars felt something like *setsuna metsu*, the continual birth and death of moments of time, in expressions that repeat a minimized motion of sound, and applied that sensibility to his exhibitions.

Byars most likely gained his teaching position at Heian Jogakuin through the expatriate community at the YMCA, where information regarding job opportunities of this sort was frequently circulated. Working multiple jobs as he did, his circle of friends, both Japanese and non-Japanese, must have expanded rapidly during this period.

Kyoto Indépendant

(March 6–12, 1963, Kyoto Municipal Museum of Art)

> "Art in Kyoto and Osaka: The Kyoto Indépendant Exhibition" by Tanaka Hisao
>
> This was the seventh *Kyoto Indépendant,* an exhibition launched by a group of young Kyoto painters and later hosted by the city of Kyoto. Over 230 participants submitted more than 480 works. With print art added this year, the show was divided into three sections: Painting, Sculpture, and Prints. Although the longevity of the exhibition reflects the undiminished desire by artists for a venue where they can freely present their work, the participant list seems to have become rather entrenched. The works of the more experienced artists in this exhibition are extremely sophisticated. Ichimura Tsukasa's *Shiro, kuro* (White, black) stood out for its immaculate finish: a dynamic design drawn with black marker pen on whiteboard. Iwata Shigeyoshi's work showcased his skill with dense compositions, while Ryo Kaori created striking images with beautiful colors. As for sculpture,

> Tanaka Kazuo presented some solid works in wood. By contrast, there were few ambitious works by new artists. Fujita Seiyo's submissions, however, succeeded because of their painstaking attention to detail. One consisted of black dots on red fabric, another of a dotted cylinder of rolled white paper, and another of tiles arranged on the floor. Kato Yumiko's *Work* resolutely exposed something of her inner self. The weirdly effective works of James Byars, who is becoming a fixture in Kyoto, also garnered considerable attention. [Translated from *Sansai*, May 1963 issue]

The record of the works Byars presented at this *Indépendant* is as follows (each "0" is the work's title):

> Room 1 (Paintings)
> 0 James Byars
> 0 James Byars
> 0 James Byars

> Curator Abe Hiromu made these notes in his diary:

> March 4: *Indépendant* installation. Byars worked hard again today.
> March 10: *Indépendant* review meeting from 1 pm. Comments and Q&A by Yanaihara [Isaku], Imaizumi [Atsuo], Hariu [Ichiro], Ijima [Tsutomu], in that order. Byars showed up partway through and raised objections, argued a bit about music, then seemed satisfied, saying "Abe-san is fair." Afterward, had a chat at the Kyoto Hotel.

According to Abe, what made this review meeting memorable was that after mentioning an artist whose work had impressed several people, Yanaihara declared, "If a picture is going to be flat, let it be flat. Like Byars's, for example." As for the argument about music, that was because one of the participating artists had played music in the venue, which was not to Byars's liking.

The works Byars exhibited were sumi ink paintings on paper. Not for the first time, they were unframed and unboxed, leaving them exposed during shipment. Since the deliverymen didn't wear gloves in those days, they were touching the works with their bare hands. Byars kept yelling "*Te! Te! Te!* (Hands! Hands! Hands!)" at them in an attempt to warn them not to soil the paintings.

Abe also recalls that Byars, by now "becoming a fixture" at the *Indépendant*, remarked of the exhibition rooms, "This is just like a locomotive!" The layout of the museum, in which a series of long galleries extended from either side of the entrance, following the square shape of the building, must have made him think of train cars linked in tandem.

The 15th *Yomiuri Indépendant* was held in Ueno, Tokyo, at the same time (March 2–15, 1963). In Akasegawa Genpei's book *Tokyo mikisa keikaku* (Tokyo mixer plan) published by Parco Picture Books in 1984, he describes Byars visiting the exhibition, wearing a bowler hat and negotiating the purchase of an art object made of packaging material by Akasegawa. It was typical of Byars, who would not hesitate to travel to Tokyo or anywhere else if something caught his fancy.

Solo Exhibition

(April 2, 1963, Kyoto Municipal Museum of Art)

In nearly every English-language source related to Byars, this one-day exhibition is described as "Two Paintings: James Lee Byars. Exhibition at the National Museum of Modern Art, Kyoto." However, the exhibition was actually held at the Kyoto Municipal Museum of Art, as the museum's records indicate:

> April 2, 1963 One day only
> James Byars Solo Exhibition
> Main Gallery
> Organizer: Taki Sachiko

Black circles of a similar size were painted in sumi ink along a long accordion-folded strip of paper 30 centimeters wide, which was set on its edge and stretched out atop a row of cube-like white pedestals approximately 70 centimeters tall. Chairs were placed in front of the work, designed to invite the visitor to sit and look. The chairs were made of metal tubing, which was curved and twisted in a Western style to form the legs and back. Byars loved sitting on them, calling them "ice cream chairs." At the time many such chairs sat in the lobby of the YMCA, so it seems likely that Byars pilfered some of them for his show.

This may have been the first exhibition where Byars presented an accordion-shaped work. As an invitation he sent out a white envelope (10.1 x 9.8 centimeters) containing a sheet of white paper (9.3 x 9.2 centimeters) with "Kyoto Museum of Modern Art 10 o'clock April 2 paintings James Byars" written on it in white letters. No doubt this is the origin of the notion that the show took place at the National Museum of Modern Art, Kyoto. Also, since there were no commas or periods between the words, "2 paintings" could easily be misread as an exhibition title, which is very likely the source of the erroneous title "Two Paintings." In fact, several paintings were exhibited at 10 am on April 2.

Byars also conducted a performance that day. It consisted of the artist holding the top of the accordion work with his fingers and slowly, teasingly, moving the paper sideways, from one end of the pedestal to the other. When he reached one end, he slowly moved it back the other way. He executed these actions in silence. The accordion was very long when stretched all the way out, so the process, as conducted in this leisurely, tantalizing manner, took considerable time. The sharp angles of the work notwithstanding, Byars's playful movements made it resemble a wriggling caterpillar.

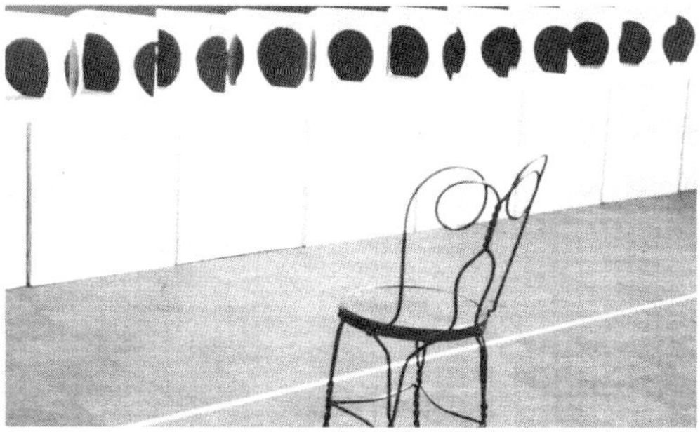

37 Installation view, solo exhibition, 1963

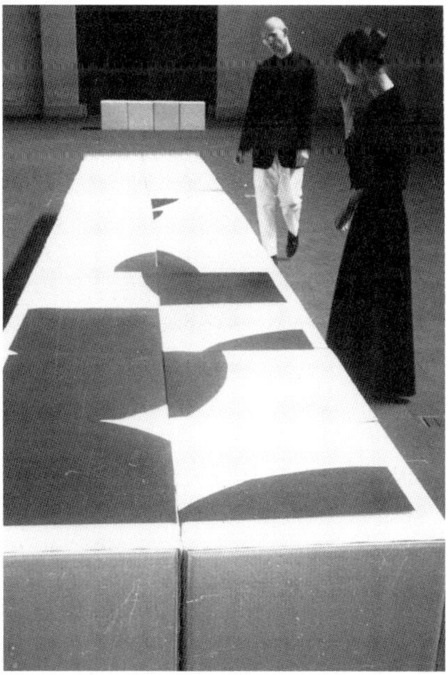

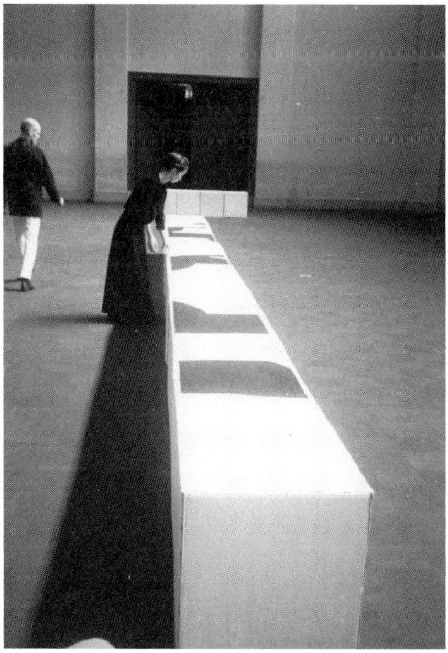

38, 39 Byars and Taki at the exhibition

Ban Fumio, an artist who participated in the *Indépendant* exhibitions and was a close friend of Byars in those days, says, "It was entertaining even from a layman's perspective." Here was a literal example of "performable paper."

There are photographs (Figs. 38 and 39) that show other works similarly laid out atop rows of white pedestals. According to Taki, Byars created these works by painting shapes in black sumi ink on large 3 x 6 *shaku* (approximately 90 x 180 centimeters) sheets of hemp paper, then cutting them into sections, which he enjoyed reassembling in new configurations. In the photos, Taki appears in a Pierre Cardin dress.

Although I cannot say with certainty that the idea for the invitation with white letters on white paper came from Kazimir Malevich's *White on White,* it surely had some impact on Byars's aesthetic sensibilities since his friend Hubbell was a fan of the work and spoke of it often. (*Suprematist Composition: White on White* is in the collection of the Museum of Modern Art, New York.) As with his "white party," Byars applied this concept of white letters on white paper to many occasions.

The Third Trip Home: Early September to Late December 1963

On November 16, 1963, Byars held a solo exhibition at Richard Bellamy's Green Gallery, located at 15 West 57th Street in New York City. It was for just the one day, however, and only from 8 pm to midnight. Another show in New York, on November 21 at the Leo Castelli Gallery at 4 East 77th Street, also lasted only four hours, from noon to 4 pm. Byars further mentions "BRECHT – BYARS – AND," an event he describes as taking place "intermittently for 21 days and nights" at 200½ East 88th Street.

At the two galleries, Byars exhibited works in sumi ink on washi, which he had prepared in Japan. They appear to have been "performable paper," incorporating such elements as expanding scrolls, interchangeable parts, and rows of white boxes. Both shows involved audience participation and were limited to four hours. MoMA's archives contain photos of both the Green and Castelli performances. According to the art historian Judith Stein, who has done considerable research on the Green Gallery, Byars "constructed a platform of 100 hand-made white boxes that ran the length" of the Green Gallery floor, and his "accomplice" was dressed in a Balenciaga gown. The dancer Yvonne Rainer "wore a black dress and heels, and danced improvisationally around [what Rainer described as] the 'sea of white boxes,' as Andy Warhol's film camera whirled."

In his somewhat sardonic review of the Green show, *Village Voice* columnist John Wilcock also mentions a young girl reading poetry by Edith Sitwell:

> A couple of hundred people turned up at the Green Gallery a few weeks ago to watch a sombrely clad artist, James Lee Byars, unroll large black and white scrolls atop a table of 100 white cardboard boxes. Occasionally the boxes were rearranged and a small girl would be sent in to read some of Edith Sitwell's poetry. The child, at least, was greeted with scattered applause. Numerically, at any rate, the show was a success, and because its venue was the important Green Gallery, it must be presumed that Byars' motives were serious. [John Wilcock, "The Village Square: An Outsider's View of the 'In' Art Scene (3)," *The Village Voice*, January 23, 1964]

In an essay titled "Accomplishments" that Byars submitted to the John Simon Guggenheim Memorial Foundation in 1964, he mentions "a four hour performance done on a change stage of 100 paper boxes January 1, 1963." In one of his diary entries, Abe writes: "January 1, 1963: Unable to go to Byars's show after all." Although he recalls that the performance in question was at a temple in Kyoto, he isn't sure. In any case it appears that Byars's four-hour performances with paper began as early as New Year's Day, 1963, and included the event on April 2 at the Kyoto Municipal Museum of Art and the two at New York galleries that November.

Also of interest is Byars's brief description of his New York events in the "Accomplishments" essay: "Oct Back to NY for exhibitions at Green and Castelli and one at 200½ East 88 which was done by stating the possibility and cancel."

In his diary, Abe Hiromu describes meeting Byars in early January 1964, just after he had returned to Japan:

> January 3, 1964: Phoned Byars. Met in the museum coffee shop, our first meeting in about half a year. Dressed all in black as usual and in good humor as usual. Gave me a single bean wrapped in cellophane as a present. Invited Byars and Ms. Taki [to my house] on the 12th.
> January 12, 1964: Byars arrived around 5 pm and presented a single poppy and a balloon as gifts.

Kyoto Indépendant

(March 7–13, 1964, Kyoto Municipal Museum of Art)

> "Fine Arts in Kyoto and Osaka" by Tanaka Hisao
>
> The *Kyoto Indépendant* (Kyoto Municipal Museum of Art, March 7–13, 1964) is held annually in Kyoto and took place again this year. The show included some 320 paintings, 23 prints, and 32 sculptures or works in

> other media. Although there were no salient changes from last year, one could see a growing trend toward pop art. However, there were exceptions. Artists such as Ichimura Tsukasa have gravitated toward the tableau style of oil painting. The participation of some avant-gardists from Nagoya was also a departure from last year. Highlights included works by Ogura Koji, Kinashi Aine, Sakamoto Masaya, and Kotsu Mitsuo, each of whom staked out a distinct domain of expression. Byars's sophisticated works also remain fresh in my mind for their uniqueness. As has happened before, some "anti-art" works were removed partway through the exhibition after a feud between the museum and the artists. Better that they had engaged in sufficient dialogue before the opening. Regardless of the reasons given, removing works in the middle of a show is an unsatisfactory solution. [Translated from *Sansai*, May 1964 issue]

The works Byars exhibited were listed as follows by the Kyoto Municipal Museum of Art:

Room 12 (Paintings)
Object L. BYARS
Object L. BYARS
Object L. BYARS

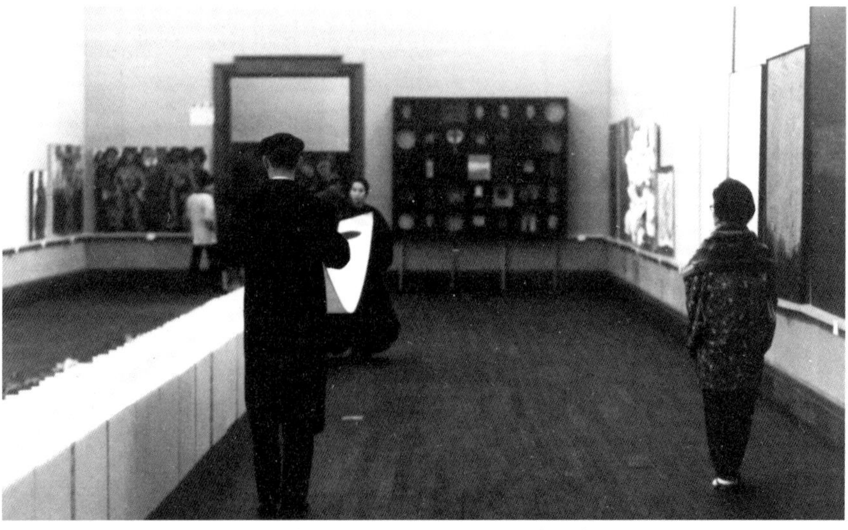

40 Byars and Taki unrolling a scroll-like work at the 1964 *Kyoto Indépendant*

A photograph from this exhibition (Fig. 40) shows Byars in a hunting cap, unrolling one of his works with Taki Sachiko. A long, scroll-like piece, it has a sumi-ink ellipse with a single, very long black line extending from it all the way to the end of the sheet. The work on top of the row of pedestals at left is made of accordion-folded *togasenshi* ("Chinese-style" calligraphy paper produced in Japan). It is not known what the third work looked like.

The bulky black dress Taki was wearing at this performance was one Byars bought in New York. He also had the performer at his Green and Castelli shows wear this outfit. Designed by Balenciaga, it consisted of a voluminous, balloon-like silk blouse and double-layered skirt. Because it was so unwieldy, Taki says, she had a rag dealer in Japan dispose of it some years later. In hindsight, she admits it was a shame she got rid of it.

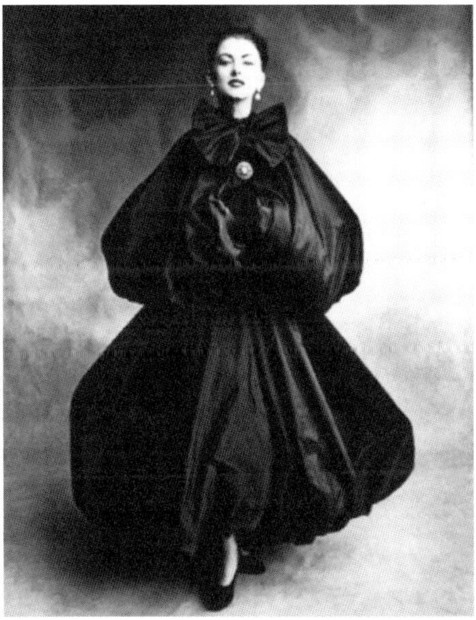

41 A model in the Balenciaga dress, photographed by Irving Penn, from the September 1950 issue of *Vogue*

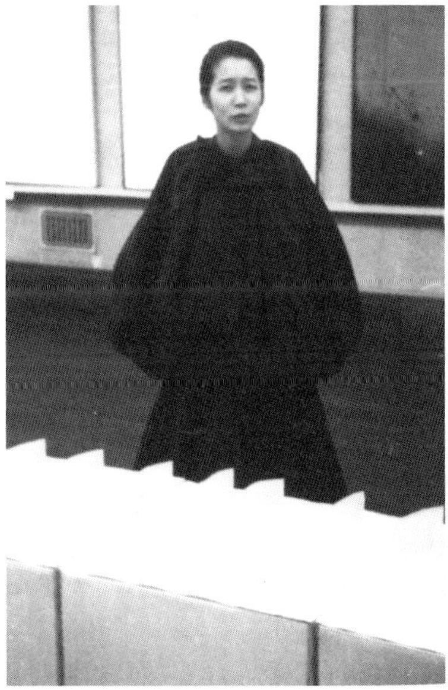

42 Taki Sachiko in the dress, standing behind one of Byars's works at the 1964 *Kyoto Indépendant*

7 Performances at Zen Temples

Shokokuji, June 21, 1964, 5–7 pm

Byars exhibited one of his accordion works at Shokokuji, a prominent Zen Buddhist temple in northern Kyoto, on June 21, 1964. The show took the form of a performance in which he expanded and contracted the work as if it were a caterpillar (Fig. 43).

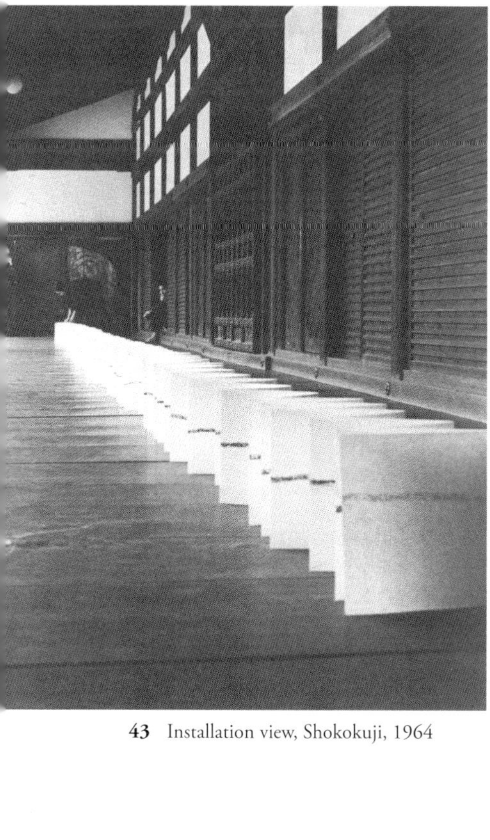

43 Installation view, Shokokuji, 1964

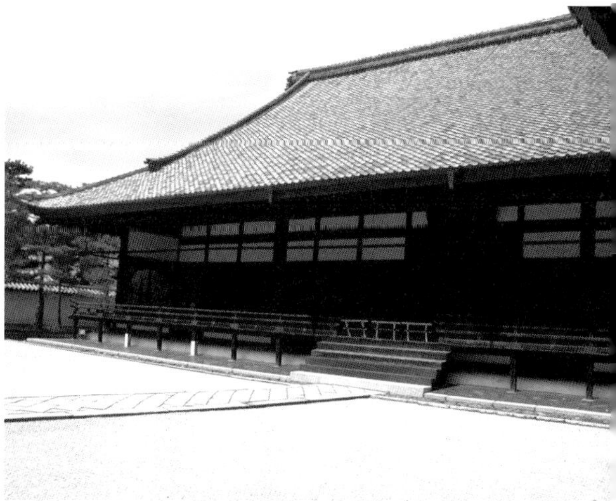

44 The Abbot's Quarters of Shokokuji today (photo courtesy of Shokokuji)

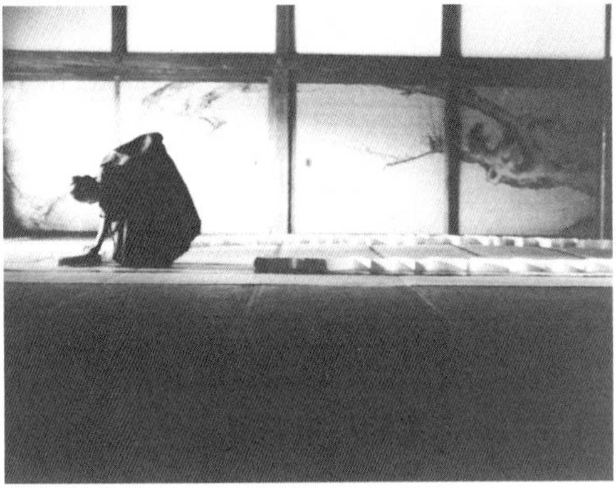

45 Installation view, Shokokuji, 1964

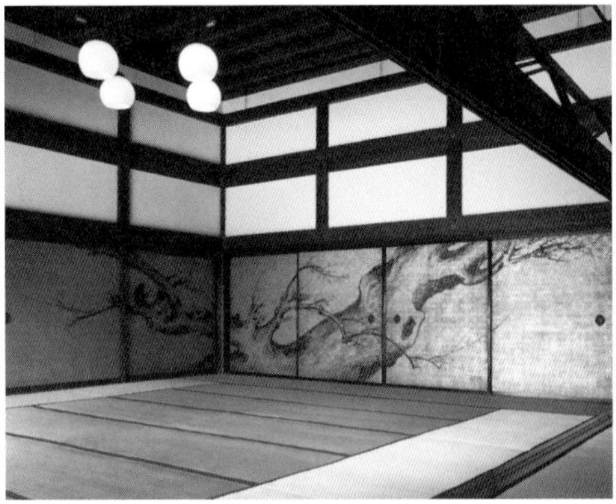

46 The same room as it appears today (photo courtesy of Shokokuji)

Taki recalls that she spread Byars's accordion piece from end to end on the long, veranda-like porch of the temple. She was wearing the gorgeous Balenciaga dress and had her long black hair tied back. Byars stared intently at Taki's movements, leaning on the wooden entrance at the end of the veranda, which carried a painting of a white elephant. A foreigner, identity not known, sat at the entrance to the room behind the porch.

There was an audience crowding close in to the spectacle, standing two or three deep in the garden and absorbed in the performance. Writhing like a snake, Byars's white "accordion" generated an exquisite tension amid the ancient architecture of Shokokuji, with its contrast of white plaster and blackened wooden doors and pillars.

1 x 200 Foot Paper was, as the title suggests, a 1 x 200 foot (approximately 30 centimeters x 60 meters) accordion work, folded every 20 centimeters or so. A line drawn with black crayon started at one end, a little below the midpoint of the paper. The 60-meter long line gradually climbed higher, finally ending a little above the midpoint. Later, Byars donated the work to the Museum of Modern Art in New York.

On another occasion, Byars held a performance in a large chamber in the Abbot's Quarters (Hojo) of Shokokuji, on tatami flooring enclosed by *fusuma* sliding panels covered with a massive painting of a plum tree. Taki, all in black, spread out a thin paper accordion work so that it formed a large ellipse, filling the room (see Fig. 45). A sliding door at one end was open and sunlight shone in, giving a bright luster to the tatami and the painting.

A 1,000 Foot White Chinese Paper, the work that Taki spread out at Shokokuji, is now in the collection of the Carnegie Museum of Art in Pittsburgh, Pennsylvania.

Its dimensions are 4 inches x 800 feet (approximately 10 centimeters x 250 meters), folded every 30 centimeters or so. The material is an extremely thin paper, probably *togasenshi*.

Among Byars's other performances in the Hojo of Shokokuji, one involved a work that expanded into a cross, while another—a huge circular sheet of paper—filled the whole room (in fact, it was too large to unfold in its entirety).

An entry dated August 2, 1964 in a journal on events at Shokokuji, kept by the head of the temple office, reads: "Two chalk pictures and three white pictures on columns were accepted as donations from Mr. James Byars, c/o Kitamura Katsusaburo, 73 Kita-Shirakawa Higashi Kubota-cho, Sakyo-ku." The "three white pictures on columns" may have referred to the works exhibited in Byars's solo show at the Kyoto Municipal Museum of Art in May 1962 (visible at left in the newspaper photo in **Fig. 33**), but it is not clear what the "two chalk pictures" were. Nor is it known if any of these works were ever displayed at Shokokuji.

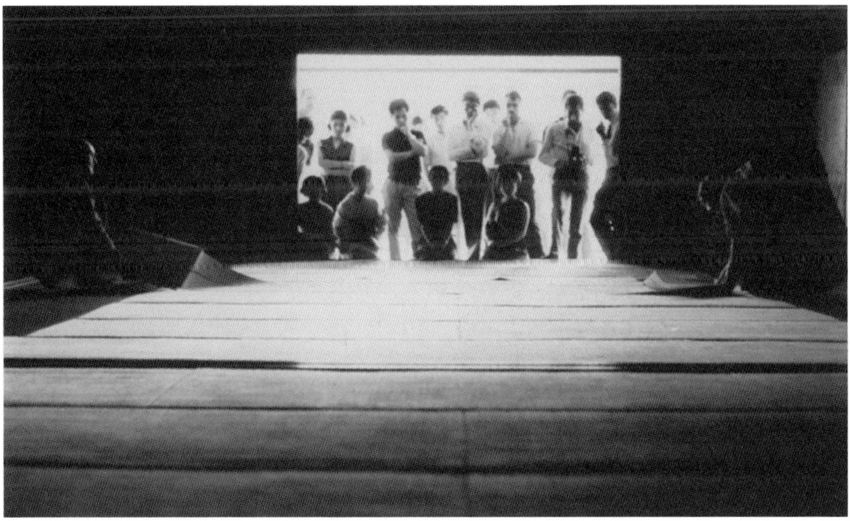

47 Byars and Taki laying out a work at Shokokuji, 1964. Image courtesy of the University of California, Berkeley Art Museum and Pacific Film Archive; bequest of James Elliott

In his 1964 "Accomplishments" essay for the Guggenheim Foundation, Byars wrote that on July (actually June) 21, he "rented a Temple Sokokuji Hojyo and did a processional using all rooms and gardens for single object presentation." Taki recalls, "For the Shokokuji performances I always wore that dress, which in itself was exhausting."

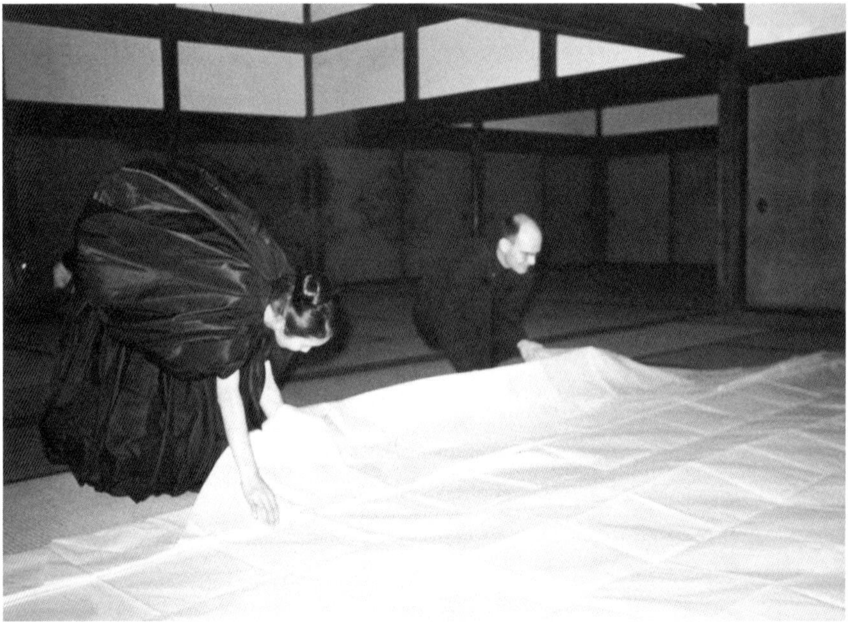

48 View of Byars's performance at Shokokuji, 1964. Gelatin silver print, 4 $\frac{1}{4}$ x 6 $\frac{1}{4}$". Photo: Simon Blackall. James Lee Byars Correspondence, I.6, The Museum of Modern Art Archives, New York, cat. no. MA2805, © 2016. Digital image, The Museum of Modern Art, New York/Scala, Florence

Performance at Daitokuji

Taki remembers that Byars also planned a performance and exhibition during this period at Shinjuan (literally, "Pearl Temple"), one of the sub-temples in the vast Zen temple complex of Daitokuji. Byars was evidently quite taken with Shinjuan, both the name and the venue. For unknown reasons, however, the performance ultimately took place in the *genkan* (entryway) adjacent to the famous rock garden at Daisen'in, another sub-temple next door to Shinjuan.

A large cardboard box, covered with white paper—probably *togasenshi*—was placed in the *genkan*. The interior of the box formed a small room. The entrance to this room was like the *nijiriguchi* entry to a traditional Japanese teahouse in that it could only be negotiated in a crouched position, one person at a time. Inside it was pitch dark. Something like a piece of paper with a small circle drawn on it hung on the far wall. The idea was that each visitor would proceed to the back and strain to see that circle.

The box with the *nijiriguchi* was quite clearly Byars's vision of a teahouse. In the act of crawling through the tiny entrance, everyone gathering for a tea ceremony in that space becomes equal. New encounters and conversations occur in the spirit of *ichigo ichie* (one time, one meeting), which lies at the heart of the tea ceremony.

Emerging from bright daylight into the unlit room, the bewildered guests would first try to orient themselves. Then a silent communication with the darkness would begin. Disruptive emotions would evaporate, the mind would calm, and the senses would sharpen. That was Byars's objective. The eyes of the guests would gradually adapt to the dark and enable them to see their surroundings. Inside the empty box, the small circle would slowly appear, beckoning the guests to approach it, wondering, "What is that?"

A circle drawn with a single stroke of the brush is a calligraphic tradition in Zen. Conjuring up the image of a window in which the painter's own mind appears, it is sometimes called a "circular window." A symbol of absolute truth, it is also described as the shape of enlightenment, or of the entire cosmos. The interpretation is meant to be left to the beholder. The name Shinjuan, with its evocation of a perfect circle like a beautiful pearl, must have charmed Byars. There of all places, he no doubt felt, enlightenment could be found in the contemplation of a simple circle.

There is an amusing anecdote about this installation. A French couple visiting Daitokuji that day encountered Byars's event by chance. According to Taki, Byars persuaded the extremely tall husband to enter the room through the *nijiriguchi*. But when his wife tried to follow him, she got stuck in the entrance because her backside was too big. Although they knew it was rude, the onlookers couldn't help laughing.

Byars wrote the following about his vision for the installation: "I WANT A PEARL TEMPLE WITH AN OPEN DOOR A COUPLE OF FEET HIGH SO THAT PEOPLE HAVE TO CRAWL IN."

An entry appears in Abe's diary about the Daitokuji event:

> February 1, 1963: Invited by Byars to a "White Plum Blossom Celebration" at Shinjuan, Daitokuji. Entered the Daitokuji grounds for the first time in quite a while. Some snow still left in the corner of the garden. Dew on the moss was lovely. Spent half an hour in the Hojo. Saw Daisen'in on the way back.

The circle, along with the ○△□ trio of symbols representing the Zen mind, are also part of Shintoism, and can even be found in ancient Egypt. They are humanity's oldest, simplest, and most evocative symbols. In Zen the triangle represents the shape of the body in seated meditation, when the self and the Buddha are one. The square suggests a frame, the constraints that no longer bind the enlightened mind.

Byars sensed a fathomless beauty in the profound meaning of these simple forms and devoted his life to pursuing it.

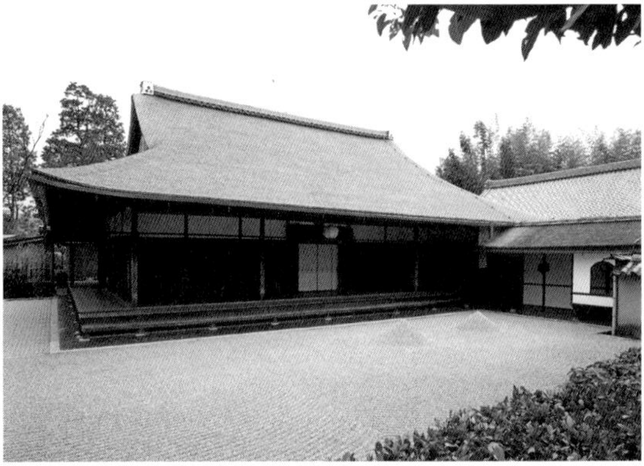

49 The "ocean" section of the rock garden at Daisen'in. Visible under the eaves at right is the *genkan* entryway, the oldest such structure in Japan and a National Treasure. Photo: Mizuno Katsuhiko, courtesy of Daisen'in

Interest in Buddhism

It appears that Byars often made unreasonable demands to hold events at temples and shrines. The exhibitions and performances at Shokokuji and Daitokuji were among those rare instances when his willfulness carried the day.

Daitokuji and Shokokuji are both Zen temples. Another American closely associated with these same two temples is the poet Gary Snyder. Part of the YMCA community and a friend of Byars, Snyder studied Zen and lived both at Shokokuji and at Ryosen'an, part of Daitokuji, between 1956 and 1968. Snyder, who had been interested in Buddhism prior to his arrival in Japan, also knew a lot about the Nishi Honganji branch of the Jodo Shinshu (True Pure Land) school of Buddhism, since he had frequented the New York Buddhist Church affiliated with Nishi Honganji.

Mas Kodani, the Japanese-American who taught English at the YMCA, was studying at Ryukoku University, which is affiliated with Jodo Shinshu, and says that Snyder and Byars often asked him questions about Buddhism. Snyder was working on a translation of *Rinzai roku (The Record of Linji)* with the American Zen Buddhist scholar Ruth Fuller Sasaki. The notoriously "wild and friendly" Snyder often held reading parties, tea parties and drinking parties at his home. It is likely that Byars learned about Zen from Snyder at these gatherings, then visited Shokokuji and Daitokuji as his fascination grew. It is unknown if the performances at these two temples were facilitated by Snyder, but his presence must have helped open their gates to a foreign artist.

That would not have been the only reason Byars gained entry, of course. Zen temples have long been intimately associated with the arts. Cultural pioneers like Zeami, who perfected the Noh theater during the Muromachi period (1336–1573), and Sen no Rikyu, who made an art of the tea ceremony during the Momoyama period (1573–1600), were both connected to Zen temples. Daitokuji in particularly had welcomed foreigners interested in Zen and Buddhism since before the war, a notable example being Jon Carter Covell, the first Westerner to receive a doctorate in Oriental art history, which she completed at Columbia University. There were also non-Japanese Zen monks. Thus it was not such a radical departure for a Zen temple to open its gate to a non-Japanese artist.

The Beauty of the Moment: *Setsuna Metsu*

Byars was concerned with introducing the concept of impermanence into art. A core element of his works and performances is the nature of passing time, viewed as *setsuna*: a series of transitory instants that could be missed with the blink of an eye. In Buddhism, the *setsuna* is the smallest unit of time; *setsuna metsu* is a Japanese phrase conveying the disappearance of every present moment just as it arrives. The previous *setsuna* vanishes as the next one appears, followed by the next; this continues on into infinity as *setsuna* come and go, moment by moment.

Art is of the moment, for it is in the moment that beauty is born, then fades away, again and again. Byars thought of art as existing for only an instant, as if triggered by the rise and fall of a single *setsuna*. It was in that spirit that he would create a makeshift teahouse and invite visitors to enter. The tea master Sen no Rikyu's philosophy of *ichigo ichie* (one time, one meeting) forms an undercurrent in the art of the tea ceremony, which is devised to encourage participants to treasure every transient encounter—in other words, to fully experience every present moment even as it slips into the past while another moment is born.

Byars's trajectory as an artist strongly suggests that the concept of *setsuna metsu* was fundamental to his aspirations. Believing that true beauty is by definition ephemeral, he wanted to make his audience aware of every passing moment.

"11 o'clock Sharp"

Byars also presented exhibitions at Kyoto temples in the form of thirty-second performances. Mas Kodani remembers a written invitation from Byars that said something like "Exhibition in front of the temple at 11 o'clock sharp."

"I don't remember which temple it was, but I'm pretty sure it was somewhere in

Higashiyama," Kodani says. He arrived a little late. When he got there, Byars's "exhibition" was already over. Byars himself was gone, so Kodani asked someone who had been there about it. He learned that Byars had appeared in front of the temple at precisely 11 o'clock and quickly unrolled something that appeared to be a painting on a hanging scroll, which he just as quickly rolled back up. That was it. Byars only had to prepare a spot to hang the scroll, then wait till 11 o'clock. The performance was less than thirty seconds long. It seems that Byars held such performances many times at various locations but always in front of temples and shrines. When asked why they would last only thirty seconds, his answer was inevitably, "Because that's life."

According to Kodani, Byars was always talking about something like the *ichigo ichie* of Buddhism: "The real thing is always just for a moment. Time is the continuation of that, but actually there is no such thing as time." Whenever Byars came up with an idea or question about something, he would ask Kodani, "What about in Buddhism?"

The *setsuna metsu* of every instant. Born, then dying. "Moment by moment. A beautiful thing is just that." It fades away in a moment, appearing only to disappear.

Taki also recalls such performances, including some details regarding the scrolls: one was just a circle drawn on paper mounted with silver leaf; another featured a black line plunging straight down. They were all quite long, approximately 2 meters, and mounted on paper of the same orange color. Byars had a string attached to the backing with which to hang it somewhere. He would quickly hang it, unroll it, roll it back up, and that was it. He did this wherever he could.

In *The Perfect Moment*, a Byars exhibition catalogue published by Instituto Valenciano de Arte Moderno in 1995, this performance is described as "the unrolling of a scroll that had been wound round three bamboo sticks. These sticks can be put together like a fishing-rod and Byars is thus able to move easily around the city and display the scroll when and where he wants."

Event in the Gosho, August 8, 1964

Byars considered August 8, 1964 to be a once-in-a-lifetime opportunity since the date could be read 8 x 8 = 64, the sort of wordplay that appealed to him. Byars never chose an ordinary day for his events if he could help it.

On the evening of the 8th he ceremoniously conducted a mysterious event, later referred to as the "Midnight Parade," at the Gosho (Kyoto's old Imperial Palace). A few days beforehand Byars prepared invitations. The words "Gosho south mon midnight 8-8-64 Byars" were printed in black on a 3 x 81 centimeter sheet of black paper, more like a long piece of paper tape, which he enclosed in a 10.5 x 82 centimeter white envelope. These invitations were handed to each participant in advance of the midnight event. Of course, the invitations were made by special order.

On the night of August 8, some twenty participants gathered at the "south mon" (south gate) of the Gosho. They were met in front of the gate by Byars, dressed in a black formal suit, and Taki Sachiko, in the black Balenciaga dress. Both of them had their index fingers to their lips, gesturing to the participants not to speak.

Midnight approached while the participants silently waited. At last, the hour came. A leisurely procession began. The group strolled in complete silence from the south gate of the Gosho to the opposite end of the precinct. Taki walked along holding up something folded into a square. The object she carried was a work by Byars entitled *The Perfect Black Circle*, a 10-meter diameter black paper circle. It had been brought to the Gosho folded up in a heavy paulownia-wood box. The box's lid was opened, the procession began, the procession ended, the lid was shut. That was the entire performance.

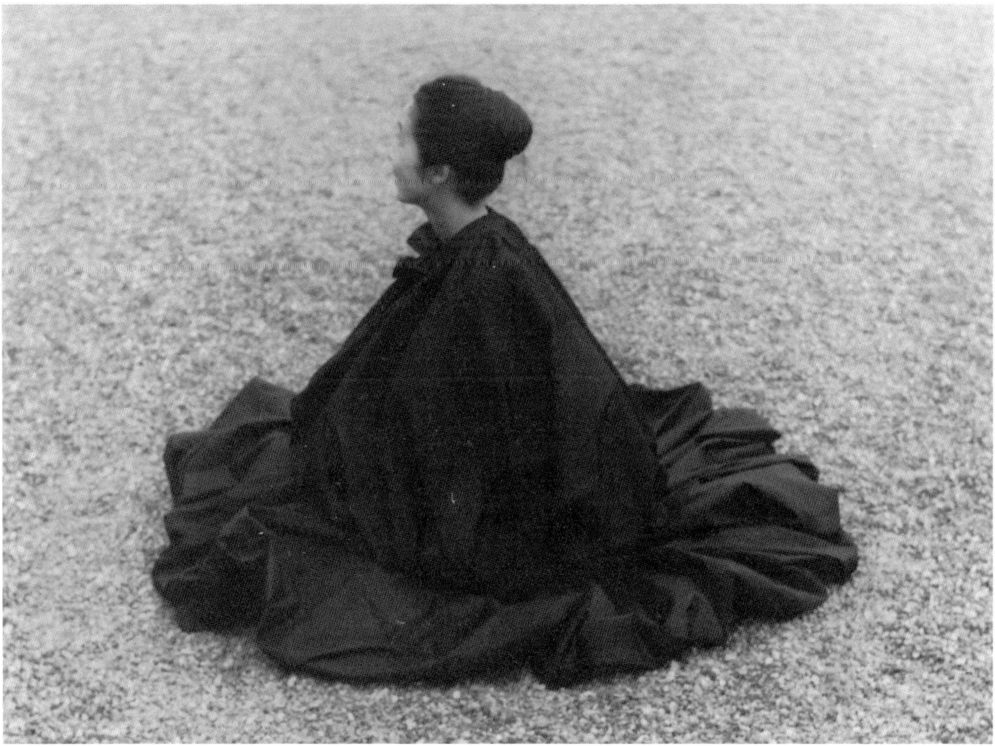

50 Taki Sachiko sitting on the gravel path of the Gosho

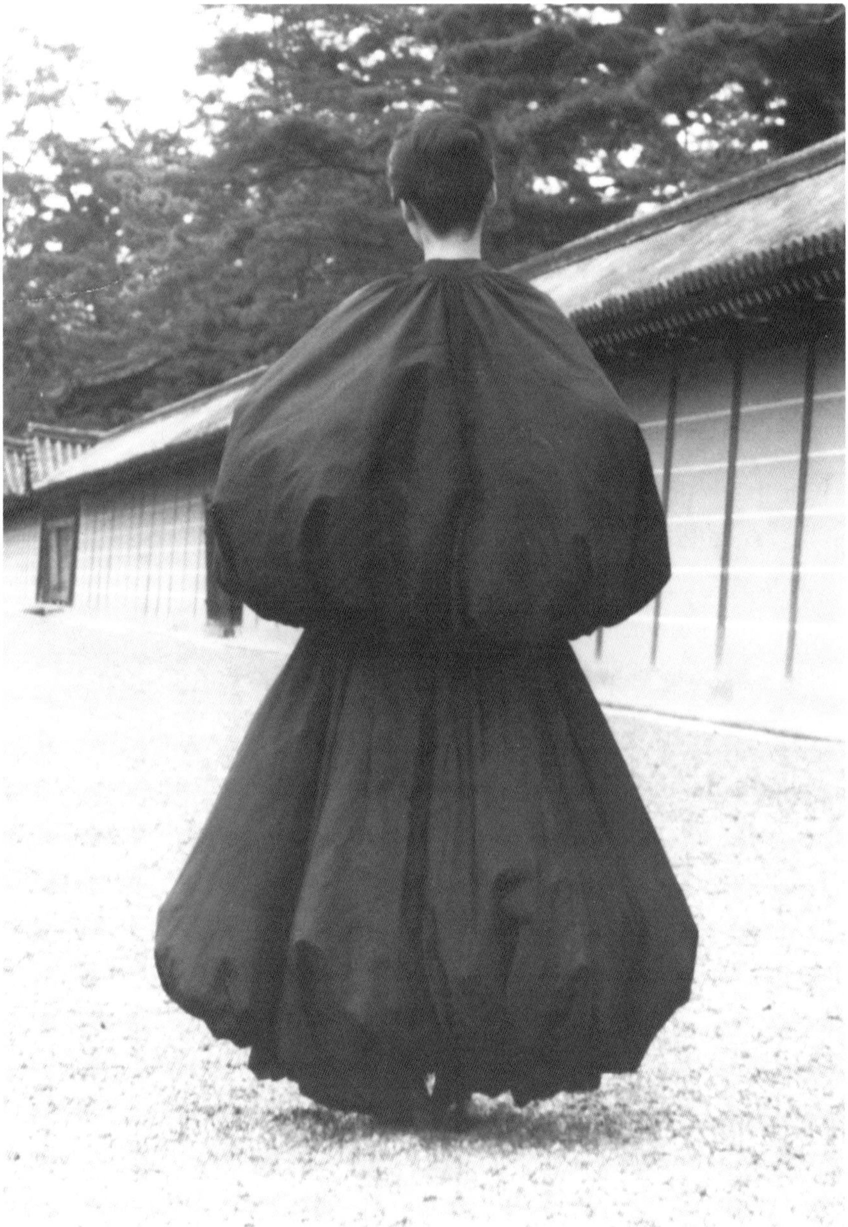

51 Taki Sachiko wearing a Balenciaga dress for the Midnight Parade, Imperial Palace, Kyoto, 1964. Image courtesy of the University of California, Berkeley Art Museum and Pacific Film Archive; bequest of James Elliott. Photo © Simon Blackall

The Gosho at midnight was absolutely quiet and pitch dark. Only the sound of footsteps on the gravel path reverberated in the air. Crunch . . . crunch . . . The sound was unspeakably beautiful and at the same time quite haunting.

With his black inscription on the long black paper invitation, Byars no doubt was suggesting a path to be walked together in the dark. In this utter darkness, the only source of illumination was the moon. As people's eyes gradually grew acclimatized, a faint sight emerged: white gravel lit by moonlight.

This was surely Byars's intended message: Hear the sound of your footsteps on the gravel. Listen carefully. Enjoy the silence. Experience something you would ordinarily not notice at all.

After closing the box, Byars left the scene, still mute. The participants, too, ended their procession and dispersed without a word spoken.

The Fourth Trip Home: Late August to Early December 1964

From the diary of Abe Hiromu:

> August 21, 1964: Byars showed up early this morning, said he was leaving today. It was around four and I was making some copies with Ito (from the photography shop) when who should arrive in a cab but Byars for a final farewell. We said a few words and he squeezed my hand so hard it hurt. Said the lotuses were beautiful and ran out.

That year, white lotus flowers had bloomed across the entire surface of the pond in the garden behind the Kyoto Municipal Museum of Art. Their profusion was something almost mystical to behold, and no one knew who had planted them there. When Abe told Byars, "White lotuses bloomed but nobody knows where they came from," Byars evidently found the notion enchanting and took a look at the blossoms before leaving for the United States.

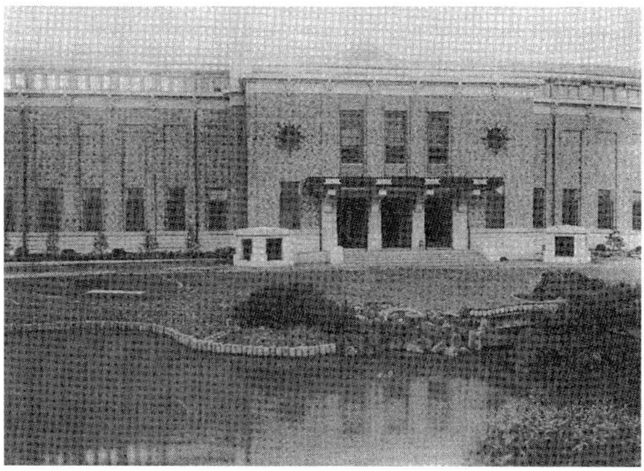

52 View from the East Garden behind the Kyoto Municipal Museum of Art, looking toward the museum's main building. The pond can be seen in the foreground. Photo: Kyoto Municipal Museum of Art, 1974

Here I would like to reproduce, unaltered and unabridged, Byars's essay "Accomplishments," which he submitted to the Guggenheim Foundation as part of a funding application. It's a valuable document that articulates his extravagant artistic vision, including some utterly infeasible proposals.

ACCOMPLISHMENTS

> My accomplishments since 1961. Willard Gallery Show Oct, Spring Show at the Kyoto City Museum. a four hour performance done on a change stage of 100 paper boxes January 1, 1963. a 4 minute exhibition at the Kyoto Imperial Palace Grounds at sunup. Oct Back to NY for exhibitions at Green and Castelli and one at 200-1/2 East 88 which was done by stating the possibility and cancel. flew Back to my English teaching position in Japan 1964. July 21 Rented a Temple SOKOKUJI HOJYO and did a processional using all rooms and gardens for single object presentation. Had a farewell parade Exhibition through the Kyoto Imperial Palace 8-8-64/Midnight. Am in NY Currently having a series of Oct shows: First "10-10 10AM 100 places 100 Men" A 5 gallery (Castelli, Elkon, Green, Kornblee, Willard) simultaneity/theoretical Oct 25 12-1 PM. To have an exact length Wall street Gold String Parade at 5 Oclock Oct 31. Have a distended event, an 8 mile long line x 4 inches which I am trying to get dropped over the US Plains from satellite after Being announced internationally, instantaneously from tel-star including a jet chartered north major city pickup of audience, including the Orient "of course it is astronomy". on my way to NY I had 18 MOBILE/BUS days for an exhibition tour stopping 8 seconds in the middle of the Golden Gate Bridge, 4 seconds at the Geographical Center of the US and 4 seconds in the Whitesands Desert. My entire Current exhibition materials weigh 16 KG, One suitcase full. I am equipped to handle time from 1/2500 MS up and single object areas 1/2 cm to 800 ground feet/10 works this is up to date with my exhibitions Oct 13 1964.

Around this time, Byars told Dorothy Miller that he wanted to donate one of his works anonymously to the Museum of Modern Art. He did in fact donate several works a few days later. A memo from Miller to Alfred Barr, then the museum's Director of Collections, describes the transaction:

October 27, 1964
Gift offered - James Byars

To: Alfred Barr
From: Dorothy Miller

Dear Alfred :

James Byars, a young man who has lived in Japan and who has been in New York for several weeks, called me this week to say that he is now leaving New York and would like to donate to the Museum one of his works. He said he wanted the gift to be anonymous and his name to be suppressed also as artist of the work.

The work is made of very, very thin delicate Japanese or Chinese paper measuring 16 x 32 feet. It is folded so that it fits into a small box. He has used this object in "exhibitions" in Japan. The exhibition consists of having a beautiful young Japanese girl, Miss Taki of Kyoto, unfold the paper in a long serpentine strip which stands up by itself on the ground.

The Carnegie International
(October 30, 1964 to January 10, 1965)

Byars held a series of three performances with "performable paper" as part of the Carnegie International (then known as the Pittsburgh International), an exhibition at the Carnegie Museum of Art in Pittsburgh, Pennsylvania. The performances took place on November 6, 1964 (during the International), and on January 13, 1965 and October 25, 1965 (after the exhibition closed).

The November 6 performance was held at noon in the museum's sculpture court. A Catholic nun, dressed in her habit, entered the court bearing, like an offering, the accordion-folded white paper work *1 x 50 Foot Drawing.* Proceeding to the center, the nun very gradually unfolded the work with her hands; when fully extended, it took the shape of a cross. She then folded the paper back to its original dimensions, again very slowly.

This work, which had been made in Japan, was shaped into a large cross by joining several sheets of paper together. Taki recalls that Byars used an inch-thick piece of black crayon to draw lines down the middle of the sheets, forming a cross with the intersecting lines as well. Naturally it was the Kyoto shop Nakamura Enshindo on whom Byars relied to join the sheets at perfect right angles. Of the many orders the shop received from Byars, this cross-shaped piece was apparently one of the most challenging, and Taki remembers that Nakamura had to go to considerable pains to get it right.

The cross-shaped work would appear to be one of the "performable papers" that Byars created with a U.S. performance very much in mind. The fact that he also arranged for a Catholic nun to unfold it suggests that he gave the overall presentation careful thought from the outset.

Byars returned to Japan while the Carnegie International was still in progress. In Abe Hiromu's diary, an entry for December 14, 1964 reads, "Byars shows up in the afternoon."

Byars was still in Japan and did not attend the second Carnegie event, held on January 13, 1965. Like the first, it was performed by a Catholic nun identified as "Sister M. Germaine, O.S.B." At 9 am she began unfolding *A 1,000 Foot White Chinese Paper*—the same work, made of very thin *togasenshi*, that Byars had exhibited at Shokokuji in Kyoto.

Though records of these events describe them as performed by "a Catholic nun," Byars told Taki that the woman was actually a former nun who had returned to secular life. In those days so many nuns were leaving convents that it was viewed as a social problem. Audrey Hepburn had won an Oscar for her lead role in the 1959 film *The Nun's Story* as a nun who renounced her vows after much soul-searching and hardship. Byars's performer, whose name was Martha, was presumably one such ex-nun. Byars thought that secularization was an extremely unfortunate thing. In his mind, to be a nun was something "inseparable from that person's nature," Taki said. "To him it was an existence to be cherished, almost like one's own mother." To be secularized, then, was akin to killing your mother; in effect, Martha had disposed of her own past life. Byars found this incomprehensible and tragic.

According to Taki, Byars caused a terrible injury to his father while still a child. His father accidentally fell into a hole young Byars had dug in the yard, breaking his leg and injuring his head to the extent that he required surgery over half his face. Byars felt tremendous guilt toward not only his father but also his mother for the emotional pain this caused her. As a result, says Taki, though he loved his mother dearly, he never called her "Mother," but "Ann." She died at age ninety-five in January 1997, four months before Byars's own death.

An article by Howard Junker in the November 1978 issue of *Art in America* describes a somewhat different accident:

> [O]ne day in 1937, when Byars was four, his father was repairing the family car, hoisted up by a chain. The chain broke. The car fell on his head. [. . .] His father survived, although terribly damaged. He had been a lawyer; for the

> next 30 years he worked washing cars. The family declined into Dickensian misery. [From "Performance as Protective Collaboration," *Art in America*, November 1978: 113]

If indeed his father met with an accident—whether involving a hole, or a car—when Byars was four, this would have occurred before the family moved to the house on Grayfield Street. According to Taki, Byars moved there when he was a bit older. In any event Byars repeatedly referred to an accident suffered by his father that adversely affected his own life, even as he altered the details over time. It seems likely that some sort of discord with his father haunted Byars as he grew up. The depth of that conflict is hinted at in his letter to Dorothy Miller alluding to how he was unable to pursue his aspirations as an artist due to his father's opposition.

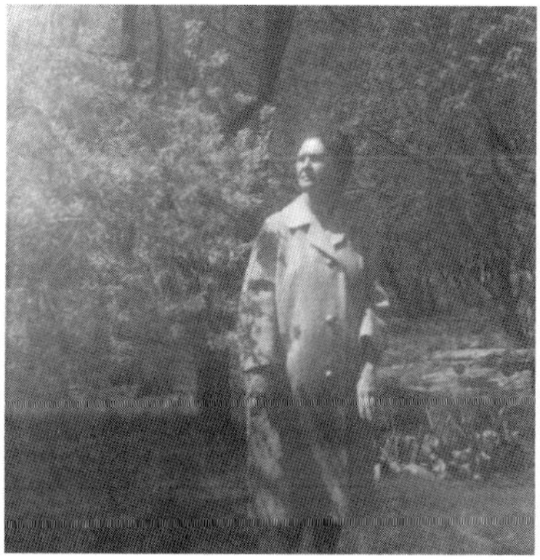

53 Ann Byars in the back yard of the Byars home, 1969

After the Carnegie International had ended, Gustave von Groschwitz, director of the Carnegie Museum of Art, sent Abe Hiromu a set of photographs and announcements of Byars's performances there, accompanied by this letter:

> PERSONAL AND CONFIDENTIAL
> 9 March 1965
> My dear Mr. Abe:
> I am indeed pleased to learn of your interest in the extraordinarily beautiful work of the artist James Lee Byars. We regard him as a person of exceptional talent and learned with enthusiasm of his "Copy of a Lao Tzu Duchamp Wait" and "Wall Street Gold String Parade" during his recent visit in the United States.
>
> It has occurred to me that you might find the enclosed announcements

of recent performances of Byars' works of art here at the Carnegie of interest. I am, therefore, taking the liberty of sending to you for your files photographs of the performance entitled UNKNOWN, January 13 which was announced in the January 1965 issue of Carnegie Magazine, page 4; and the announcement of an earlier performance which was presented in our Hall of Decorative Arts at Noon on November 6, 1964. This appears on page 338 of the December 1964 Magazine.

The paper object which was presented on January 13, 1965 is now a part of the Permanent collection of the Museum of Art, Carnegie Institute.
With every good wish for you in the year ahead,
Sincerely yours,
Gustave von Groschwitz
Director

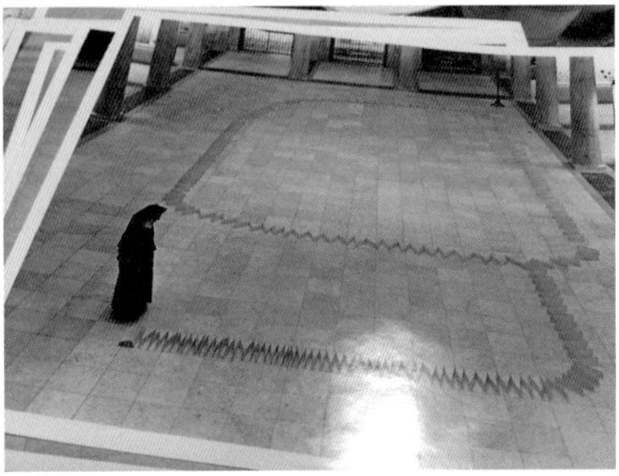

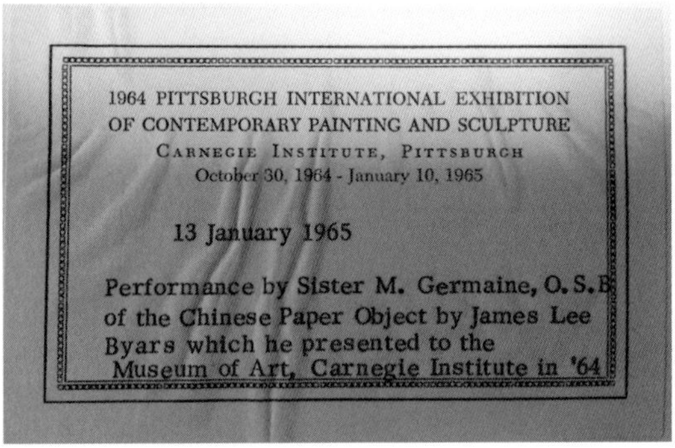

54, 55 A set of photographs from the Carnegie (Pittsburgh) International, kept at the home of Abe Hiromu, 1965

8 A "Mature Period" in Kyoto

Kyoto Indépendant

(March 5–11, 1965, Kyoto Municipal Museum of Art)

According to the museum's exhibition record, Byars displayed the following works (titles were given in English) at the 1965 *Indépendant:*

Room 12 (Paintings)

THE EXACT LENGTH	James Byars
3 OCTOBER PROJECTION	James Byars
THE 9 MONTH	James Byars

It is not known what these works looked like. No newspapers could be located that mention Byars during this period.

After the *Kyoto Indépendant,* Byars wrote two letters to a friend, the artist Ban Fumio. Ban was a regular participant in the *Indépendant* and had exhibited that year as usual.

The two envelopes that Ban received from Byars did not enclose any actual missives. The first was a square white 14 x 13.8 centimeter envelope with five 2-yen postage stamps affixed to it. Byars's address was written in pink pencil. Inside was a folded 24-centimeter square sheet of cellophane paper with the word "Cool" written on it, again in pink pencil. That was all Byars enclosed. The second one was a business envelope inscribed with the name and address of a machine shop: "Japan Kyoto Iwashiya Iwasa Kikaiten, Teramachi Sanjo-agaru." Ban's address on the front was written in blue ballpoint pen, and on the other side was Byars's address, in the same blue ballpoint; glued to the envelope were ten 2-yen postage stamps. The envelope enclosed a scrap of transparent nylon in the shape of a hand.

Iwashiya Iwasa Kikaiten sold medical devices, so this hand-shaped piece of nylon was probably used for some purpose by doctors. Perhaps Byars was inspired by Ban's work at the *Indépendant*, and these letters were his response. The *Indépendant* served not only as a venue where artists could show their work, but also as a community in which they could interact with one another.

Performable Square

(August 4, 1965, Kyoto Municipal Museum of Art)

Byars's solo exhibition *Performable Square* was held at the Kyoto Municipal Museum of Art on August 4, 1965. The invitation consisted of the following text:

IT IS WHITE
IT IS A FIFTY FOOT SQUARE
IT IS A STRIP DIVISION
IT IS TOP HINGED
IT IS STRIP MATCHED
IT IS REVERSE FOLDED
IT IS KINETIC
IT IS AT KYOTO MUSEUM
IT IS FORMAL
IT IS AUGUST 4
IT IS NOON

The exhibition record preserved at the museum is as follows:

August 4, 1965 One day only
James Byars Solo Exhibition
Main Gallery

The exhibition featured his work *A 50 x 50 Foot White Chinese Paper*. Unfolded, it measured approximately 15 meters square. It was made out of white *togasenshi* and folded into a cube a little under 50 centimeters on a side, which was placed atop a 2-meter square sheet of glass. A white *uchiwa* hand fan was handed out to each visitor. It was a hot day, and photos taken at the event show people waving the fans to cool themselves while viewing the work (see Fig. 56).

All of the "performable papers" that Byars had previously exhibited were not merely displayed but also activated in performances of unfolding and refolding, just as the word "performable" suggests. In this show, however, no performance accom-

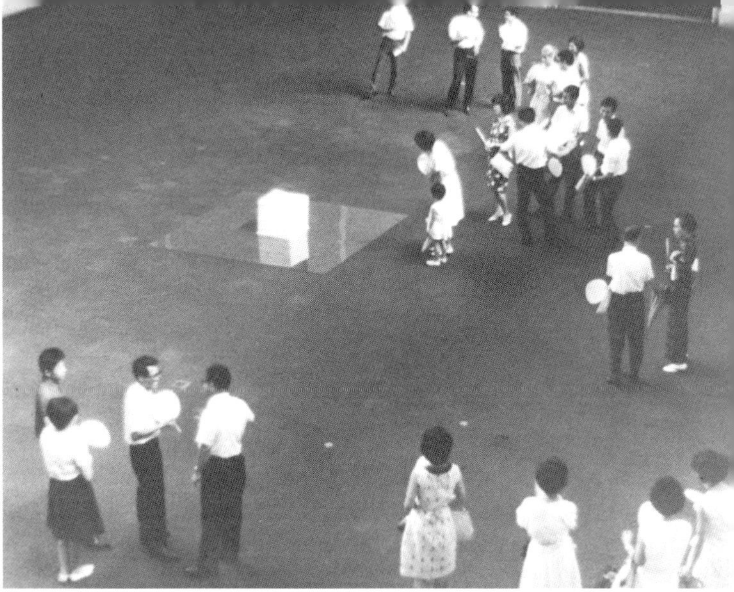

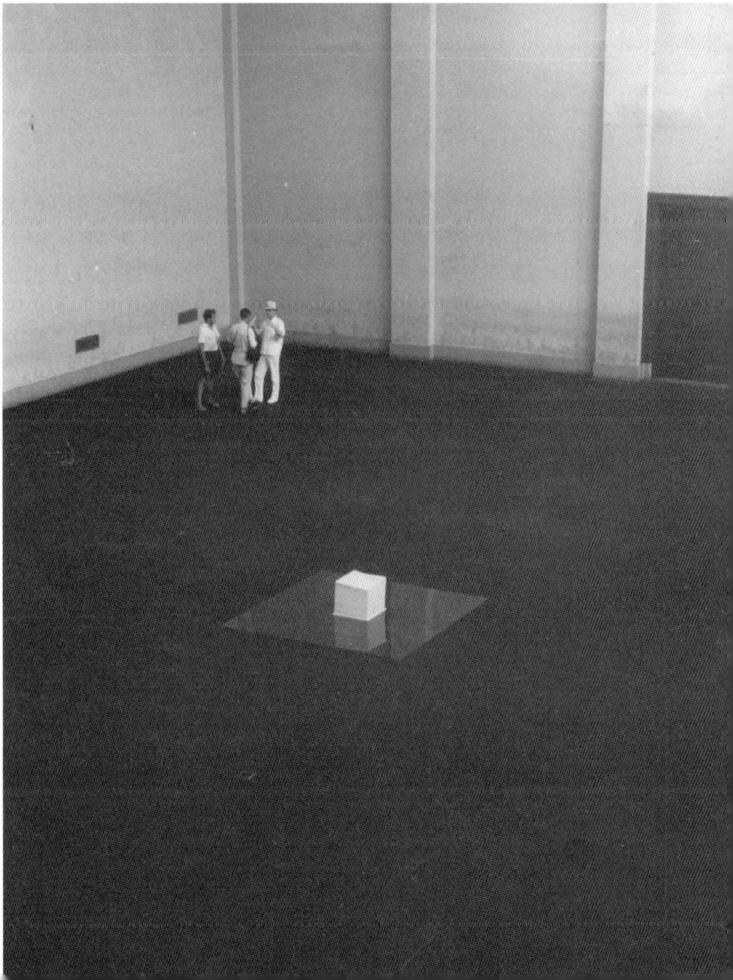

56, 57 The *Performable Square* exhibition at the Kyoto Municipal Museum of Art, August 4, 1965; photos by Abe Hiromu

panied the display of the folded work. It was only thirteen years later that this same piece was finally unfolded—at the U.C. Berkeley Art Museum for three days, from March 24 to 26, 1978. This was as part of the solo Byars show *The Perfect Kiss*, which ran from March 1 to 31.

According to Taki, the folded work shown at the Kyoto Municipal Museum of Art took the shape of a square pillar not quite 50 centimeters high. It was composed of large sheets of *togasenshi* that Nakamura Enshindo had joined together. Nakamura was also asked to make a 50-centimeter square cardboard box, which had a rough inner surface like a typical packing crate and was covered with something like white *gasenshi* paper to make its exterior more attractive. *A 50 x 50 Foot White Chinese Paper* was usually stored in this box, which was a type of container that Byars used often.

During the exhibitions at the Kyoto Municipal Museum of Art, as on other occasions, Byars incessantly pestered the curator Abe Hiromu with requests and complaints. At this particular show, Taki clearly remembers Byars assiduously explaining to Abe, "This work is very long, but it's folded up here. That's why it looks like a square. But it's actually quite long!" Despite Byars's quirks, Abe had always maintained a genial attitude toward him. But Imaizumi Atsuo, who had recommended Byars for the *Adventure in Today's Art of Japan* exhibition in 1961, had by this time grown tired of Byars, and would say to Abe with an astonished look, "What, are you still dealing with Byars? He's too eccentric for me, I can't deal with him anymore."

In Fig. 57, Byars is the man dressed in white who is chatting with someone in the far corner of the gallery. Around this time he was always seen in a white Panama hat and jacket, white shirt, white training pants, and white tennis shoes. Many of his Kyoto contemporaries recall seeing him strolling the gravel paths of the Gosho, dressed all in white.

Incidentally, the Kyoto Municipal Museum of Art's Main Gallery, where the exhibition took place, had been used as a factory for making balloon bombs toward the end of World War II, and as a basketball and darts court by American soldiers during the Occupation.

The Fifth Trip Home: Late August 1965 to Early February 1966

From the diary of Abe Hiromu:

> August 20, 1965: Byars phones
> August 21, 1965: Byars says goodbye

Byars sent the following letter to Abe, postmarked October 6, 1965 in New York. It was written on white paper and sealed in a red envelope.

> Dear ABESAN Thank you for your dream wishing it were a more available Reality the distance and energy to bridge could come more easily! Mr. VonGroschwitz was delighted with your Letter and photos We are in process of planning Oct 25 for a showing of my "piece" It is very complicated procedure but excellently. Im in NY to attend to show means here then? My father is OK But weak and my immediate departure to Kyoto would be unwise so wait I must! I miss the still tranquil city and the elegant Noh and of course Miss "T" and my other gentle friends Maybe By spring I will be free????? It is a brilliant scene in NYC One work of exceptional interest is an aluminum lamination 1 by 300 feet to be filled with Helium and floated perpendicular as column from a ground chain at the Modern Museum in Stockholm (I may ?send a piece?) Wish you could get a chance to witness the "City" We have a new and excellent Asian Wing in the Metropolitan just opened. An extraordinary hand Broken off a China Buddha in the 8th century upon a column—Hope your "talk" goes well! fondly JLB
> c/o Landsmans Hall 249 CPW Apt 8 NYC NY USA

The return address was that of the apartment of the architect Robert Landsman, who lived in New York. Byars usually slept in the hallway there—hence, perhaps, the "Landsmans Hall" in the address. "Oct 25" refers to the third of Byars's performances for the Carnegie International. According to accounts of this event, the dancer Lucinda Childs, covered from head to foot in a white ostrich-feather suit, very slowly unfolded a work titled *A Mile-Long Paper Walk* in stately, unhurried, Noh-like fashion. The work is now in the permanent collection at the Museum of Modern Art, New York.

A few months later Abe received a letter from Byars postmarked January 18, 1966 in Detroit, in which Byars congratulates Abe on the birth of his son. The return address is that of Byars's family home.

> ABESAN thank you for the lovely cards. "Omedeto" to the Beautiful Baby Boy. Also to you, your wife and other child. Regret I'm not there to say so personally. Hope your year of the "Horse" is a good one, Bringing joy and hope to you. With deep appreciations JB
> P.S. It snows like that day your "Noh Mask" came!
> 15167 Grayfield Det 23, Mich

Abe also wrote to Byars while the latter was in the United States. He remembers sending a black and white postcard with a picture of a long-nosed Suikoju mask from the ancient Gigaku masked drama that is stored in the Shosoin treasure house in Nara. Byars mentions in his letter that it is snowing like the day that postcard arrived. He also wishes Abe a good "Year of the Horse." Byars was intrigued by the Chinese zodiac and often asked people he met which animal year they were born in.

Over the span of a decade, Byars made the round trip between the United States and Japan seven times. According to Abe, nearly every time Byars left Kyoto, he told people, "This may be my last time. I might not be able to come back to Japan"—but everyone who knew him took this with a grain of salt and fully expected him to return.

This time, Byars got back to Kyoto in February 1966. Apparently he had already moved out of the Kitamura house in Kita-Shirakawa. The following entry appears in Abe's diary:

> February 19, 1966, around 11: Met Byars, who has called the past few days. Lunch at Arena. He was in the front corner writing a letter. Looked quite tired, said he had arrived on JAL a few days ago and was staying at Higashiyama Kaikan, and that it was the eleventh time he had crossed the Pacific. Parted ways after about thirty minutes.

The Sixth Trip Home: March or April to Late July 1966

Before this particular trip, Abe Hiromu and his wife invited Byars and Taki out for a final pre-departure dinner party. Abe's diary says: "March 11, evening: Chat with Byars and Miss Taki." The dinner took place at a small machiya-like establishment in the Shimogyo district. Byars and Taki apparently thought the ambience "mysterious," as Byars mentions in a letter that arrived at Abe's in an airmail envelope postmarked April 20, 1966 in New York:

> Hello ABESAN Thank you for the mysterious departure dinner! I'm sorry it had to be that way and as I wander about N.Y.C. streets my mind stays half in Kyoto. It seems I live there in rumor even now. Maybe since I doubt that I can change my attention much I will return someday and go back to my paper constructions which I feel are beautiful. Fate is not to be understood by intent, I see, as I live on and wish to pursue my inspirations. It is a very strange event that I should be so held by Kyoto and of all the endless materials be only able in paper to express myself. I dream

> of vast white expanses and uses of time and potentiality in exhibitions of great purity. Kyoto remains an isolated place of great meaning to me and if I sell some works I might be there again in '66. (Hopefully) to stay. Taki is so great as a performer of my pieces. I wonder how she has such a profound understanding of my experiences with them? ABESAN, my friend, I do hope we will meet again one day soon, perhaps by summer who knows.
> With fondness
> J. Byars
> P.S. Kyoto must be exquisite by now in pink.
> c/o Reynders 214 East 11 St. NYC, NY, USA

The "Reynders" of the return address is probably Judith Reynders, whose name appears in a handwritten note on the back of a photograph in the archives at the Museum of Modern Art:

> at Green Gallery
> purchased by Judith Reynders
> 5-24-66

Reynders most likely purchased the work shown in the photo on the indicated date. The photo shows the paper scroll placed atop the "sea of white boxes" that Yvonne Rainer danced around at Byars's one-day, four-hour exhibition at the Green Gallery on November 16, 1963, two and a half years before the date of Reynders's purchase. Always short of money, particularly in high-priced New York, Byars would often rely on the good offices of Miller or other MoMA staff to find lodging for him with collectors who had purchased his works.

During most of his New York sojourns, however, Byars would stay for several months in an apartment owned by the architect Robert Landsman, located on Central Park West. According to Taki, Landsman was a friend of Byars and a very generous man. He usually lived in a rented apartment and let Byars stay in this other apartment, which he owned. It was in an ideal location on the Upper West Side, close to Central Park and the American Museum of Natural History. At the time Landsman worked as an architect at Webb & Knapp, a real-estate development company, and participated in projects by I.M. Pei, who also worked there. Byars and Taki frequently met up with Landsman in Kyoto. Years later, when Taki came to New York, Landsman often visited her and they would have dinner together.

One more letter of interest that Byars wrote to Abe during this period was postmarked May 23, 1966, New York. It was written on yellow paper and enclosed in a white envelope.

> Dear ABESAN
> I wonder often of you. Hoping you are well. Suppose you often go up your nearby mountain to think and refresh your spirit. I miss you and all of Kyoto.
> P.S. I'm living in Marcel Duchamp's old studio. It is all white and square with one wall of opaque grey glass. I have an old Kannon's hand out in the middle with nothing else but white.
> It is a strange romance. I shall never be free of your sensitive attitudes, and will likely never pass a day without longing. So if at all I can manage #7 to Kyoto, I will.
> Hope it can be by summer. Hope we can with Taki san have a dinner out. Hope to not leave Kyoto again if I can make it back. Many works I dream of.
> With deep fondness
> James Lee Byars
> c/o Reynders 214 East 11 St. NYC, NY, USA

Abe recalls: "Byars was genuinely fond of Kyoto. He always spoke of how beautiful the mountains looked at sunset . . . the silhouette of Mt. Atago . . . the sun going down . . . the trees. . . ."

Byars returned to Kyoto at the end of July that year. Abe's diary contains these entries:

> June 18, 1966: Phoned Miss Taki, who says Byars will be back in July.
> August 2, 1966: Met Byars at Kyoto Kaikan at noon. Dressed in white suit and hat, seems well. Says he was delayed by airline strike.

A Midnight Happening

(October 15, 1966, Kyoto)

A rather unique performance, referred to after the fact as *Peace*, took place at the Kyoto house of Lindley Williams Hubbell, who taught Shakespeare at Doshisha University. This is the same midnight "happening" that Hubbell described in one of his answers to Howard Junker's postcard questions about Byars.

Very late one night, Taki Sachiko, wearing a dress entirely covered in white feathers, showed up in Hubbell's garden. She said nothing, but handed Hubbell a piece of paper that said "PEACE" in tiny, barely legible lettering, then left. Thrilled by this occurrence, Hubbell promptly wrote a letter to Dorothy Miller, the MoMA curator, recounting the event in detail. (Interestingly, he uses Japanese reckoning for the year, Showa 41.)

> 10/16/41
> Dear Dorothy:
> I can't resist writing to tell you about one of Jim Byars' "works of art" because I was the only person who saw it, and I hate to have it lost and forgotten.
> Last night at midnight …
> I know it was midnight because I always turn my radio on just before twelve, to set my watch (it goes ping-ping-ping-PING at midnight) and then when they go off the air they play the national anthem which I like to hear, so …
> just as turned off my radio at 12 I heard someone knock on my window. I went to the front door and opened it and there, in the dim light of my garden, with a little light from my window lighting her, stood Taki-san (Jim's lovely Japanese fiancee) completely enveloped in some sort of robe, from her neck to the ground, composed entirely of white feathers. On her head was a sort of huge turban, also consisting entirely of white feathers. There she stood, in the dim light, like a great white cloud. She handed me, without a word, a tiny piece of paper. I took it, bowed, and she disap peared in the shadow and left. I went back to my living room and looked at it – it was a little round piece of paper, about as big as a dime, and on it, in almost microscopic letters, was the word PEACE.
> That's all. It was one of what Jim calls his "presentations." All that time and preparation and effort (and expense!) goes into something to be seen for only a moment and by only one person.
> Sometimes not even one person. Once he wrote asking me to come and see one of his "presentations" which was to take place at 5 a.m. in the grounds of the Imperial Palace. I refused to get up so early. Afterwards he wrote me, "It was quite nice. It was witnessed by a policeman and a dog."
> Fortunately he has been given a teaching job in an art school in Osaka, where they seem to really appreciate him. I'm so glad. I'm giving a show of his "objects" at Galerie 16 in Kyoto, tentative date Jan. 9, will of course send you the catalogue.
> Hope you are well. Hello to John. It's almost time for your annual letter.

Looking forward to it …
love
Lin

For Byars it was an absolute imperative to conduct performances punctually and as planned. Because of that, Taki had to take a taxi that night to make sure to be at Hubbell's house at exactly 12 o'clock midnight. In those days, Hubbell lived on the hillside of Mt. Kujo, which was between Kyoto and Yamashina (the address was 17-12 Ebisudani-cho, Kujoyama, Yamashina, Higashiyama-ku, Kyoto). Neighbors referred to Hubbell as "the hermit of Mt. Kujo" because he descended from the mountain to the university each day. When he passed by, children would chant, "Here comes the hermit! Here comes the hermit!"

Living far from town as he did, Hubbell naturally had no idea that Taki would be visiting him. As instructed by Byars, she knocked on his door at precisely midnight, and stood there silent, expressionless. She gave him the piece of paper saying "PEACE" and departed without a word.

Hatano Kazuko, a former student of Hubbell who currently teaches at Mukogawa Women's University, still remembers Hubbell talking about it: "There was a beautiful moon that night."

This sudden visit to Hubbell's house was not a singular occurrence. Taki recalls several such occasions. On one, Byars gave Hubbell a work that consisted of a large heart cut out of something like wrapping paper, with a golden thread hanging down from the cleft in the heart. For gifts, he often took a type of dark blue paper used for hand-copying sutras and attached gold thread to it. After seeing sutras lettered in gold-colored sumi ink on this dark blue paper, Byars was inspired to make his own version.

9 1967 in Kyoto

Exhibition from the Collection of Lindley W. Hubbell
(January 14, 1967, galerie 16, Kyoto)

The exhibition of Byars's "objects" mentioned by Hubbell at the end of his October 16 letter to Dorothy Miller took place at galerie 16 on January 14, 1967, from 11 am to 7 pm. Consisting of objects by Byars collected by Hubbell, the show included invitations to exhibitions and performances that Byars had sent to Hubbell as well as ordinary letters they had exchanged. Hubbell viewed these items not merely as invitations or letters but as works of art.

The show was Hubbell's brainchild. He had approached Mizutani Yoko, who worked at galerie 16, and told her, "I want to do a one-day exhibition. What do you think?" Mizutani's family was prominent in Kyoto's antique art circles and had connections with the Metropolitan Museum of Art. On the postcard-size invitation, which consisted only of text giving the title, date, and place of the event, it was described as *Exhibition of Work by James Lee Byars from the Collection of Lindley W. Hubbell.*

Information about the show also appeared in the art listings of the *Kyoto shinbun*:

> galerie 16 (Teramachi Sanjo-sagaru Higashi-iru) — James L. Byars exhibition: Works from the collection of Hayashi Shuseki. The artist is a lecturer at Naniwa Junior College. (Date: 14th) [Translated from *Kyoto shinbun*, January 14, 1967]

Hubbell provided a typed checklist of the exhibited items, and Ban Fumio took photos of the exhibition on 35-millimeter half-frame film. The mounted slides were discovered at Ban's house in 2007, forty years after the fact, along with an invitation, the typed list, and an envelope containing the slides.

Hubbell's list of twenty-two items and Ban's photographs of the installed objects

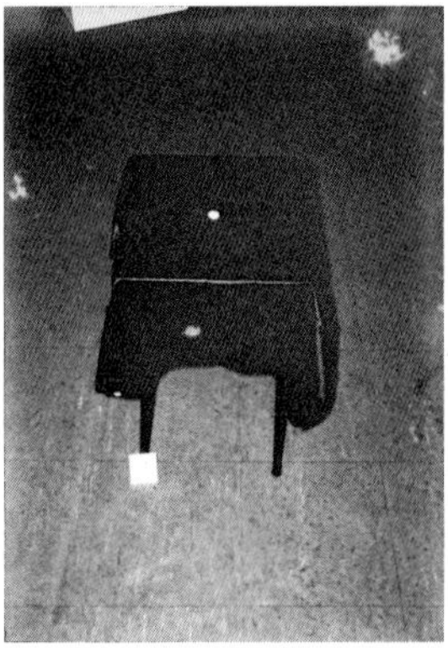
58

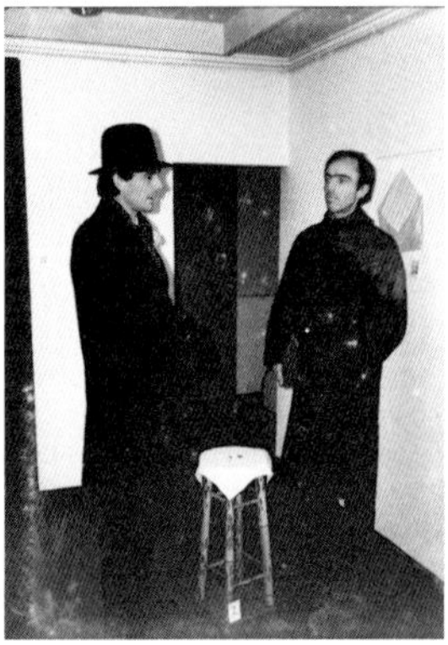
59

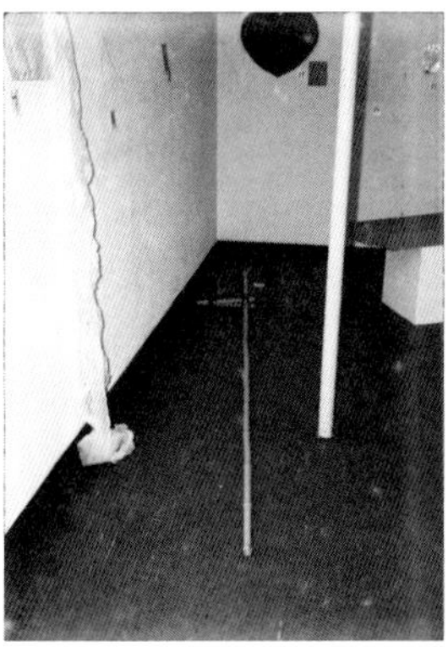
60

constitute an invaluable record of Byars's work from this period. Below I have reproduced Hubbell's numbered descriptions verbatim, together with photos of the works by Ban (Figs. 58–72). My own comments follow Hubbell's descriptions.

Fig. 58

1. Peace (white paper disk, 1.7 cm. diameter, black lettering.)

A circular paper inscribed with the word PEACE. Taki Sachiko handed this to Hubbell during the midnight "happening" at Hubbell's house in 1966.

Fig. 59

2. Stones (three flat pebbles from Lake Erie, approx. 2 x 1.4 mm., 1.5 x 1 mm., .75 x .6 mm.) [*sic—mm should be cm*]

At left is Byars. On the right is Gerow Reece, who would later marry Taki Sachiko. The three small flat stones on the white cloth were found on the shore of Lake Erie, one of the Great Lakes not far from Detroit. Byars often talked about stones when he was immersed in Mingei folk art in the early sixties. Taki received several pebbles from Byars and still keeps them. He would pick up and present as gifts small stones of various sorts: round, flat, smooth, some with visible fossils. Hubbell, who had given himself the Japanese name Shuseki, which means "autumn stone," also loved stones and always kept some round pebbles on his desk.

Fig. 60

3. Stilt (two bamboo poles, 3.025 m. & 36.5 cm. long, tied cruciform with black rope.)

As the title indicates, this appears to be one of a pair of stilts. A split bamboo stick was fastened with black rope around one end of the long bamboo pole.

Fig. 61

4. Rock (oblate spheroid, 40.6 cm. circumference, painted white.)

5. Stick (cedar wood, 92 cm. x 8 mm. x 8 mm.)

At lower left is the stone, which was painted white. On the stool is the pole made of cedar.

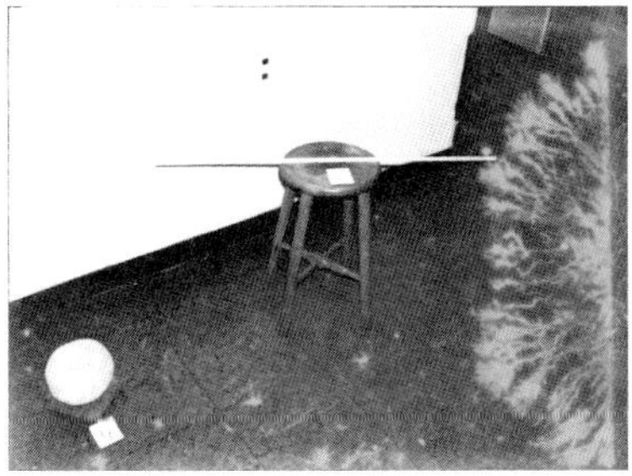

61

Fig. 62

6. Visitor (button, 5 cm. diameter, in corrugated paper box, 1.07 m. x 17 cm. x 9 cm.)

Byars most likely placed a small button in this large box and sent it to Hubbell.

7. Thank you (white paper, 9.16 m. x 12 cm., crumpled in white envelope, 31 cm. square. 50 1-yen stamps.)

The long white paper, which appears to be tissue paper, can be seen hanging down the wall in Fig. 60. One end is crumpled up in the square envelope in which it was mailed to Hubbell with fifty 1-yen stamps affixed to it.

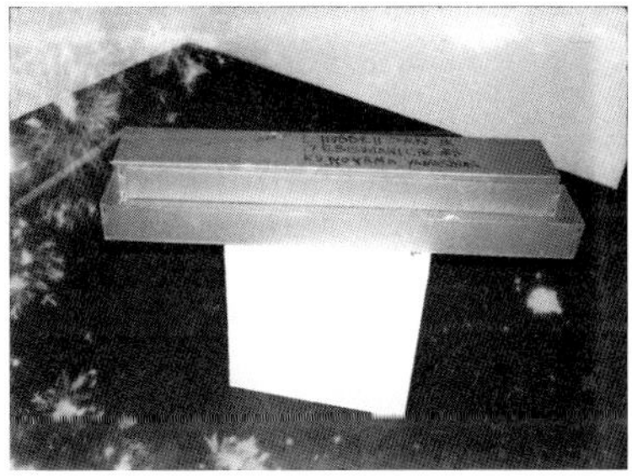

62

Fig. 63

8. Orange envelope (41.6 x 39 cm., formerly containing black feathers.)

Byars was partial to the reddish-orange paper of which this envelope was made and used it frequently.

63

Fig. 64

9. Hanger (pneumatic clothes hanger, inflated.)

A clothes hanger inflated with air. It appears to be decorated with a black-on-white

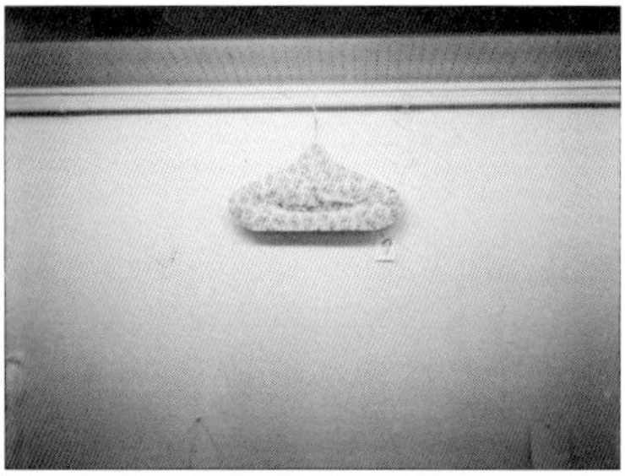

64

pattern of some sort, but this is not clear in the photograph.

10. Letter in box (white paper, 1.935 m. x 6 cm., in white cardboard box, 6.5 x 6.5 x 6 cm.)

The long sheet of paper was presumably folded into an accordion shape to fit in the box.

11. 000000000000000000000000000 0000000000000000000000000000 0000000000000000000000000000 0000 (telegram.)

Byars sent a telegram consisting of this row of zeroes.

12. 0 (telegram.)

He also sent a telegram consisting of a single zero.

65

Fig. 65

13. Postcard (14.8 x 10 cm.)

The content of the card is not discernible in the photo. Hubbell, too, frequently sent postcards containing only commas or periods, for example, to his close friends. He and Byars clearly shared an artistic sensibility.

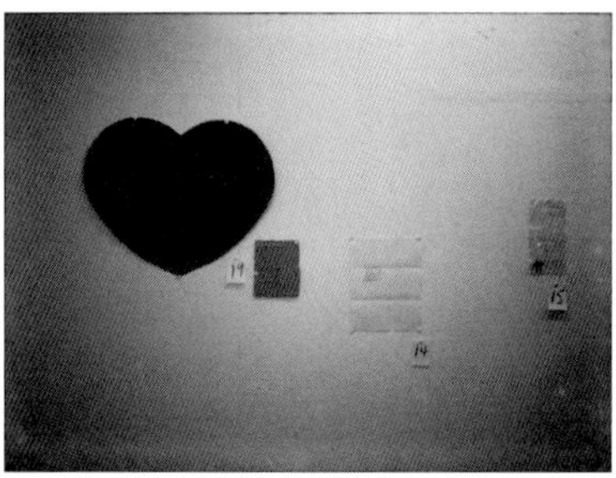

66

Fig. 66

14. Same old duties for 100 years (newspaper clipping, xerox.)

Probably a copy of a newspaper article, but it is unclear what the article was about.

15. Blue balls (two spherical pieces of blue chalk, 22 mm. circumference, in

cellophane slip.)

The balls, which are on the far right in the photo, were actually made of crayon, not chalk. Byars often drew with crayon of the kind used to take rubbings of stone Buddhist statues; he was partial to the medium because it did not run on paper. Before starting to use crayon he almost exclusively used sumi ink, which he ordered in powdered form from Nara via the Kyoto shop Kobaien and mixed with white Elmer's Glue. He always purchased sumi powder and glue by the gallon, and used a large brush to paint with the mixture.

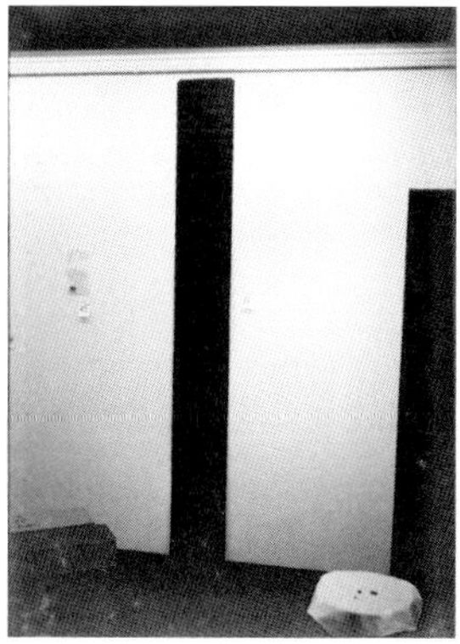

67

Fig. 67

16. Black on black (letter, 2.325 m. x 27 cm.)

Black letters written on a long black sheet of paper. There remain the traces of accordion folds.

68

Fig. 68

17. Kyoto Museum of Modern Art [*sic*] 10 o'clock April 2 paintings James Byars (white on white, 9.3 x 9.2 cm., in white envelope, 10.1 x 9.8 cm.)

An invitation Byars made for an exhibition that was actually held at the Kyoto Municipal Museum of Art on April 2, 1963.

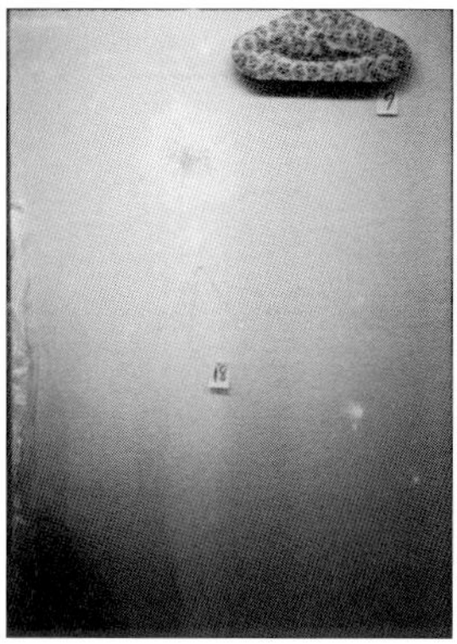

69

Fig. 69

18. The Green Gallery 15 West 57th Street New York November 16 1963 from 8-12 PM Byars. The Castelli Gallery 4 East 77 Street New York November 21 1963 from 12-4 PM Byars. Intermittently for 21 days and nights at 200 1/2 East 88 Street New York Brecht-Byars-and. (Three plastic strips isinglass 23 cm. x 6 mm. each, black lettering.)

The three plastic strips were attached with fish glue. The date, place, and time of each of three exhibitions or performances that Byars conducted in the United States in 1963 were written on the strips in black.

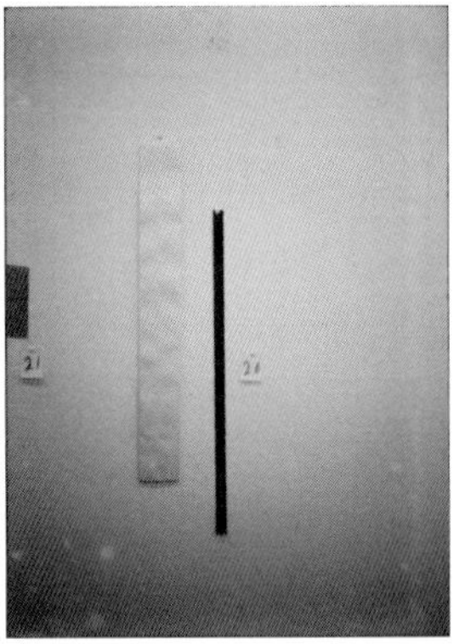

70

19. Purple heart (paper, 57.4 x 40 cm., in red envelope, 16.5 x 13.5 cm.)

The heart, made of dark blue paper, can be seen in Fig. 66.

Fig. 70

20. Gosho south mon midnight 8-8-64 Byars (black on black, 81 x 3 cm., in white envelope, 82 x 10.5 cm.)

An invitation Byars made for the midnight procession performance at the Kyoto Imperial Palace on August 8, 1964.

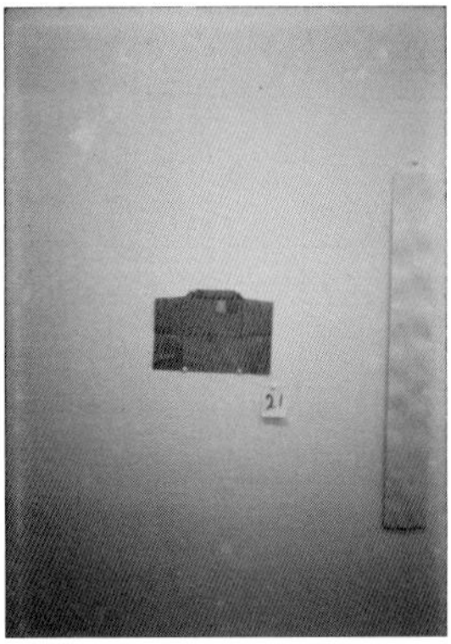

71

Fig. 71

21. Dyed letter (aerogramme from Byars to Guggenheim Museum, letter scored out, paper dyed orange.)

Fig. 72

22. Pentagon (letter, yellow crayon on white paper, 80 cm. square, folded pentagonally.)

The person standing in front is Byars, dressed completely in black. He had a pink carnation in his breast pocket that night and wore a checkered scarf around his neck.

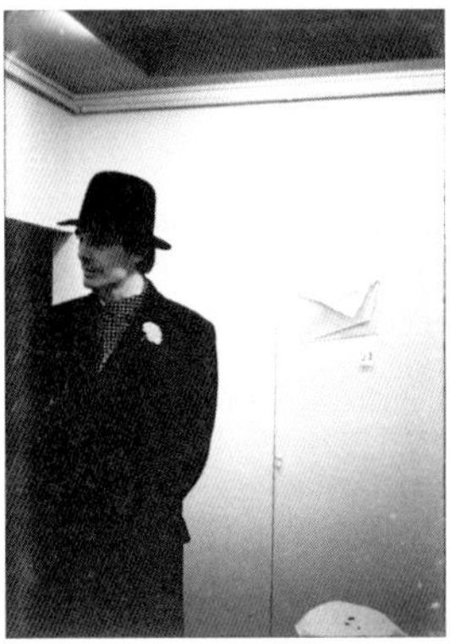

72

Later, the audience was directed to stand in a line in the gallery and do a sort of performance. There is a photograph (Fig. 73) that captures this scene, but it is hard to tell what the performance entailed.

Fig. 74 is a diagram I prepared of the layout of the exhibition, based on Ban's photos.

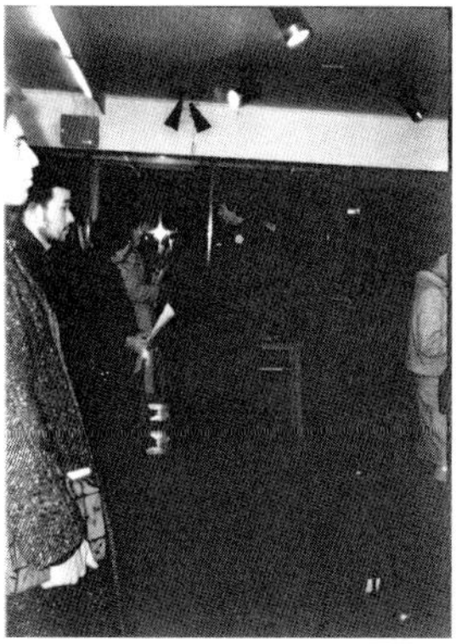

73 Photo taken at the exhibition by Ban Fumio

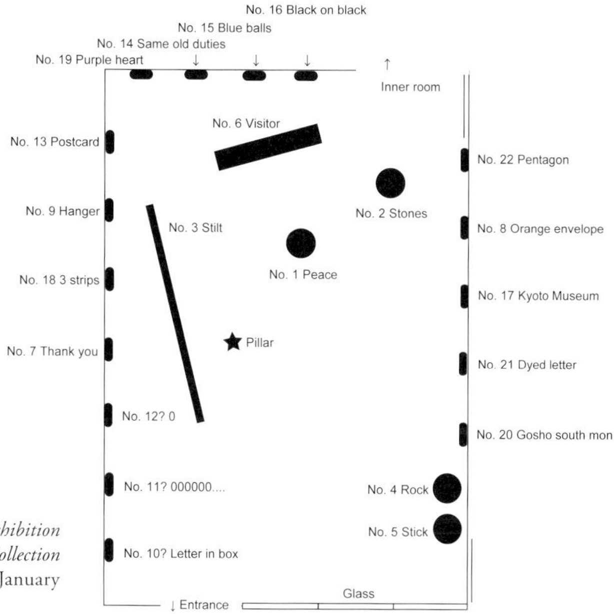

74 Diagram of the layout of the *Exhibition of Work by James Lee Byars from the Collection of Lindley W. Hubbell* at galerie 16, January 14, 1967 (by the author)

Performances at Naniwa Junior College

(January 25, 1967, noon: weaving; January 28, 1967: Rand Castile "Murasaki" exhibition; February 1, 1967, 12:30 pm: Ban Fumio, Mitsuda Takako)

From late January to early February 1967, Byars held a series of performances on the campus of Naniwa Junior College (Naniwa Tanki Daigaku, now Osaka University of Arts Junior College), located in Yata, Higashi-Sumiyoshi-ku, Osaka. He had started working there in the autumn of 1966 as an English teacher and was now also teaching art, including performance art. It is not known who helped him get the position, his first ever as an art teacher. Perhaps it came about as a natural consequence of his increasing visibility as an artist. He appeared to be very excited about teaching art.

Presumably the college was expecting him to be an art teacher in the conventional sense: teaching students how to draw and paint, or giving lessons in art history. There is no record of what kind of classes he actually taught, but before long he began to do performances involving the students on campus. This eventually cost him his job and ultimately led to his departure from Japan, developments that I will discuss below.

Byars's plan for performances at Naniwa began with the construction of a white room measuring 120 x 210 x 240 centimeters. One is reminded of the white room he installed in the *genkan* of Daisen'in at Daitokuji. In that instance, the interior of the room had been pitch dark and a piece of paper with a small circle drawn on it was hung in the back. This time, the room served as a space for performances by several people in turn.

A request was mailed soon after the New Year holidays to each person Byars was asking to participate. One of the recipients, Ban Fumio, still treasures the one he received. The Japanese text, in Taki Sachiko's hand, was written on a special-delivery postcard postmarked January 5, 1967 in Kyoto at Sanjo-Hiromichi, the post office near Taki's parents' house. Here is an English translation:

> Happy New Year.
> I hope your year is off to a good start. I know this is on very short notice, but I have been asked to inform you of the following. I [Byars] am planning a *hyakunin* ["100 persons"] exhibition in a *hokokushitsu* ["reporting room"], a 4 x 7 x 8 *shaku* [1 *shaku* = approximately 30 cm] white room (it is also all right to use the courtyard) at Naniwa Junior College (Yata, Nishi-Tanabe) between January 10 and 20(?), between noon and 1 o'clock (any time of any day is all right). Although I call it a *hyakunin* exhibition, each of the participants will use the space for their own exhibition, production, or performance. As the presenter you may plan anything you like. However, exhibited works may not be left on display. You can present your work there during your preferred time, but not after that. The presentation is to be viewed by the students of the college and invitees only. This is a busy time for everyone and I realize you have other obligations, but I'd very much like you to participate in this event. I believe this will be an enjoyable and opportune learning experience for both the students and ourselves. I hope I'll receive a favorable response from you. Do you have any plans to come to Kyoto? I'd be happy to see you. I'll be going to the College on the 10th so I would appreciate it if you could let me know your situation by then. I hope this Year of the Sheep will be a good one for you.

The return address in Japanese read: James Byars, 361 Kamigoryobaba-cho, Kamigyo-ku, Kyoto. This address was the home of Abe Masao, a distant relative of the curator Abe Hiromu. It was located about five minutes' walk north of Shokokuji, the temple where Byars had conducted "performable paper" events. Byars presumably lived in a *hanare*, a smaller house detached from the main one. A prominent religious scholar, Abe Masao at the time was teaching philosophy at Nara University. After retirement from Nara, he taught at the University of Hawaii. He published many works about Zen and Buddhism in both Japanese and English, including the book *Zen and Western Thought*. Byars must have welcomed the opportunity to pelt Professor Abe with numerous questions. Abe Hiromu recalls being queried frequently about Byars by his relative.

After that, Ban received a letter postmarked January 23, Yamashina. In a square white envelope measuring 18.8 x 18.8 centimeters, there were three red hearts, large, medium, and small, each folded in half. The Japanese text, written by Taki, read as follows:

> Dear Mr. Ban,
> I hope everything is going well for you.
> Regarding Byars's exhibition, he is going to display a white carpet (hand-woven) next Wednesday. After that, his friend Castile (art critic of the Japan Society) is planning a Murasaki exhibition in the room. That is on Saturday the 28th. For your show, I'd like to ask you to present a Rainbow as the finale on February 1. I look forward to hearing from you.

Ban began his performance at 12:30 pm on February 1. Although he arrived at the designated time, Byars was not present. That's fine, not a problem, Ban thought. Having brought with him seven spools of rainbow-colored sewing-machine thread, he entered the white box as directed and started constructing a rainbow that stretched from one wall toward the middle of the space. Ban had been working on a piece titled *Rainbow shinbun* (Rainbow newspaper) at the time, for which he was painting newspapers in seven colors. This performance was an extension of that. He worked for thirty minutes, until his time was up, without any appearance by Byars.

The next performance was by the artist Mitsuda Takako, who had accompanied Ban there. She stood in the box, holding a piece of paper for thirty minutes. It appears that Byars's students took pictures of Mitsuda standing there, but these have not been found. Byars never showed up.

The poet and translator Sato Hiroaki was in attendance at one of the performances in the white box. He later remarked, "If I hadn't met Byars, the life I have now would have been very different." At the beginning of his book *Amerika honyaku-musha shugyo* (A knight errant of translation in America), published by Maruzen Library in 1993, Sato writes about his encounter with Byars at the event on January 28, 1967:

> It's already twenty-five years ago, and I'm not sure which month it was. At the time I was in the master's program in English literature at Doshisha University.

One day an elegant female upper-class student asked me to participate in a white-themed happening by an American. I think there may not be many people who remember happenings, which were popular back then. Unlike painting and sculpture, which are semi-permanent, they're a form of artistic expression that comes to an end on the spot. What Christo does in various parts of the world are happenings of a sort but on an extremely large scale.

The organizer of the happening I was asked to join was James Byars. The location was on the campus of a university located between Kyoto and Osaka.

Why did I—a person who was naturally conservative and had almost no interest in art—agree to participate? In hindsight, it was probably because Byars himself was such an eccentric. Back then he was teaching English at various universities, including Doshisha. He walked with a brisk stride, always in a tailcoat, with a red carnation in his breast pocket, and a top hat that reminded me of Lincoln. It was as if he were about to go to a ball. In style he was the complete opposite of the then-fashionable hippies, with their habit of dressing down on purpose. Also like Lincoln, he was very tall.

One day a friend of mine introduced me to Byars. He handed me a large cardinal-red envelope he was holding in his hand. When I opened it, there was a small white envelope inside. That was all. I was told, however, that Byars had a famous paper craftsman make these envelopes.

It was raining heavily when my alarm clock woke me from less than three hours of sleep that particular morning. When it rains, I get wet since I use a crutch. If it were merely to skip a class, I might have chosen to go back to sleep. But if I had skipped the happening, I wouldn't have met Rand Castile. If I hadn't met Castile, I wouldn't have come to the United States. And if I hadn't come to the United States, I wouldn't have persisted in the work of translating my mother tongue into the foreign language of English.

Instead, I ventured out in the rain to Shijo-Kawaramachi station and took the Keihan train to the university, where I found the site of the happening—a little shack. Byars had painted it all white inside and out. A weaving loom from the Nara period was installed in one corner of the shack, and the girl who had invited me was learning how to use it. The loom was painted white, the fabric being woven on it was white, and the weaver was dressed in a white kimono. I've forgotten what other "props" there were in this vein, or who else was there. However, one of the few other visitors was Castile.

What was my first impression? What comes to mind is a shadow to the right of a quiet young fellow, not much taller than me, standing with his back to the wall of a dimly lit room with white floor and walls. Other than that, I'm not sure what was part of my first impression and what was not. I'm certain I was not the one who initiated the conversation. Castile was a handsome young man with an intelligent look in his eye. He spoke a curious English that was refined, yet in a different way from the gently decorous New England English spoken by my poetry teacher, Hayashi Shuseki (his Japanese name; he was born Lindley Williams Hubbell). There was something about it that we usually associate with British accents, but without the staccato delivery. His English continued to captivate me for a long time.

Later on Castile rented a civic hall, one of the newer buildings in Kyoto, and held a poetry reading that didn't include his own work. I don't recall, though, if he was at Byars's happening to read white-themed poetry as I was. In the course of our conversation he found out that I was studying English, and asked me to do some translation from Japanese. He said he was researching *chanoyu* [tea ceremony] on a Fulbright scholarship. One day he had parked his motorcycle outside of a bank to withdraw some cash. When he came back, the briefcase tied to the back of the motorcycle had been stolen. The briefcase held a loose-leaf binder full of detailed notes on the history and procedures of *chanoyu* that Castile had gathered from various people, as well as depictions of teahouses he had visited. He had to make up for this loss quickly, he said. Later, I heard that he had gotten a long article published in the *Kyoto shinbun* with the help of Urasenke [the famous Japanese tea ceremony school], urging the thief to keep the inconsequential briefcase but appealing for the return of the notes, which were meaningless to anybody else. Apparently, however, there was no response.

That is how I began translating, with the shaky English of a graduate school student. But my association with Castile did not become something cut and dried, like meeting occasionally just to hand in translations. He took me with him to visit teahouses around Kyoto and Nara. In this way, I got to visit temples I had never even heard of despite having lived for over five years in Kyoto. I visited some pottery studios too. I even went to *omizutori* [a water-drawing festival that occurs before dawn], waiting for the first train of the morning, warming myself over some sort of charcoal

> stove at the station. At the poetry reading I mentioned, I ended up sitting next to Castile and apparently wore a painfully solemn expression the whole time. Afterwards Byars teased me, saying, "You looked like a shrine dog."

Rand Castile is the person who once said of Byars, "If I were not convinced he is a genius, I would think he is a madman," the quote with which this book begins. After his stay in Kyoto, Castile returned to the United States and became one of the foremost exponents of Japanese art abroad, serving as the founding director of the Japan House Gallery at the Japan Society in New York and later as the director of the Asian Art Museum of San Francisco.

While he was in Kyoto on a Fulbright, Castile attended Urasenke and later published a book on the tea ceremony, *The Way of Tea*, in 1971. It was while studying at Urasenke, in 1966 and 1967, that he became a close friend of Byars. His wife, Sondra, later trained at Oka Bokkodo, the venerable art restoration studio in Kyoto. After they returned to the United States she worked for the Department of Asian Art Conservation at the Metropolitan Museum of Art in New York.

In Kyoto, Castile was known for driving around on a motorcycle, often with his briefcase stuffed with documents. The incident of the stolen briefcase that Sato mentions occurred near Yamada Gallery, where Byars had his first solo show in 1960, and received a lot of media coverage at the time. There are many people who still recall that episode: "Oh yes, the documents stolen from the motorcycle. . . ." whenever Castile's name is mentioned.

According to Sato, the Castiles "exuded the air of a refined, intellectual gentleman and lady." At a "black party" to which they were invited by Byars, Rand arrived in formal attire complete with cummerbund, an item normally associated in Japan with orchestra conductors, while Sondra appeared in a fashionable dress that could have come straight from the latest issue of *Vogue*. Indeed, this is how they typically dressed in public, suggesting an affinity in fashion tastes between Byars and the Castiles. Also at Byars's black party that day was Sato, wearing what he says was his only business suit. Sato recalls that Byars's house was dark and that he and the Castiles appeared to be the only guests. One of his most vivid memories is of Sondra kneeling in formal *seiza* posture on the floor of the dark room and placing a lit candle next to a large wine glass, so that the flickering, wavering candlelight was projected through the glass across the floor.

The invitation that Sato received to the Naniwa performance was on white paper in a red envelope (see Fig. 75). The paper may have contained the following printed message, which appears on a copy of the same invitation found in a closet at Taki's parents' house:

> A WHITE CARPET
> IN YATA
> ON WEDNESDAY
> AT NOON.

A WHITE CARPET
IN YATA
ON WEDNESDAY
AT NOON.

75 Invitation to the January 28, 1967 event at Naniwa Junior College, found in the Taki family home

After the performances at Naniwa, Ban received a letter postmarked February 10 from Byars. The envelope was identical to that of the letter of request postmarked January 23, a white square measuring 18.8 x 18.8 centimeters. Inside was a letter written on three sheets of A4-size paper, along with a single golden sewing-machine thread.

> O Mr. BAN Your Rainbow show was excellent. On the first day at 1230 PM I looked out of the school window and saw Hubbell walking up the Yata Road. It was a second miracle for he almost never gets up before 4 PM. It was a rare honor, he'd been up at 9.
> The event was so pure The feeling of idea moving all around the Little Room. But then coming in to the fact that the thing was very beautiful. Its suggestions in Yata were strongly felt. Its arrangement was simple pinned in Red Orange Yellow Green Light Blue, Blue and Purple from the ceiling edge. The reverse bend or horizontal bow was a pleasure to me – also the suggestive rearrangements. But more to be said in thanks and compliment to you for participating in the series of shows, a pleasure to realize that your pleasure is in the event.

Thankfully J.B.
P.S. your invitation was very good – And I will kept your pieces for you until we meet – soon.

The golden thread inserted in the envelope must have been a kind of complimentary response to Ban's seven colored threads. By this time gold was Byars's signature color. The event in the white shack at Naniwa is still etched in the memories of those who were there. That day in February was one on which Byars's art truly blossomed, simply and splendidly.

However, the college's bureaucracy viewed with disfavor the fact that Byars had enlisted a large number of students in his own performance, and before the end of February they had dismissed him. This incident directly contributed to his decision to leave Japan.

Kyoto Indépendant

(March 8–14, 1967, Kyoto Municipal Museum of Art)

Since 1961, Byars had exhibited work at every *Kyoto Indépendant* except 1966. The 1967 show was the last in which he would participate. He presented an approximately 90-centimeter wide, 30-meter long work on paper in a scroll format with a single hole punched in the middle. It was titled *Hyakushaku no ugoki* (Movement of a hundred *shaku*).

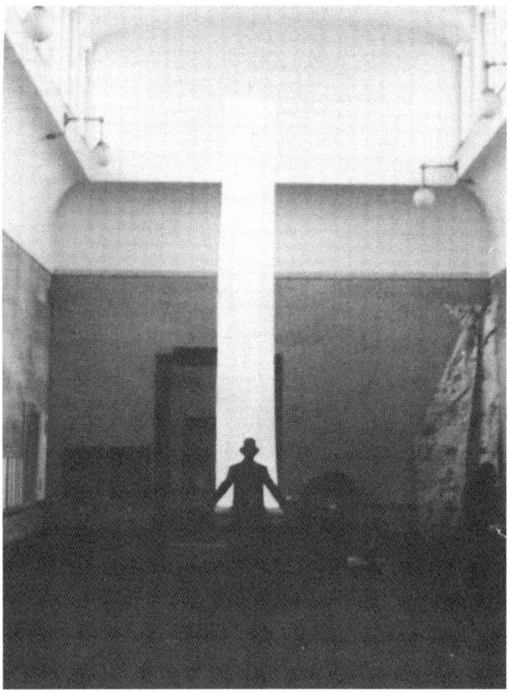

76 Performance at the 1967 *Kyoto Indépendant*

77, 78, 79, 80 (right page) Photos of the performance at the 1967 *Kyoto Indépendant*, courtesy of Ban Fumio

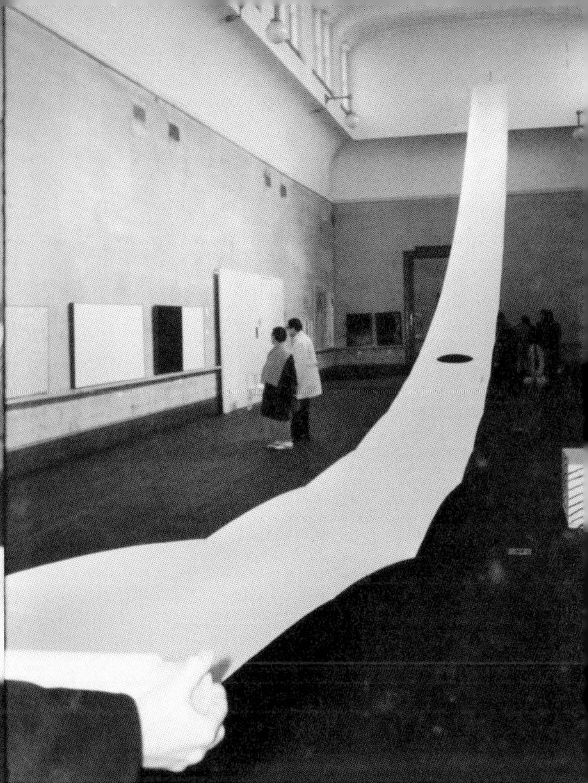
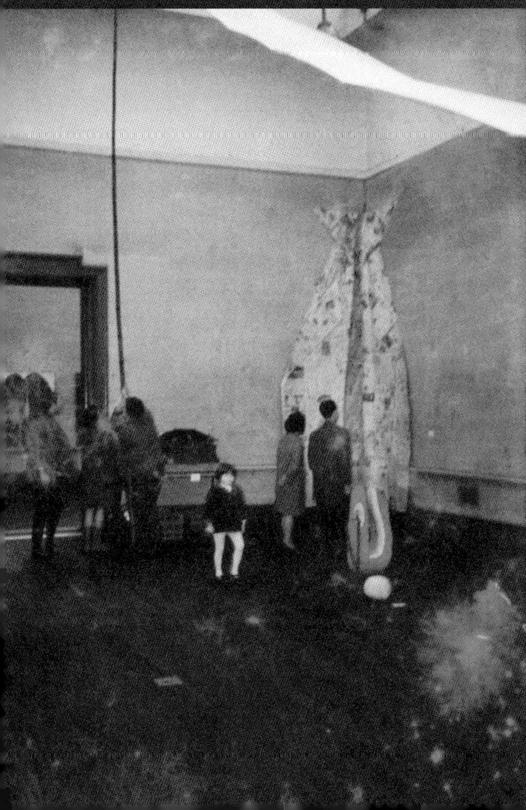
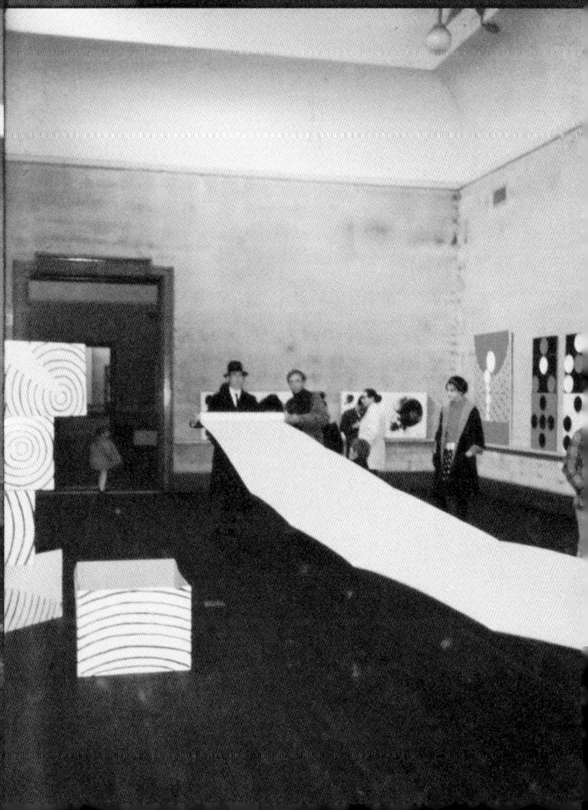

On the first day of the exhibition, Byars stood alone, quietly, at the entrance of the museum in a black suit, black tie, and black top hat, holding the work rolled up in a cylinder. His performance had already begun. A friend, Rem Stone, attached a cord from the edge of the work to a hook at the end of a 12-meter long pole, which he held upright while Byars very slowly unrolled the work. The long white scroll of *Hyakushaku no ugoki* gradually emerged, standing out vividly against the dull ocher wall and sooty brown floor of the Municipal Museum. The dazzling white scroll seemed to radiate its own light. Arrestingly beautiful, the sight stole everyone's breath away.

The work to the right of Byars's was an oversized origami "squid" airplane made out of newspaper by Ban Fumio, titled *No.19673516*. It was named for the publication date and time of the newspaper used as material: March 5, 1967 at 16:00. Upon seeing this paper airplane, Byars brought a clipping from an English newspaper and showed it to Ban one day during the exhibition. Byars said, "There's an ad calling for submissions of paper planes, so I brought it for you. Since you're working on super airplanes, why don't you apply?"

Ban recalls, "I often met Byars at the *Kyoto Indépendant* exhibitions and we spoke to each other, without words. His *Hyakushaku no ugoki* was a truly wonderful thing. I think it's still a cutting-edge work today. Even now I can't get his Eastern sensibility out of my mind."

From the records of the *Kyoto Indépendant* that year:

> Room 5 (Sculpture)
> Hyakushaku no ugoki James L. Byars

From a written reminiscence by Byars that appears in *The Palace of Perfect*:

> I REMEMBER THE 100 FT SCROLL IN THE INDEPENDENT SHOW IN JAPAN. THERE WAS A HOLE IN THE MIDDLE AND SOME ARSEHOLE PUT HIS HEAD THROUGH IT.

And from a letter by Hubbell to Dorothy Miller, dated "3/22/42":

> Jim Byars (f.s., Jim Byars) was represented by a piece of white paper, 2 feet wide and 100 feet long, on a heavy wooden roller. One end of the paper was attached to the top of a pole 40 feet high and was supported by another young man called Rem Stone (f.s., Rem Stone.) One afternoon they stood there for three hours without moving (Jim was holding the other

end) and when we had coffee together later their arms were almost paralyzed.
The other enclosure has nothing to do with the Independants. Still another young American, Rand Castile, is giving a poetry reading, and I enclose the invitation as it shows the influence of Jim Byars.

The Last Trip Home

As I mentioned earlier, following his performances at Naniwa Junior College Byars was fired from his position there as both English teacher and art teacher because the school found it problematic that Byars had put his students to work. Everyone around him worried what would happen to him. Here is a letter that Hubbell wrote to Byars, postmarked February 16:

2/16/42
Dear Jim
Any news about the job?
Thank you so much for directing me to Tennoji. I had a wonderful time. The shokubutsu-en isn't much compared to Kyoto, but the dobutsu-en is superb—the lions and tigers roaming around out doors, and that wonderful Earthly Paradise with deer and birds wandering around together. Then I went to the top of the tower where I had a birdseye view of the whole thing. That neighborhood is a delight—every other building is a strip show—yakuza everywhere.
The next day I went to Kobe, and visited Suwa Jinja . . . Suwa Koen . . . Suwa Yama. It's one of my favorite places. Some day you and Taki-san must go there with me.
I thought of you on St. Valentine's Day.
I was too shy to write to Ban-sensei. Some day please tell him how much I enjoyed his show.
Today I saw the print biennial. I thought that Great Britain and West Germany had the best shows, but my favorite work by an individual was Josef Albers' three lovely prints, and my very favorite print was one by Antonio Calderara (Italy) called "Measure of rectangle" —it's a double white on white.
I'm not on the street at night much lately—I'm too busy and it's too cold. Why don't you come here some evening? But please let me know first, otherwise that is sure to be one of the rare evenings when I do go to the

> Kagetsu or the Yachiyokan.
> love
> Lindley
> Went to Galerie 16 today. Liked Kotsu-san's show.

In the decade following his first arrival in Japan, from 1958 to 1967, Byars returned to the United States seven times. Every time he left Japan he quit whatever position he held as an English teacher. Each time he went home he was planning to come back to Japan, and whenever he came back he had a new job lined up, whether at the YMCA, Doshisha University, Heian Jogakuin, or Naniwa Junior College. But in the spring of 1967, when he got fired from Naniwa, he had no other job to fall back on.

Byars had a veritable mental breakdown from the stress of not being able to find a new job. He was so depressed that he had to receive counseling from an American social worker at Doshisha. After that he made the decision to return to the United States for good, completely withdrawing from Japan.

This entry appears in Abe Hiromu's diary:

> June 3, 1967: Went to the [Kyoto National] Museum in the afternoon and met Miss Taki for the first time in a long while. Viewed the Oriental Exhibition together, then went to the café at the bottom of the stone steps. She said she's worried about him, he can't find work and seems to be depressed.

Says Abe, "Byars did well to return to Japan so often. He'd come by plane, by ship, hop on a freighter and get off in Nagoya. When he arrived he always looked for a house to live in, and always in Kyoto. In the end he lost his job. I remember meeting Miss Taki at the museum in 1967. Byars was still around then. It's in my diary—Miss Taki talking about how he'd become depressed."

10 1967 in the United States

Byars left for the United States in June 1967. Everyone he knew in Japan fully expected him to come back again. For his part, Byars gave no hint that he would not return. But with the expiration of his visa, he could no longer remain in the country, so he headed for Los Angeles.

The biographical notes that appear in the English-language exhibition catalogues mentioned above provide the only substantive records of Byars's activities subsequent to his return to the United States. I have referred to those sources for the following account, in which I focus on activities that relate to his work in Japan and his exposure to Japanese culture. The quotations are primarily from *The Palace of Perfect* (Serralves Foundation, 1997), which, like other Byars catalogues, borrows heavily from James Elliott's "Notes Toward a Biography" in *The Perfect Thought: Works by James Lee Byars* (University of California at Berkeley, 1990), to which it adds a few supplementary details.

Upon first alighting in Los Angeles, Byars stayed for about a month at the home of Stanley and Elyse Grinstein. At the suggestion of the Grinsteins he prepared an all-white meal at their house, much like his previous "white parties" in Japan. *The Palace of Perfect* adds, "The choice of white food suggests the influence of Satie but Byars was, in fact, simply repeating the kind of meal that he had previously prepared in Japan, using red or black rice. This idea is derived from the Shinto practice of setting out 100 little dishes on a table." In fact there is no such tradition in Shinto, but Byars may have said this because he was fond of the number 100. *The Palace of Perfect* also notes that after taking leave of the Grinsteins, Byars stayed for 100 days at the home of Jim Butler, whose wife, Eugenia, ran a gallery. Byars had already moved to New York by August, however, suggesting that the "100 days" reference was another Byars embellishment.

"A White Paper Will Blow Through the Streets"

At some point in 1967 Byars handed out 10,000 white circular sheets of tissue paper with this statement printed on them: "A WHITE PAPER WILL BLOW THROUGH THE STREETS." He had conducted similar performances in Kyoto, sometimes with round sheets, sometimes with square ones. Years later, several of the square sheets were found in a closet in Taki Sachiko's home.

Four in a Dress

This work consisted of a 16-foot diameter circle of silk with four holes cut in the middle for people to poke their heads through. According to *The Palace of Perfect*:

> A white version of *Four in a Dress*, a silk circle with holes cut in the material, is exhibited at the Eugenia Butler Gallery, Los Angeles. People are invited to take off their clothes and get in. Byars sees these dress pieces as a form of "socialising." A black version of this same piece is shown at the Green Gallery, New York, where Byars also presents an action [titled *Poodle Paper*]: shredded white tissue paper that looks like snow covers [gallery owner Richard] Bellamy's small office that is lit by a single small light bulb.

Though listed as a 1967 event, the actual time frame for the "black version" is uncertain, as the Green Gallery was no longer open in 1967. What appears to be a prototype for *Four in a Dress*—a 6-meter diameter circle of *gasenshi* with four round holes in it—was later found in the closet at Taki's house. Taki recalls that it was constructed in 1966 or 1967.

Byars arrived in New York that August, and immediately headed for the Museum of Modern Art to see Dorothy Miller. Although he was unable to meet with Miller, he did see Alicia Legg, who reported the encounter to Miller in the following memo, which reflects her astonishment at the change in Byars's appearance:

> August 4, 1967
> Dear Dorothy:
> Yesterday James Byars telephoned to say he urgently wanted to see me. I gather he had already called your office and heard you are away. I am leaving tomorrow for approximately 3 weeks but I asked him to come in this morning. While this incredible interview is fresh in my mind, I'll try to tell you something of what he said. First, though, I haven't seen him in

several years, actually since his happening at Green Gallery, so I was totally unprepared for his bushy fringe of black hair emerging under his tall white Panama hat. Without the hat, of course, he is fairly bald on top but I'd never seen his head anything but completely shaven. He was wearing yellow shantung trousers and a stiff-front evening shirt without the collar. He has two propositions that he is eager to get underway immediately. When I told him most people are out of New York now he said "all the better," it would be more impressive for what he plans, to have an almost empty city, but what I meant was most people who could help him are away. He took out a purple silk cloth and unfolded it to reveal a twisted length of gold paper thread, 1,000 feet long which he would like to attach on one building such as the Museum and extend to another, such as Philip Johnson's office in the Seagram Building. Apparently he telephoned Philip immediately on his arrival two days ago and Philip did not react to this idea.

He also has a paper ellipse 100 feet long and two feet in diameter with a thread 100 feet long. When these are folded up he proposes they be pasted on a building 100 feet high and let unravel. Tom Messer at the Guggenheim apparently refused the use of the dome for this. He uses north Chinese calligraphy paper which is fairly sturdy, I gather.

He has been in Los Angeles and says that Maurice Tuchman received him with great enthusiasm and although the museum officially did not sponsor him, one of the ladies of their equivalent of the Junior Council did, in putting on a happening of some sort with 500 people dressed in white doing something or other with a cord or scroll between the City Hall and the Los Angeles Times Building which is 1,000 feet. Somebody named Isador Zufferstein, a psychiatrist, was extremely enthusiastic and put him in touch with a Mr. Fink, a Los Angeles dress manufacturer. Fink loved the idea of making a million dresses—four people to a dress. This consists of a huge circular piece of cloth 16 feet in diameter with four holes for heads. The skirt comes to the ankle and presumably the subjects wear nothing underneath. This piece of cloth can also be cut like a pie, in halves or quarters to accommodate two people, or one, respectively.

His final and global proposal is what he calls a "galaxy show" which would consist of a one minute presentation of all means of expression, such as a work of painting or sculpture, a piece of prose or poetry, a phrase of music—almost anything—to be assembled in one place, hopefully MoMA or Santa Barbara (apparently Tom Leavitt has expressed interest). He calls the whole thing "global spontaneity" and even hopes to get Dr.

Werner von Braun to help enlisting Telstar for a verbal-visual announcement.

Byars is presently staying with Gordon Washburn until this Sunday night. He then goes to Mr. Douglas Overton, director of the Japan Society, who lives at 1270 Fifth Avenue. How long he stays there is indefinite.

He ended by saying that being short of funds he is willing to sell a lot of the material he has with him, including yards of folded paper and enormous lengths of string, etc., each item for $1,000 apiece.

Bring this to an end, I can now report that I just talked to Philip Johnson to check his reactions and he says he heard the whole thing on the telephone and is entirely opposed to any participation on his or our part.

Dress for 100

Byars presented this work as part of the *Made With Paper* exhibition (November 15, 1967 to January 7, 1968; sponsored by the Container Corporation of America) at New York's Museum of Contemporary Crafts (now the Museum of Arts and Design). A huge piece of cloth with many holes, from which participants were to protrude their heads, it was "big as a baseball diamond" according to one review by a UPI writer:

> Group Dress Makes Debt In New Body Covering Show
> by Patricia McCormack
> NEW YORK (UPI) — In this era of group insurance, group therapy and group everything, make way for—the group dress.
>
> Such a thing, big enough for four, at once will help serious bridge players to keep their minds on the cards. They won't have to squander mental energy evaluating clothing of fellow players.
>
> The maiden model of the group dress is on view at the Museum of Contemporary Craft's body covering show. But it's just a starter.
>
> James Lee Byars, the designer, also offers a group dress for 100. It's big as a baseball diamond. Dress might be the wrong word. You see, males also may wear it. [. . .] [Newspaper clipping in the possession of Lindley Williams Hubbell; publication name and date unknown]

The Giant Soluble Man

Byars offered this work (see Fig. 28) as an opening performance for the *Made with Paper* exhibition. According to James Elliott's account it was "made of four hundred feet of Dissolvo, a water-soluble paper most often used as 'spy paper'." The manufacturer, the Gilbreth Company of Philadelphia, made a gift of the paper to Byars. The performance, by art students from the Parsons School of Design and members of a boys' choir, consisted of unrolling the title work—a giant human effigy—and laying it across Manhattan's 53rd Street, whereupon passersby were invited to sit, walk over, or lie down on it. Later, two streetcleaning trucks arrived and washed the paper away, at which point the performance ended.

According to Taki, the idea for this work had been incubating since Byars's Kyoto days. He envisioned making a larger-than-lifesize human figure out of *oblaat*, a thin, water-soluble, edible layer of starch used to wrap candy or medicine in Japan. His notion was that the figure would dissolve in the rain. Byars had even begun negotiating with an *oblaat* manufacturer and working on a prototype. The idea originated, apparently, with the solid sumi-ink blocks that Byars used, which arrived wrapped in *oblaat* that gradually dissolved over time. This transformation fascinated him.

As mentioned earlier, paper doll-like *hitogata* effigies (see Fig. 27) have played a role in Shinto rituals since time immemorial. Serving as a stand-in for their donor, they take on impurities and misfortune, which are washed away with them in a river or the sea. Today it is still a common practice to write one's name, age, and a wish on a *hitogata*, blow on it, and submit it with a prayer to a Shinto shrine. At some places, like Jishu Shrine in Kyoto, the supplicant dissolves the *hitogata* in water after blowing on it.

11 1968 in New York

In 1968 the Architectural League of New York awarded Byars a J. Clawson Mills Grant for $6,000, which Byars used to produce a series of events. His opening performance earned coverage in an article in the *New York Times*:

> A Mile of Red Acetate Parades Here
> By Grace Glueck
> Was it a protest? A love-in? A graduation procession? Or maybe—heaven forbid—a Shriners' convention?
>
> Those were some of the questions blasé upper East Siders asked last evening as they watched some 130 people march up East 65th Street toward Park Avenue, turn north on Park and wind around the block. What caught their attention was the marchers' garb. They were joined together in a mile-long communal garment of red acetate, heads poking through holes cut at three-foot intervals.
>
> "It's probably the world's biggest dress," said James Lee Byars, an artist who masterminded the parade and was himself separately enfolded in a pink silk "pants suit" that tied at the chin and could expand to include five persons.
>
> "Call the parade what you like. I'm tired of words like 'event' and 'happening,' with their open-ended definitions. I simply call this one 'Do.'"
>
> Actually, the divertissement was intended to celebrate the opening of "Mr. Byars and Six Pays [*sic*]," a series of audience participation events dealing with communication and behavior that will run through Oct. 3 at the Architectural League, 41 East 65th Street, where the procession originated.
>
> The events—or "plays" as Mr. Byars prefers to call them—will include "100 in an Airplane," in which 100 volunteers will be asked to pretend to fly a 100-foot-square silk airplane; "Twelve in a Pink Pants," in which a dozen people will don a continuous silk suit to discuss their life styles with

Mr. Byars, and "Construction of a Mile-Long Strip," in which a Chinese tailor will sew a mile of acetate into a single strip.

As a kickoff event, last night's procession of volunteers was stately but far from staid. As it left the league building, it moved to strains of Bach's E-Flat Fugue, played by a tuba quintet (maybe the world's first) known as The Substructure. The quintet was echoed by Janet Farrell, a flutist, playing on the building's balcony.

Shere Hite, a blond model and friend of Mr. Byars, led the procession and soon shucked off her blouse under the enveloping garment ("It's delightful to feel the wind"). Peter Flynn, a Columbia student, walked backward in the parade ("Why not? It's releasing") and met Cara Goalstone, an administrative aide at the Cornell College of Architecture who occupied a head-hole behind him. And four-year-old Charles Beckman, who came with his parents and 2-year-old brother, ducked out of his head-hole and ran through the garment tickling people's legs.

"I feel slightly silly, but it's a lot of fun," said Bob Lanier, a young architect as he marched near the head of the line. Reginald Perry, another young architect, from Tennessee, reported that he felt "kind of young—like the first time I was taken to the fair. You don't know what to expect. There's a lot of color and a bit of confusion."

Suddenly, a large section of the strip emerged from the league building with head-holes untenanted, and a number of people deserted their positions up front to run back and fill them.

"Hey, is that a demonstration?" a taxi driver asked a policeman assigned to parade duty as the line rounded 65th Street onto Park Avenue. At 630 Park Avenue Dennis Moloney, a doorman, asked, "It's just for fun? You mean they're not advertising anything?"

"We're Klan members," said David Pratt, a Columbia student, to a questioning bystander. "We're having an adventure in communication," he informed another, gravely.

As the marchers turned on to Madison Avenue, friends of Mr. Byars cut sections of the garment apart, and participants were released into clumps of five. At a postparade cocktail party back at the league, the garment was further divided, and soon nearly everyone was wearing a piece of it, separately or in doubles.

Mr. Byars, who has been given a J. Clawson Mills grant of $6,000 by the league to do the series, will hold an all-day session there today to discuss last night's activities with participants and others. He said one of the ques-

> tions he hoped to explore in connection with the block-encircling parade was "What does it mean to put a ring around something?"
>
> John Lobell, who is in charge of the league's exhibition program, explained, "We're interested in such vital questions as 'What is man and what's happening to him today?' Artists can do the most adequate job of exploring such questions." [*New York Times*, September 13, 1968]

An accompanying photo of Byars draped in fabric is captioned: "James Lee Byars wore expandable suit in the event."

Mr. Byars and Six Plays

The title of the league-sponsored series, *Mr. Byars and Six Plays*, is explained in *The Palace of Perfect* as follows:

> Byars uses the term 'plays' to describe these actions since he found that the twenty-eight definitions of the word 'play' in the Oxford English Dictionary applied to his work. He later adopts the term 'actions.' The six plays scheduled were *Do, Fly, Can't, Talk, Breathe* (also called *Two in a Hat*) and *Try*.

The number six has a special significance in Buddhism. The Six Realms (*rokudo*), for example, are the six domains of existence—gods, demi-gods, humans, animals, hungry ghosts, and hells—into which unenlightened beings are reincarnated. The Six Great Elements (*rokudai*) that form the basis of all creation are earth, water, fire, wind, space, and consciousness. Also in Buddhism, the number 666, of which Byars was fond, represents the six faculties or sense organs, six objects, and six consciousnesses. The six organs (*rokkon*) are the eye, ear, nose, tongue, body, and mind; the corresponding six objects (*rokkyo*) of the senses are forms, sounds, odors, flavors, textures, and phenomena; and the six consciousnesses (*rokushiki*) are sight, hearing, smell, taste, touch, and thought. Collectively these are referred to as the Eighteen Elements to which human beings form attachments. Only by freeing oneself from these attachments can one become enlightened. Yet at the same time these elements are already empty and devoid of form. Hence, ultimately, all is emptiness—a fundamental tenet of Buddhism.

Pink Silk Airplane

Many of Byars's 1968 performances at the Architectural League involved long pieces of fabric with numerous holes in them. One of these, *Pink Silk Airplane*, is described in *The Palace of Perfect* as having "holes for 100 people to stick their heads through."

> Presents *Pink Silk Airplane* and other events at the Architectural League. Byars 'like a pink pilgrim' sits on the floor and talks to visitors. He tells one visitor: 'I want people to come and develop an awareness about their perceptions, their behavioral cycles, what they eat, their life styles.' He also presents what he calls 'plays' in which he poses open-ended questions such as 'What does "pretend" mean?' And 'Is self-conscious option enough?'

Breakfasts with Howard Junker

The Palace of Perfect describes what appears to have been a series of breakfasts with Howard Junker, the New York–based writer who corresponded that same year with Lindley Williams Hubbell, sending him questions about Byars on postcards.

> Breakfasts with Howard Junker. Presents *Life's Six Likes* (Life is like a dream, like a vision, like a bubble, like a shadow, like dew, like lightning) and speaks of his favourite three: Stein, Einstein, and Wittgenstein. Howard Junker notes: "The first days Byars appeared at appointed hour 'at eye level'; as I looked out my window at the park across the street, there he was standing quite still, looking at me, waiting to be noticed. He had several days before, knowing my address, stood at various levels waiting for me to notice him. 'How interesting' that it is so difficult to see who you do not expect. The second day he brought me a golden pencil."

Byars's "six likes" are a quote from the Diamond Sutra: "All conditioned phenomena are like a dream, an illusion, a bubble, a shadow, like dew or a flash of lightning; thus we shall perceive them." These episodes involving the number six suggest that Byars was beginning to use it as a symbol signifying awareness of the unseen.

By now a year and a half had passed since Byars's departure from Japan. In his activities during that period, he seems to have set aside paper as a medium in favor of large pieces of fabric, as well as carrying out other performances that might be said to revolve around the concept of "consciousness." His output in both categories was nothing short of astonishing. Byars himself is quoted in *The Palace of Perfect* as saying he was "amazed by the reception my ideas had in New York, when I first came back from Japan."

12 1969 from the U.S. and Canada to Europe

100 People in a Dress

From *The Palace of Perfect*:

> *Electric Art*. Exhibition at the Dickson Gallery, University of California at Los Angeles. Byars scheduled to do an opening night performance, *100 People in a Dress*. This piece consists of one hundred nude people in a single red garment that shows only their heads. At the last moment the performance was moved to the Dwan Gallery in Westwood. January 19th to March 23rd.

It should be noted that the Dwan Gallery, a prominent champion of conceptual art, had closed its Los Angeles space in 1967, although a New York branch remained open until 1971. It is possible that the actual venue was the ACE Gallery, which occupied the former Dwan Gallery premises by 1969.

The Art and Technology Project

Further excerpts from the *The Palace of Perfect* chronology for 1969:

> [Curator] Maurice Tuchman invites Byars to take part in the Art and Technology project at the Los Angeles County Museum of Art. Byars's first proposal involves sending a rocket to Mars with the help of the Jet Propulsion Laboratories in Pasadena. This project is rejected. Later he is accepted as the artist-in-residence at the Hudson Institute in upstate New York where he works with Herman Kahn. [. . .] Byars conceives of the *World*

> *Question Center* and begins to implement it through letter writing and by using a telephone WATS line provided by the institute. [. . .] Also while at Hudson Institute produces *The Book on Edible Paper*, which had been conceived before 1967 when he first worked with soluble paper. While attending a meeting at the Pentagon with Herman Kahn Byars proposes that he be appointed *Artist of the Pentagon*. [. . .]
>
> Invited by David Askevold to be visiting artist at Nova Scotia College of Art and Design in Halifax [Canada] during the fall term [. . .]. Does several multiple garment events around Halifax with student participation: *100 in a Hat*; *Cake*, a disc-shaped piece of fabric with openings for twenty heads; and *Two Consciousness Pieces*, a one-hundred-foot strip of red silk covering all but the eyes of the performers who remain still for one half hour. In the city Byars passes out white index cards inscribed *Mr. Byars is the artist in the Pentagon*.

Tuchman's Art and Technology program, which introduced artists to corporations and think tanks for collaborative projects, began in 1967 and continued until 1971. Byars's invitation to the Hudson Institute, a think tank founded in 1961 by the futurist Herman Kahn, was part of this program. While at the institute Byars submitted a variety of proposals, including numerous ideas for participation in Expo '70 in Osaka. However, *The Book on Edible Paper* appears to be the only project that reached fruition while he was there.

In Europe

Elliott mentions that around this time (1969), "Rumors spread in Europe that Byars works for the CIA, a misunderstanding that caused a degree of difficulty for him among European artists for some years." He attributes this to Byars's self-proclaimed association with the Pentagon during his Art and Technology project. As we will see later, however, this was not the only aspect of Byars's behavior that sparked rumors of CIA involvement.

1969 was also the year when Byars first began working in Europe. From *The Palace of Perfect*:

> Anny de Decker, director of Wide White Space, Antwerp, invites Byars to exhibit for the first time in Europe. The gallery is renamed *The Institute for the Advanced Study of James Lee Byars*. He exhibits the *Pink Silk Airplane*

(only the body is used), later used in the *World Question Center* (November) and begins to draft his first book.

Isi Fiszmann introduces Byars to Joseph Beuys at the Dusseldorf Academy of Art. Byars gives spontaneous *Performance of Pretension* with the *Pink Silk Airplane*, which Beuys and his students helped to recreate. 100 students fill the plane. Byars tells them to "pretend to fly" and to remain silent. At end of action they cut up the plane into fragments.

From Elliott's chronology:

This Is a Call from the Ghost of James Lee Byars. Performance with participants in Antwerp and Los Angeles. Creates a triangular paper work imprinted "Please limit all talking to the sound of O, as preview given by W.W.S. Antwerp to This Is the Ghost of James Lee Byars Calling." The paper was to be worn around the head.

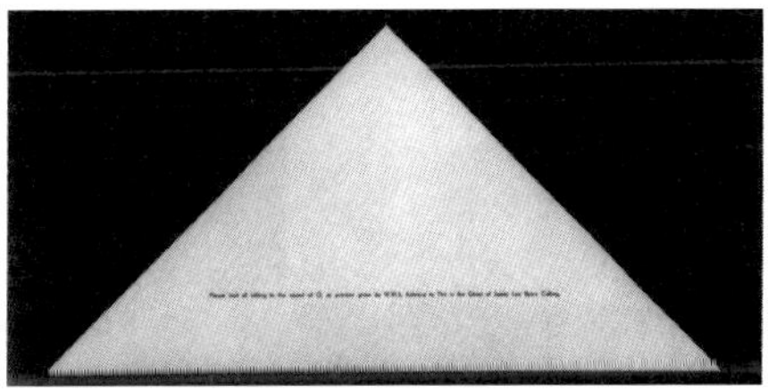

81 The triangular paper from *This Is a Call from the Ghost of James Lee Byars*, with a printed request to "Please limit all talking to the sound of O"

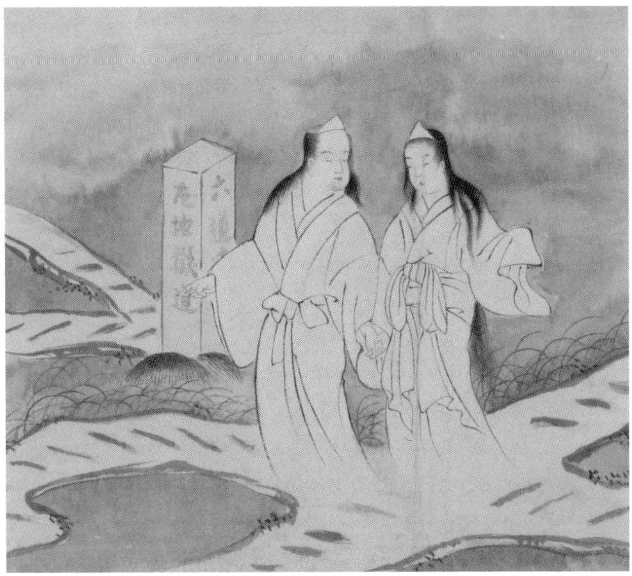

82 *Hell Scroll (Jigoku zoshi emaki)*, courtesy of the International Research Center for Japanese Studies

A triangular sheet of paper is customarily placed on the head of the deceased at Japanese funerals. Paintings of ghosts also frequently show them wearing a triangular paper on their foreheads. See Fig. 82, in which two spirits of the recently departed stand at a crossroads in the afterworld, unsure which of the aforementioned Six Realms to proceed to. The triangular image is also reminiscent of the pyramids, the great tombs in whose shadow Byars died in Egypt.

Also from Elliott:

> Live broadcast on Belgian national television of the World Question Center, held at Wide White Space. The center consisted of several scores of students from the University of Brussels dressed in a plural garment, telephoning celebrated intellectuals and asking them to state what questions they are asking themselves. November.

Among the "celebrated intellectuals" who participated, either in person or by phone, were the composer John Cage, the architect Hans Hollein, and the artist Marcel Broodthaers. Byars's World Question Center project has survived online to this day, collecting questions from around the world via the internet.

The *Fundoshi* of 1969

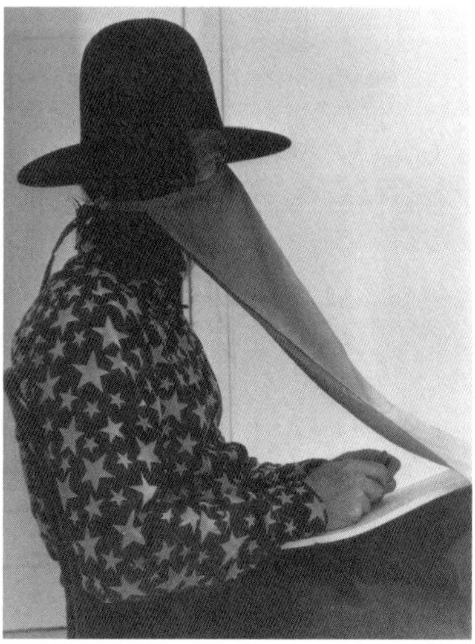

83 Byars wearing his *fundoshi* in *1/2 an Autobiography*

There was at least one more European event in 1969, this one involving underwear. Before returning to the United States, Byars had asked Taki Sachiko to make him a *fundoshi*—a traditional Japanese men's undergarment, in the form of a loincloth—from silk. Like a standard cotton *fundoshi*, it had cords attached to one end for tying. In 1969 Byars used it in a performance in Antwerp, at Anny de Decker's Wide White Space. Perhaps not too surprisingly, Byars appeared wearing it tied around his face. Records suggest the performance was titled *1/2 an Autobiography* (see Fig. 83).

Taki also recalls seeing a photograph in an American newspaper of a Byars show in which a model performed some sort of action with the *fundoshi* hanging from her neck. It would seem that Byars drew inspiration for this work from the sartorial culture of Japan, in which a single piece of rectangular fabric can be sewn into any number of articles of clothing.

Byars's use of the *fundoshi* in performances began as early as 1968. A fashion column in the *New York Post* dated November 12, 1968, about a Manhattan boutique opened by photographer Bert Stern, suggests that Byars's *fundoshi* had even become a marketable fashion item:

> For the new boutique Bert Stern also has an artist in residence, James Hilary [*sic*] Byars, who looks like a Mennonite father with shoulder-length hair, a wide-brimmed black hat and a frock coat. His job is to furnish ideas, usable or not. In Bert Stern's office the other day, dozens of his ideas were sketched on circles of pale pink paper and scattered over the floor for him to look at.
>
> Byars' first saleable idea is a long strip of fragile silk with ties at the top. It's called Mask or Underwear, and it's no smiling matter.
>
> Mask or Underwear is the small start of a new trend in fashion. [. . .] Dozens of Bert Stern's friends are already wearing the silk thing in different ways. [Eugenia Sheppard, "Inside Fashion," *New York Post*, November 12, 1968]

The Hidden Side of Success

Since returning to the United States, Byars had stopped communicating with Taki. In 1969 she traveled to the U.S. to see the country and to find a sponsor for her study of psychology, which she wished to continue in America. Also at the top of her list, of course, was to look for Byars, whose career as an artist appeared to be gaining momentum. However, she was unable to ascertain his whereabouts, perhaps because he was traveling between the U.S. and Europe so frequently at that point.

In the course of her travels, Taki visited Byars's family home on Grayfield Street in suburban Detroit and accepted his parents' invitation to spend the night there. It was a very small house, she recalls. Byars's mother expressed indignation at her son's treatment of Taki, saying, "You've come all this way, and yet Jim won't give you the time of day. That's inexcusable." Taki vividly remembers that the elms that lined the street were being killed off by a blight, that a stream flowed behind the property, and that Byars's parents took her on a picnic to a nearby park with a small lake.

Taki was subsequently fortunate enough to find a job in the U.S. related to clinical psychology. By 1970 she was working at a New York hospital when she received a single letter from Byars. It was written on a sheet of thin pink paper in the shape of a large heart, but consisted of nothing more than superficial greetings.

Rand Castile, who had returned to the United States about the same time as Byars, was extremely helpful to Taki during this period, she says. He told her, "These days Jim is big in the newspapers and magazines. He's also attracting a lot of critical attention. But since he left Kyoto and came back to America, he seems to have gotten quite wild. He's not like he used to be. It's as if he's lost some of his peace of mind."

Katharine Ormiston, the British artist who had lived in the same neighborhood in Kyoto and treated Byars and Taki to meals of *oyako donburi* (chicken and egg on rice), visited Byars in San Francisco for old times' sake, but came away deeply distressed by the meeting. That was in 1972. Though Ormiston did not go into details, Taki remembers that she sounded shocked by what she had encountered. The change in Byars was so profound and painful to see, Ormiston said, that it put her at a loss for words.

According to a friend of Lindley Williams Hubbell, the individual who had the greatest impact on Byars during his Kyoto days, Hubbell once remarked, "After Byars returned to the States, he grew harder and harder to make sense of." There is no way to know what transpired between the two men. However, a student of Hubbell who cared for him in his final years says that he eventually disposed of all the items he had retained that were associated with Byars—this despite having treated even the most mundane letters, presents, and invitations from Byars as works of art when he had exhibited them in January 1967.

The Spy Rumors

When Byars first arrived in Japan in 1958, the country was finally emerging from the aftermath of World War II and the Occupation (1945–52), entering a period of surging economic growth triggered by the "special procurements" boom that had accompanied the Korean War. In 1959 Tokyo won the rights to host the 1964 Summer Olympics, and construction of the first Shinkansen "bullet train" line commenced the same year. "The postwar era is over" was a popular catchphrase, and tourists from the United States began pouring into the country. America's Cold War with the Soviet Union had brought the two nations closer, to the extent that Japan was sometimes referred to, either proudly or disparagingly, as "America's 52nd state" (the "51st" being Canada). The country's drift toward vassal statehood under the American umbrella was accelerated by the Vietnam War. As presidents Kennedy and Johnson committed growing numbers of troops to the conflict, Japan became the de facto supply depot for U.S. military forces. Now the most pro-American nation in Asia, Japan not surprisingly attracted so many individuals engaged in espionage that it became known as a "spy's paradise."

Within the ten-year period from 1958 to 1967, Byars returned to the United States no less than seven times. As someone who barely eked out a living from part-time English teaching jobs, and appeared to spend virtually his entire salary on art supplies, how did he manage to make so many cross-Pacific trips? It was their sheer frequency that gave rise, more than anything else, to rumors in Japan that Byars was a spy for the CIA.

Yet people who knew Byars well unanimously rejected that allegation. Any time it was brought up, Lindley Williams Hubbell was known to retort, "Jim is absolutely not a spy! I can say that with complete certainty!"

Taki Sachiko, who was close to Byars for most of his decade in Japan, declares emphatically, "He did not have the kind of personality capable of espionage. Jim was someone who paid no attention to what other people said, or to their intentions, unless there was some direct and immediate benefit to him involved—someone offering to give him a show or buy his work, for example. A spy has to infiltrate a group of strangers in a foreign country and do it without bringing attention to himself or divulging his true identity, doesn't he? Jim lived his life on the exact opposite terms. To produce his art or carry out his plans he would work himself to death to make money, then spend it all on his art. You might say he was the ultimate egoist. It's inconceivable that someone like that would act in a spirit of service to his country or anyone else other than himself."

Whatever the source of the funds that enabled Byars to travel so often to the United States and back during his Japan sojourn, one particular acquaintance was instrumental in facilitating his final return home to a "soft landing" in Los Angeles by introducing him to Maurice Tuchman, curator at the Los Angeles County Museum of Art (LACMA). It was also the Tuchman connection that led to his joining the Art and Technology project in 1969 and resulted, however inadvertently, in the spy rumors that later dogged Byars outside Japan as well.

The friend who introduced Byars to Tuchman was Anne Truitt, a sculptor who was married to James Truitt, the Tokyo bureau chief for *Newsweek* magazine. She came to Japan with her husband in 1963 and lived there until 1967, holding solo exhibitions of sculptures, paintings, and drawings at Tokyo's Minami Gallery in 1964 and 1967. In 1974, while preparing for a retrospective at the Whitney Museum in New York, she destroyed all the sculptures she had made in Japan, saying she no longer liked the work. Distancing herself from sculpting and art in general, she later became known for her superb writing in a series of highly introspective journals. She died in 2004 at age eighty-three; a posthumous retrospective of her art was held at Washington's Hirshhorn Museum in 2009.

In an extensive interview that took place in 2002 and is preserved in the Smithsonian Institution's *Archives of American Art,* Truitt speaks at length about her friendship with Byars, whom she regarded as "one of the very first minimal artists":

> He was fascinating. And a friend of mine whom I'd known from Big Sur [an artist colony on the California coast], Louisa Jenkins, gave me his name and wrote him a letter, and he wrote me letters and we became friends. He's about the only friend I had in Japan. He used to come up from Kyoto and stay with us, he and his girl, Taki San. [. . .] And he went back and forth to America. [. . .]
>
> I have some of his work [. . .] which he gave me with the instructions for me to destroy it, and I said, "I'm not going to destroy it." [. . .] So he gave it to me anyway and I have it. [. . .] Imagine destroying it. I wasn't going to do that. But that was the whole essence of what his work was about, coming into being and going out of being, and about the passage of time. [. . .] A very interesting man and a real friend, and the only person in all of Japan that I found with whom I could really talk. We used to converse back and forth. [. . .] He was compatible. Mad. Quite mad, but compatible.
>
> Finally, he ran out of money, but that was usual; he never had any money. But he ran out of his visa, and that was a serious matter. Then they were going to deport him, so I called Maurice Tuchman at the Los Angeles County Museum. And greatly to his credit and forever to his credit, he met [Byars] at the airport. I put him on the plane in Japan and Maurice Tuchman met him in L.A. and took him under his wing and launched him into America. [. . .] I'd only met [Tuchman] once before in my lifetime, and I called him up from Tokyo. He could perfectly well have ignored me. [. . .] And he could have ignored a perfectly unknown artist. [Oral history interview with Anne Truitt, April–August 2002, *Archives of American Art,* Smithsonian Institution]

As Alicia Legg noted in her memo to Dorothy Miller of August 4, 1967, Tuchman, who had been hired as LACMA's first curator of twentieth-century art, encouraged Byars to produce performances in Los Angeles and later invited him to be one of the artists in the museum's Art and Technology program. This gave Byars an unprecedented opportunity to come up with one outlandish idea after another and a platform for gaining exposure in American art circles. Ironically, however, it was

Byars's irreverent claim to the position of "artist in the Pentagon," inscribed on cards he handed out at performances, that gave rise to the spy rumors.

Taki recalls meeting Louisa Jenkins, the mosaic artist who introduced Byars to Anne Truitt. Jenkins visited Kyoto in 1963, staying at a Zen temple there for a period of time. It makes sense that she thought Truitt would enjoy meeting another idiosyncratic American artist living in Japan.

In 1973, six years after Byars had left Japan, the art critic Hariu Ichiro happened to run into him in Berlin. In his book *Hariu Ichiro jihitsu nenpu* (Hariu Ichiro's personal records), published by Wako University Press in 1996, he describes how he was invited to participate in a five-day series of talks in Berlin about producing an international exhibition, and encountered Byars at the venue (participants included Joseph Beuys, Richard Hamilton, and Achille Bonito Oliva; however, the exhibition never took place).

Their first meeting, Hariu writes, was over a meal he was having with Beuys and the other participants. Beuys asked Hariu his opinion about something, whereupon Byars, who was sitting close by, interrupted: "In this situation a Japanese usually won't say anything at all." Then he went on: "Strawberry cultivation is very advanced in Japan. They grow big strawberries in plastic greenhouses. They even have special boxes on Japan Airlines for keeping strawberries under the seats, and they export them overseas in all seasons." Hariu retorted, "When I went to your country, America, they didn't want to give me a visa. They finally gave me one for just one week, and wrote 'Only to survey the art museums and galleries' in my passport. In other words, your country is the kind that begrudges even a visa like that. What's more, I despise the industrial development in Japan that you are talking about. You're the one who's really Japanese." Byars stared long and hard at Hariu, then responded, "You're a leftist VIP, maybe on a par with Khrushchev or Chaplin. Are you sure you can return safely to Japan?"

According to Hariu, the belief that Byars was a spy for the CIA was widespread in Europe at the time. Hariu himself saw Byars's works as a kind of code, which he associated with that rumor. While we may never know for sure if there was any truth to it, any such activities by Byars certainly had no discernible impact on his artistic vision.

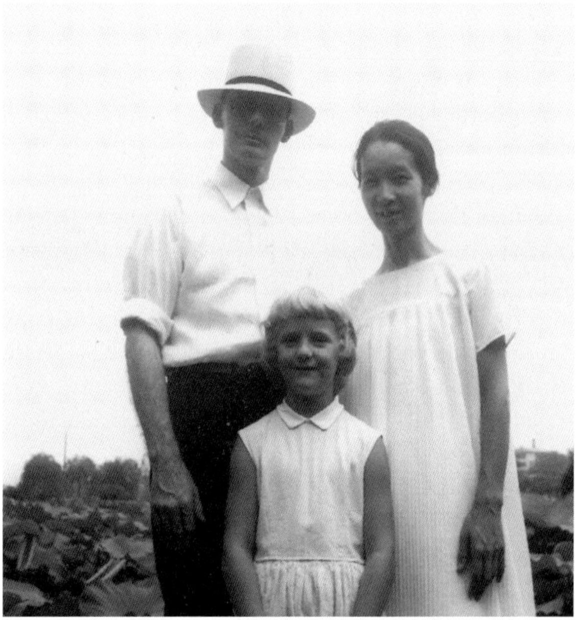

84 Byars and Taki with Anne Truitt's daughter in Kyoto

13 *Documenta* in Kassel, Germany

In 1972, a year before the artists' gathering in Berlin, Byars's visibility in Europe took a quantum leap with his participation in *Documenta 5*, the contemporary art exhibition held in Kassel, Germany. The artistic director was the legendary Swiss art critic and curator Harald Szeemann. In 1969 Szeemann had curated an exhibition titled *Live in Your Head: When Attitudes Become Form* at the Kunsthalle Bern, where he was director. This show drew attention for its incorporation of happenings and performance art by permitting artists to bring in steel, oil, and other raw materials to produce their works on site and in public. Szeemann was known for questioning the very nature of art by prioritizing the creation process over the finished work, arguing that meaning was to be found in the message inherent in that process. Szeemann's activities as director of *Documenta 5* were not without controversy, as Hariu Ichiro noted in a 2010 essay, "My Encounters with This Region," in the art journal *Aida*:

> Szeemann filled the three exhibition halls with some 500 works that skirted the edge of mediocrity, incorporating elements of the sensational popular culture of the day, primarily through happenings and conceptual art. The entirety of *Documenta 5* thus had the appearance of a hodgepodge of oddities. For example, James Lee Byars, an American who lived in Kyoto for some years after the war, dressed in a crimson robe and turban and stood atop the portico of the Fridericianum, yelling out nonsense syllables ("Eu," "Au," "Pus") through a megaphone in a performance he titled "Calling German Names." The German artist Joseph Beuys took up a position at the entrance to the same building, where he spent every day, from opening to closing time, answering visitors' questions on all manner of topics, from differences between East and West Germany, to religious issues, to discrimination against women. Moreover, these lectures were the sum total of his participation in the show. Meanwhile, Ben Vautier of France placed a bed in the middle of the room next to that of Beuys and slept there, do-

> ing nothing for the entire duration except to get up to go to the toilet. The American La Monte Young brought a multi-member band that performed an interminable drone of Indian-like music, while most of the audience lay sprawled on a carpet. The exhibition also featured countless paintings that resembled posters or pornograffiti. [Translated from *Aida* 174, July 20, 2010]

After the exhibition, the city of Kassel and the state of Hessen threatened to sue Szeemann for incurring huge losses by displaying nothing but oddities and trivia. He was able to avoid charges only by resigning from the Kunsthalle and forfeiting his severance pay to compensate for the show's losses. Yet this particular *Documenta*, which seemed to be a sure recipe for controversy, also earned an unprecedented degree of attention.

Szeemann had invited Byars to Bern and loaned him his Bern apartment for the summer. Thanks to Szeemann's good offices, Byars acquired an image in Europe as the "face of *Documenta*" and was able to establish a foothold on the continent. From that point on, Byars's reputation in Europe, and particularly in Germany, would continue to grow, and he went on to participate in *Documenta 6, 7, 8*, and *9*.

14 Return to Japan: Tokyo, 1993

In 1993, Byars returned to Japan for the first time in twenty-seven years. The occasion was a solo exhibition at SCAI The Bathhouse, a contemporary art gallery opened by Shiraishi Masami (SCAI stands for Shiraishi Contemporary Art Inc.) in a converted public bath in the Yanaka district of Tokyo. The show took place from November 5 to December 18. Byars and Shiraishi first met in 1992 at *Documenta 9*. Byars had placed *White Figure*, a white cube of marble, in the middle of a completely white room, creating a mystical space that generated a blurry, halation-like visual effect. In the wall behind the work was a window through which trees and leaves could be seen swaying and rustling in the wind. The sensation was of a reality too dazzling to bear. To Shiraishi, it was a space the likes of which he had never encountered before. At the time he was in the midst of renovating the 200-year-old bathhouse near the Yanaka Cemetery where he would open his new gallery. He decided that his inaugural show had to be by Byars. Through negotiations with Michael Werner, the Cologne gallery owner who represented Byars, Shiraishi was able to acquire two works on consignment: *Eros* (1992) and *The Spherical Book* (*Q Is Point*) (1990).

Arriving in Japan before the show with his second wife, an American said to be from a wealthy family, Byars produced a work about his own size and shape from gold-colored paper on site. Cutting the paper into a long, rectangular strip rounded at the top, he framed and hung it just inside the entrance to the bathhouse.

On November 4, at a pre-opening event, Byars, in a golden suit, stood in front of the framed work greeting visitors. Every ten minutes or so he would disappear. When Shiraishi asked him where he had gone, he replied that he was visiting a neighborhood temple to absorb "the spirit of the atmosphere."

During the exhibition Byars also put on a performance in which he scattered small circular pieces of gold paper printed with the words "Your Presence Is the Best Work" or "A Presence Is the Best Work."

Byars introduced his wife as belonging to "the very wealthy Gulbenkian family of Portugal." Shiraishi had booked the couple a tiny three-mat room in a cheap hotel frequented by young travelers. The room was so small that Byars woke up to find his feet protruding from the air vent in one corner, a story the couple told with much laughter. Byars was already suffering from cancer and said that he had had a tumor weighing several pounds removed from his stomach, but he appeared to be in good spirits and enjoying his sojourn in Japan.

One of the facilitators of the SCAI exhibition was Nishida Kosaku, owner of the Nishida Gallery in Nara. Like Shiraishi, Nishida saw Byars's *White Figure* at *Documenta 9* and was deeply affected by it. Before returning to Japan, he visited Seoul to attend the opening of an exhibition by Murakami Takashi and Nakamura Masato. There he met Koyama Tomio, who was then working for SCAI, and told him, "If you go to Kassel, be sure not to miss Byars."

Once the opening of the SCAI show was out of the way, Byars and his wife traveled to Nara, where Nishida, having been asked by Shiraishi to look after them, met Byars for the first time. The couple, who were getting along well at the time, spent two nights at the Tenpyo Hotel, a Japanese-style inn near the Sarusawa Pond that Nishida had booked for them. They ate udon noodles, saw the sights, and generally seemed to thoroughly enjoy their first trip to Nara. Nishida recalls Byars saying he couldn't believe that he had never once visited Nara despite living in nearby Kyoto for nearly ten years.

Byars also visited Kyoto for the first time since 1967. One of his frequent haunts, galerie 16, had moved to a different location. His old friend Hubbell, now ninety-two, was hospitalized and bedridden. Byars, galerie 16 owner Inoue Michiko, and Mizutani Yoko, who had served as intermediary between the gallery and Hubbell when he first proposed his 1967 Byars show, shared a cab to the hospital and visited Hubbell. The three gathered around his bed and chatted for some time. Then Mizutani and Inoue quietly left the room so Byars and Hubbell could talk alone. The two men spent an hour together; no one knows what they said to each other, but there was surely a tacit understanding between them that this would be their last meeting.

Hubbell had been one of Byars's best friends in Kyoto. He introduced Byars to Noh, Kagura, and other hallmarks of Japanese culture, but also whetted his interest in Shakespeare and Stein. Their many mutually stimulating conversations had a tremendous impact on Byars. At the same time Hubbell encouraged the younger man in his art, recognizing its value from the outset and even hosting an exhibition for him. Hubbell passed away on October 2, 1994, less than a year after their final encounter. Byars and his wife returned to the United States sometime before the end of 1993.

The seven photos on the following pages were taken by Anzai Shigeo at the November 4 pre-opening party at SCAI The Bathhouse.

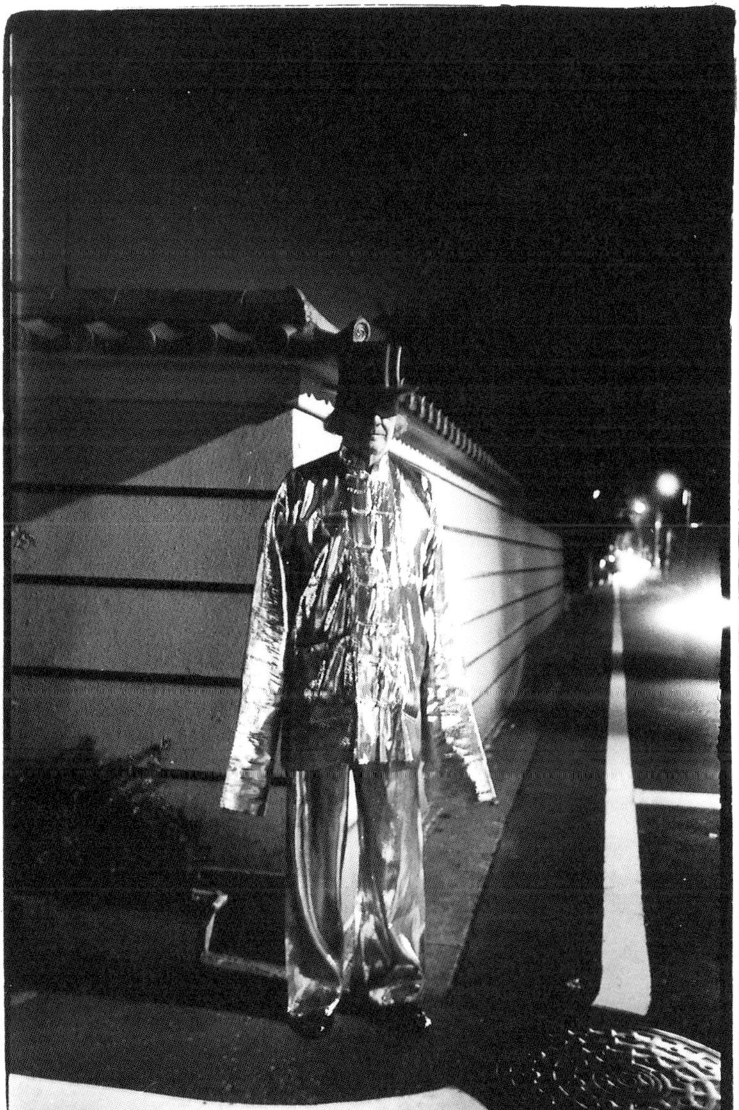

James Lee Byars
Nov 4 '93 Ueno, Tokyo

85

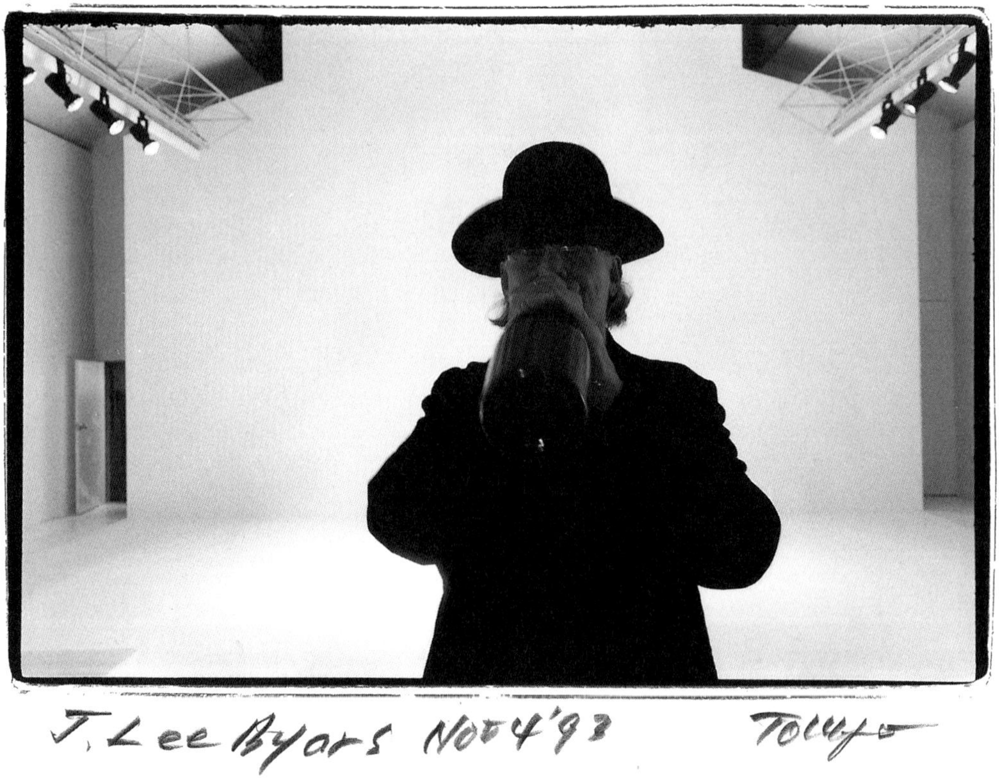

86

85 - 91 Photos by Anzai Shigeo, November 4, 1993

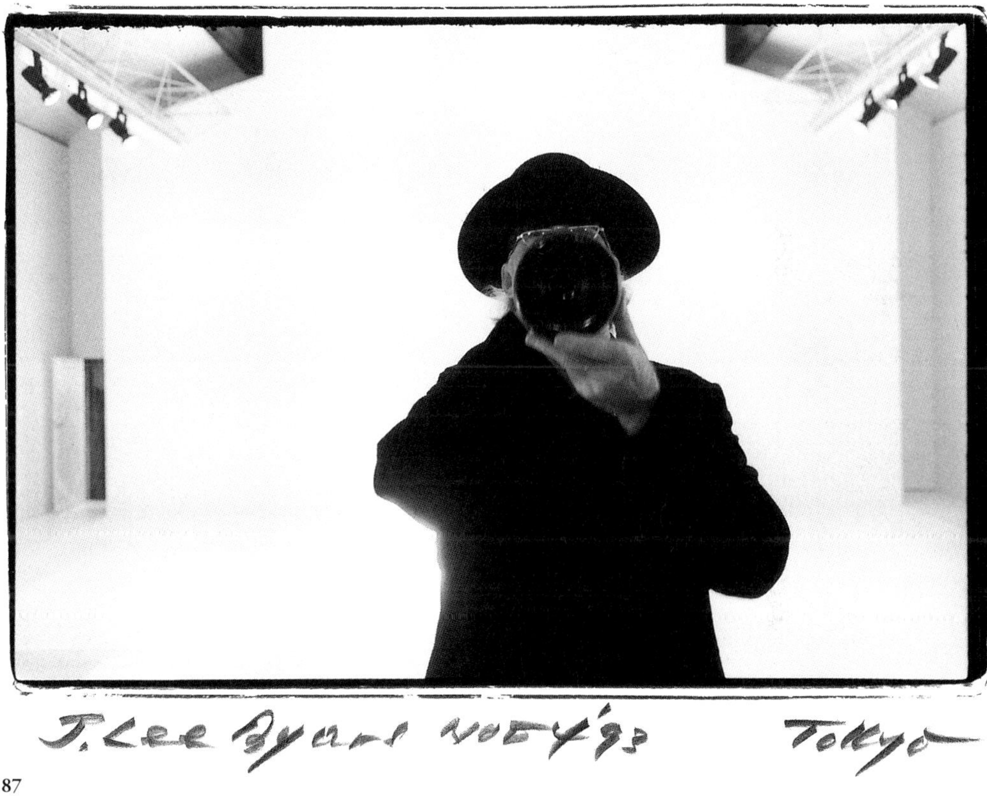

87

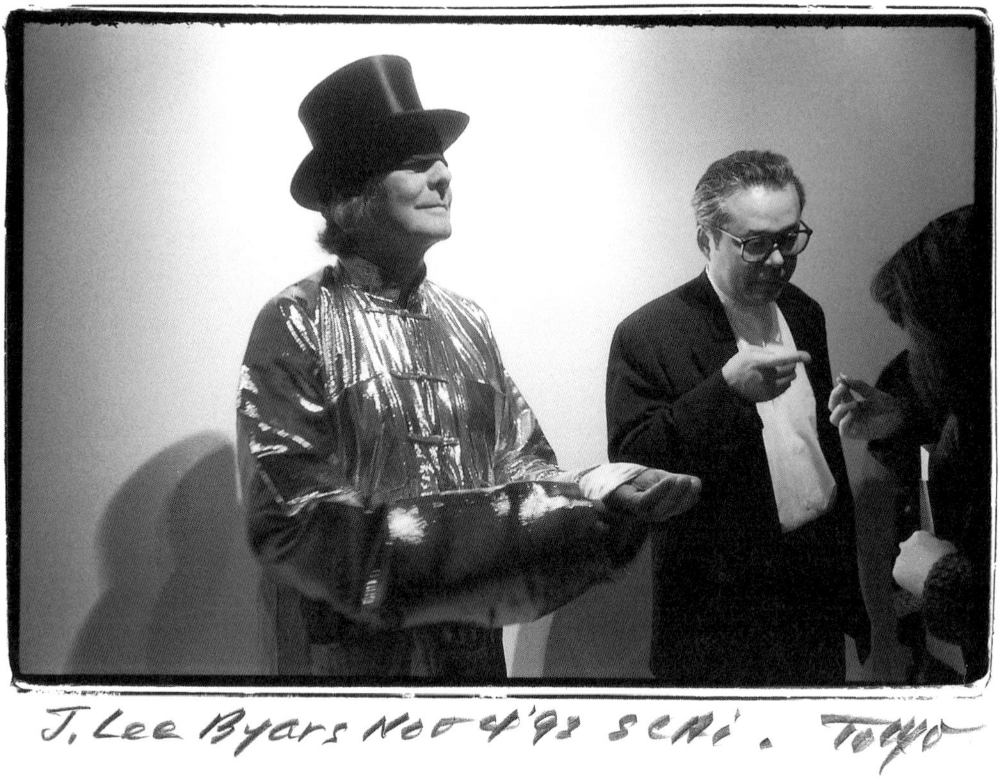
J. Lee Byars Nov 4 '93 SCAI. Tokyo

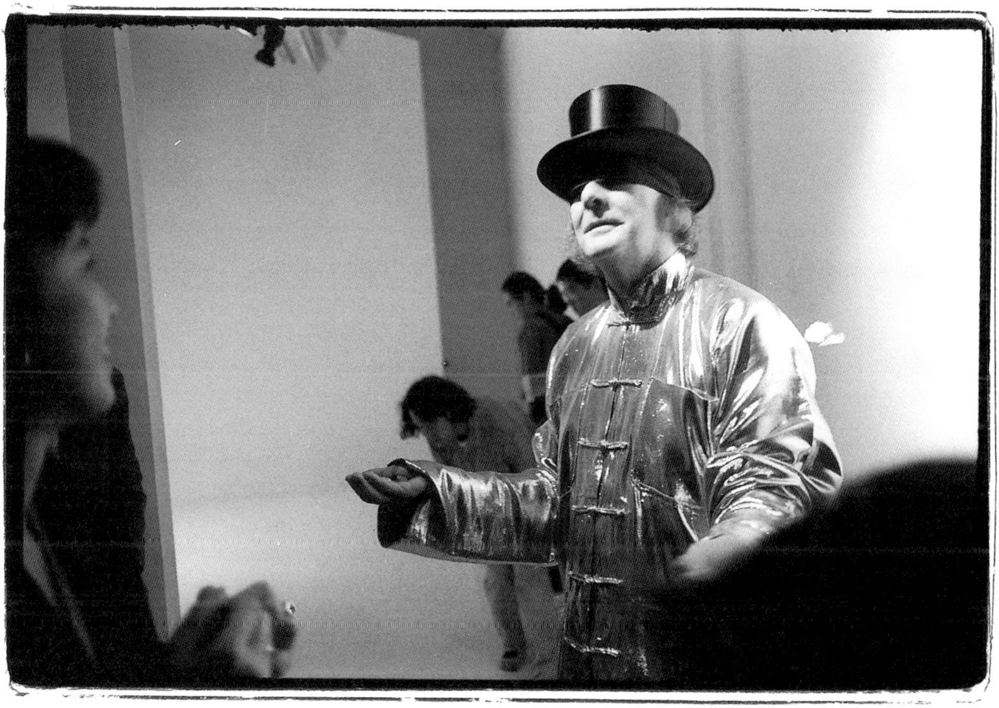

T. Lee Byars NOV 4 '93 SCAI

89

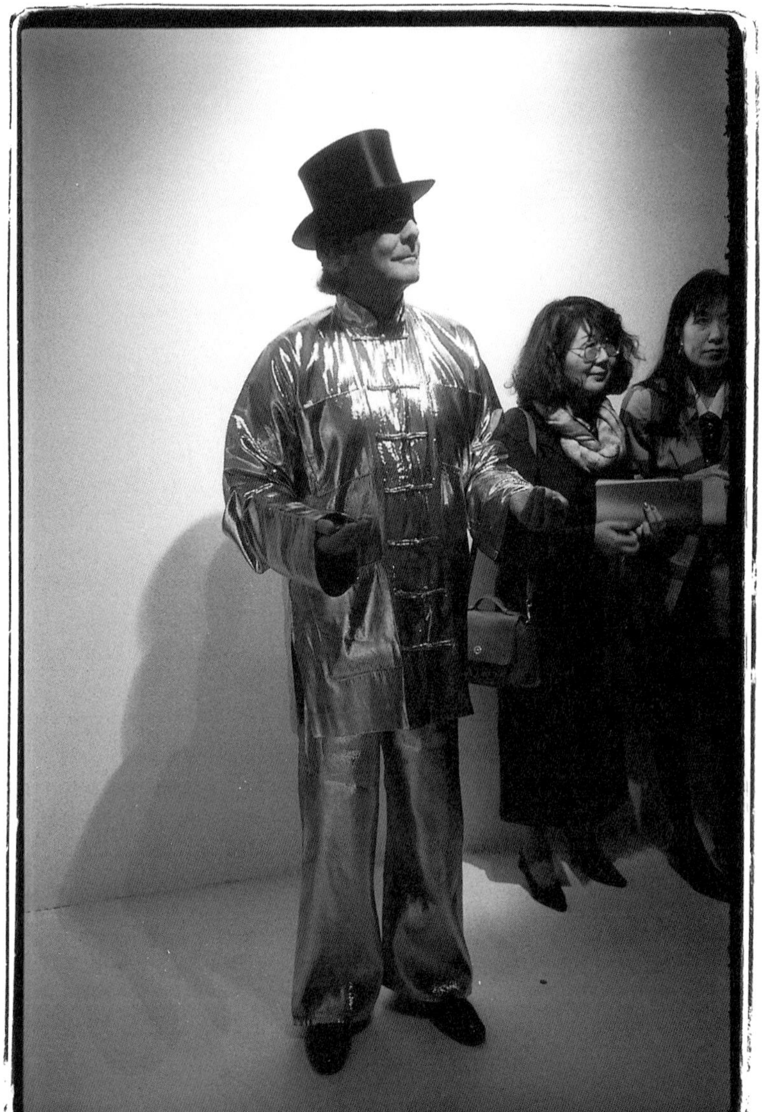

T. Lee. Byars NOV 4 '93
SCAI". Ueno Tokyo

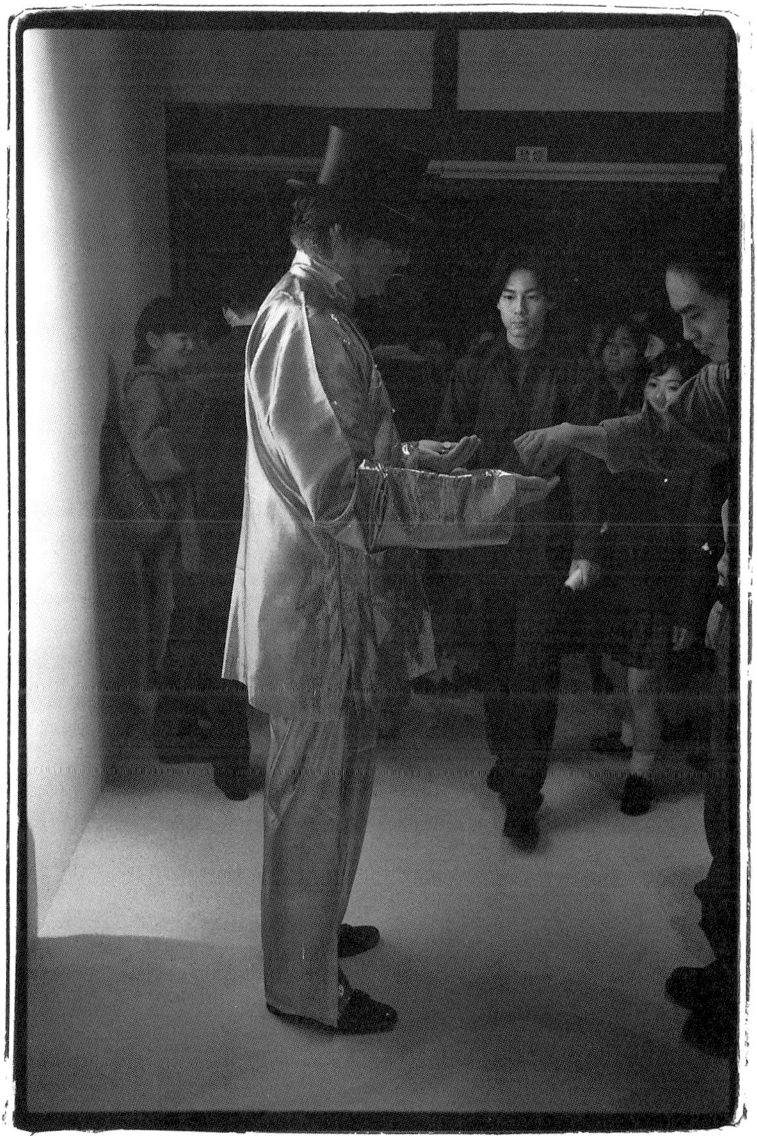

T. Lee Byars Nov 4 '93
SCAI. Ueno. Tokyo

91

15 The Last Japan Trip

November 1996

Byars came to Japan once more, flying in from Cologne, Germany, where he had been staying in an apartment owned by his dealer, Michael Werner. He arrived on November 21, 1996, to discuss plans for a solo exhibition, *Treasures of James Lee Byars*, to be held at the Toyama Memorial Museum near Kawagoe in Saitama prefecture, northwest of Tokyo. (The exhibition took place posthumously, from April 1 to 16, 2000). The museum is located next to the former residence of Toyama Gen'ichi (1890–1972), the founder of Nikko Securities Inc. Toyama had spared no expense on his home, hiring the most skillful carpenters and plasterers of the day, gathering the finest building materials from all over the country, and taking two and a half years to construct it. Completed in 1936, it was later used as a guest house for Nikko Securities and was designated a National Registered Cultural Property. The museum, which houses Toyama's collection of Japanese and oriental antiquities, opened in 1970.

The man who planned the exhibition, Gen'ichi's grandson Toyama Koichi, was the museum director as well as a professor of art history at Keio University. According to his article "James Lee Byars: His Last Exhibition" in the July 2000 issue of *Bijutsu techo*, Toyama and Namioka Fuyumi, who worked for the Japan Foundation at the Japan Cultural Center in Rome, visited Byars in Venice, where he was then residing, in the winter of 1995–96 to propose that he exhibit at the museum. Toyama writes that Byars, who had already undergone surgery twice at that point, watched a video of the Toyama residence—an expansive tatami-floored manor that included a large thatched-roof *minka* farmhouse–style east wing, a *shoin* study–style central wing, and a *sukiya* teahouse–style west wing—and declared that he wanted to show his work in just such a traditional Japanese space once more before he died.

The project soon began to expand in a manner that could accurately be described as delusional. "In the course of visiting stonemasons and lumber dealers on a near-daily basis, Byars began thinking about creating new works in Japan and would place one order after another with different artisans. These orders grew to preposterous proportions," writes Toyama. Byars's ideas included "arranging several thousand black-granite spheres in multiple concentric circles, the diameter of which kept expanding in 1, 3, 5 meter increments [from an original plan of 25 meters]; he also proposed covering in gold foil an entire airplane, in which he would arrive for the show's opening, or covering a huge gas storage tank in gold foil and floating it on Lake Hamana."

Of his consternation at these developments, Toyama notes, "We might have been able to predict this outcome, given that Byars had once [in 1969] proposed flying a rocket to Mars. But we were naïve and simply attributed his speech and actions to eccentricity. He would do things like print up business cards portraying himself as an associate of the museum, present these at shops and bring back various items. He drove us crazy."

Though Byars was expected to stay in Japan only two weeks on this visit, he extended his stay of his own accord and ended up spending three months in Nara.

Struggling with Illness

While in Nara, Byars happened to run into Inoue Michiko, the owner of galerie 16 in nearby Kyoto. Inoue was vacationing in Nara with two friends when she put in a phone call to the gallery and was informed that Byars had called and wanted to speak to her. His message was that he was staying at the Nara Hotel and hoped that Inoue would phone him there. Inoue immediately called the hotel but Byars was out.

That same evening, Inoue and her friends were strolling along Sanjo Street, one of Nara's main thoroughfares, when one of her companions, the artist Hidaka Rieko, suddenly cried out, "Isn't that Byars over there?" Indeed it was Byars, wearing a bright-red hat. He was standing in a shop that sold sumi, inkstones, and washi, just the sort of establishment that would attract him. Overjoyed at this chance meeting, Inoue and her friends rushed into the store. However, the mood inside was weirdly tense. Byars had already accumulated a pile of merchandise he wished to purchase, but the shopowner did not look happy about it at all. Evidently Byars had been arguing with the owner. He said to Inoue, "I want to buy all this. Could you bargain with the owner to give me a discount?" Byars had brought with him a man who was ostensibly interpreting for him, but when Inoue suggested he ask his friend to interpret, Byars turned a deaf ear. Inoue gave up and spoke directly to the shopkeeper: "He says he wants to buy all these items. Couldn't you consider giving him some kind of discount? I realize a reputable business like yours isn't accustomed to such requests. Suppose you offer him the lowest price you feel comfortable with, and if he says no to that, then we'll just forget about it?"

A compromise was finally reached, but now Byars said, "Ask if he'll accept an Amex card." The answer was no, so Inoue suggested that Byars withdraw some cash at a bank and return to the shop the next day. They then left the shop without Byars.

The establishment where Byars created a scene was Isshindo, a maker and seller of sumi brushes that had been a Nara fixture since the early 1900s. Byars would grow fond of this shop and visit it several more times; the owner, Kojima Masamichi, remembers delivering goods Byars had ordered to his room more than once. He recalls Byars purchasing "an extremely expensive brush with a red lacquer handle, and another quite pricey light-colored brush—I think it had white hairs. . . . He bought brushes, sumi, and colored paper, which was mostly black—nearly a box full of that. He was very particular about the color black. He even wanted the cords on the brushes switched to black ones. Normally the cords are brown or dark blue. Black doesn't look good. It was impossible to switch all of them so I gave him a black cord for just one brush. Hardly anything he said made sense to me. But I could tell how strongly he felt about certain things."

Byars spent a total of ¥230,000 (about $2,500 at the time) at Isshindo. He was nearly penniless at this point, yet he spent extravagantly on credit, badgering acquaintances into paying on his behalf. In the United States or Europe he would rely on Michael Werner, the German gallery owner who handled his work, or on other patrons; in Japan the burden fell on Toyama or Nishida.

As mentioned above, the purpose of Byars's trip to Japan this time was to lay the groundwork for an exhibition at the Toyama Memorial Museum to be held in the near future. However, he was already suffering from abdominal cancer at an advanced, perhaps terminal stage, and was in no condition to concentrate on preparations for an exhibition. His personal life, too, was in upheaval, particularly relations with his wife; indeed, he appeared to have welcomed the invitation to visit Japan as an opportunity to escape from troubles at home. Thus it was that he willfully extended his stay from the intended two weeks, and instead of boarding his scheduled flight home, traveled to Nara.

Let us take a look at Byars's itinerary during this trip:

November 21, 1996
Arrives in Japan; attends exhibition planning meeting at Toyama Memorial Museum

November 26
Evening: arrives in Toyota, Aichi prefecture. Visits Toyota Municipal Museum of Art; stays two nights in Toyota in room 1223, Meitetsu Toyota Hotel

November 27
Visits Toyota Municipal Museum of Art
November 28
Visits Toyota City Folk Craft Museum; views works by Enku. Evening: travels to Ise in car driven by Stephan Kohler; stays at Ise Kokusai Hotel
November 29
Travels from Ise to Kyoto; stays at Miyako Hotel
November 30
Kyoto at Miyako Hotel
December 1
Travels from Kyoto to Nara; stays in room 222, Nara Hotel
December 2–25
Stays in room 138, Nara Hotel
December 15
Performance at Nara Hotel
December 26, 1996–February 4, 1997
Stays in room 311, Nara Three-M Hotel
February 4–12
Stays in Kyoto in room 536, Miyako Hotel
February 12
Travels from Kyoto to Tokyo; leaves Japan

Byars's original itinerary had him flying out of Japan on December 1 and returning to Germany. The plan was that a fan of his, Stephan Kohler—a young German artist who lived in Gifu prefecture—would meet him in Toyota and drive him to Kyoto on November 28. There he would meet with a group of Kohler's Kyoto acquaintances. On November 29 he would meet Hirano Kazuyasu, an assistant to Toyama, as well as Shiraishi Masami and his wife, travel with them back to Tokyo, and fly from there to Germany.

However, while he was riding in the car from Toyota to Kyoto on November 28, Byars suddenly changed his mind, telling Kohler, "There's no reason for me to go to Kyoto today. I want to worship at Ise Shrine." Kohler protested that there were people waiting for him in Kyoto, but to no avail. They drove to Ise and stayed overnight at a hotel there.

The next day, Hirano and the Shiraishis were at the Miyako Hotel in Kyoto awaiting Byars's arrival. They were planning to put Byars on the Shinkansen train for Tokyo on November 30. But once again, Byars changed his mind en route from Ise, telling Kohler that he wanted to go to Nara instead, and instructing him to phone the group and tell them to reserve rooms at the Nara Hotel and wait for him there. Shiraishi et al. hurriedly contacted the hotel and traveled to Nara to wait for Byars. Now, however, Byars and Kohler headed from Ise to Kyoto instead of Nara, and checked into the Miyako Hotel. Knowing that Byars had a reservation on a flight leaving for Germany on December 1, Shiraishi and the others rushed back to Kyoto from Nara to try to catch Byars in time. If he did not board the Shinkansen from Kyoto on November 30, he would miss his flight. But once again Byars refused to cooperate. Telling them he felt unwell, he refused to budge on the 30th. Instead, he said, he would fly to Tokyo the next morning, the same day as the return flight, and had them book a seat for him on a flight to Tokyo out of Osaka's Itami Airport, the nearest airport to Kyoto. On the night of the 30th, the Shiraishis and Hirano left Byars in Kohler's care and took the last Shinkansen of the day back to Tokyo.

On December 1, Byars and Kohler drove to Nara. Byars never boarded his flight, necessitating a same-day cancellation of his first-class ticket to Germany. Despite being completely out of money at this point, Byars stayed on in Japan. For over two months—from the end of November to early February the following year—he lived in Nara, with Nishida picking up the tab. The following are Nishida's recollections of this period:

> December 1: I had business at Todaiji temple, so I walked there with my son, who was three at the time. In the distance I saw Byars being pushed in a wheelchair in front of the Chumon [Inner Gate] of the temple. In his silk hat and black coat, there was no mistaking him, even from a distance. But since I was in a hurry, I didn't try to catch up with him. I hadn't even known he was back in Japan.
>
> December 2: Byars phoned me and said he was at the Nara Hotel. I went to see him, and learned that the person who had been pushing his wheelchair the day before was Stephan Kohler. He and a Mr. Izumi, a bamboo artisan from the city of Sakurai who I presume was a friend of Kohler, were looking after Byars together, I was told. I learned that Byars had traveled from Tokyo to Kawagoe, Toyota, Ise, and Kyoto, and, postponing his return home, originally scheduled for December 1, had come to Nara instead.
>
> On December 2, Byars moved from room 222 to room 138. The rate for room 222 was ¥37,000; for room 138 it was ¥24,000 (tax and service charges not included).
>
> I advanced nearly all the costs Byars and his assistants incurred for services, meals, champagne, wine, cheese, souvenirs, and phone calls, both up to that point and for the remainder of Byars's stay in Nara, until February

4. I had no choice. According to my records [as of December 2014], his receipts totalled ¥3,293,345.

December 5 or 6: I was contacted by Mr. Suzuki, who was in charge of accommodations at the Nara Hotel. He told me that before coming to Nara, Byars had stayed at the Miyako Hotel in Kyoto. The Miyako had introduced Byars to the Nara Hotel, which was under the same management. When he first arrived at the Nara Hotel, Byars had been able to use his Amex card. But when Byars expressed a wish to stay longer, they contacted Amex and discovered that a hold had been put on his card. Around this time I was visiting the hotel fairly frequently on business, so Suzuki and I knew each other's faces, even though we had not spoken before. Noticing that I had visited Byars's room, he decided to consult with me.

Regarding Byars's physical condition:

When I met Byars in his hotel room, he was dressed in a yukata. His cheeks were sunken. He looked like a skeleton, like skin stretched over bones. There were no muscles left on his legs. It's amazing he can stand and walk, I thought. For a moment I wondered, is this really Byars? But his voice sounded the same as ever. When he had phoned me, I immediately knew it was him.

Fluid had accumulated in his abdominal cavity, causing his belly to bulge out. The cancer tumors protruded like icebergs under the skin. He told me to touch them, so I did; they felt rough and lumpy. But he did not complain of pain.

I took him to the hospital several times, including a large one in Osaka. I made one appointment for him at a famous hospital where the doctor said he was at a stage where he might die any time. It would not have surprised me if they had found him dead in his hotel room on any given morning.

Byars told me he wanted to go to the hospital and have the cancer surgically removed. He'd been told it was too late for that in America and Europe, but he thought that Japanese doctors might have a different opinion. But here, too, even before they'd examined him they told him it was pointless to operate. Better to leave things be than to cut him open. Byars accepted their explanation. All they did was to keep him on an intravenous drip.

I also took him to a dentist.

He was terribly afraid of being hospitalized and no longer able to move freely. If he went back to America or Germany, he said, people around him would toss him into a hospital. I suppose that's one reason he didn't want to leave Japan.

He told me that his visa would expire after three months, so he wanted to get an extended visa with me as his guarantor. I told him I would be his guarantor, but he would have to deal with the Immigration Bureau himself. He never did.

Sometimes he would walk on his own; sometimes he used a wheelchair.

Nishida also describes the situation at the Nara Hotel during Byars's stay, through December 25:

He made phone calls all the time and sent numerous faxes too.

One day, on the spur of the moment, he took a taxi to Kyoto. The fare would have been several tens of thousands of yen. He said he was going to a certain gallery to purchase a woodblock print. I got a call from the gallery—"Who's going to pay for his purchase?" "I will," I said. I think it came to 40 or 50 thousand yen. Byars immediately cut the print up, so I don't know what sort of work it was. He took only the section of it that he wanted. Then he said, "This is my work." He was using someone else's work as a part of his own.

He often walked off with works from my gallery. I don't know what he did with them after that.

He wore golden bifocals. He also owned a fine pair of scissors, and another pair colored gold.

He would pour wine into the bathtub and dye his underwear in the wine. The tub was stained red.

He would order things from room service even after hours. The staff would respond, even if they had already shut down the kitchen and put everything away.

He kept a stone garden lantern in his room. I remember that we were driving in the car and passed an antique shop or something where he saw the lantern, liked it and bought it then and there. He couldn't get the entire lantern into his room so he only kept the top part, as I recall.

The Nara Hotel kicked him out on the pretext that all their rooms had been booked in advance over Christmas and the New Year holidays. But I'm pretty sure their real reason was that he had wreaked havoc on the room in the month he had been there. They told me that the room was in such bad shape it would take a day or two just to clean it up.

December 15, 1996: Performance at the Nara Hotel

Byars gave the final public performance of his life on December 15, 1996, in the Chrysanthemum Room of the Nara Hotel. He invited twenty-one people to attend the event, but over forty actually watched it, many of them standing. Guests presumably invited by Byars included Toyama Koichi, Nishida Kosaku, Shiraishi Masami, Inoue Michiko, the art critic Nakamura Keiji, Hubbell's student Yamamoto Shigeki, the poet Iida Yoko, Isshindo owner Kojima Masamichi, and the assistant priest at Yakushiji temple, Murakami Taiin. They sat around a U-shaped arrangement of tables and waited in breathless anticipation of Byars's every word and action. Three people, dressed in the ninja outfits that Byars had taken a liking to, served as *kuroko*—black-clad, "invisible" Kabuki-style stagehands: Stephan Kohler, Aoki Masahiro of the Toyota Municipal Museum of Art, and Aoki's friend Kunishima Makiko.

Ravaged by cancer, Byars could no longer stand up without difficulty, yet he made his entrance into the Chrysanthemum Room in his usual style, dressed in a gold suit and black hat. To some people in the audience, his gaunt visage had the "look of death." But on this day he appeared to forget his illness, cloaking himself in the stillness of the space and focusing mind and body on the performance at hand.

Byars began by reciting this line from Lindley Williams Hubbell's 1971 book *Autobiography in Fifty Sentences*: "The first sentence I ever read was 'I can see you.'" To "see," in other words, is more important than any other action. As Iida Yoko later noted, "What Mr. Byars was saying, I think, is that it is essential to see what lies behind phenomena of every kind."

As he often did during performances, Byars wore a black blindfold over his eyes. A blindfold, of course, suggests that "I can't see you"—and yet "I can see you" in your essence, which is what really matters.

Now Byars began asking his audience questions: "How do you translate 'Is is?' into Japanese? What does 'Is is?' mean?"

At the outset of his performance, which lasted about forty minutes, Byars did look like a sick man, frail and emaciated, his legs unsteady. But as his interrogations intensified, he became increasingly excited, even angry. His voice rose and he began berating his audience, as if intent on tormenting them with endless questions. The atmosphere grew weirdly, unbearably tense.

These are Nishida's recollections of the event:

> The Nara Hotel had a policy of renting its banquet rooms for only one

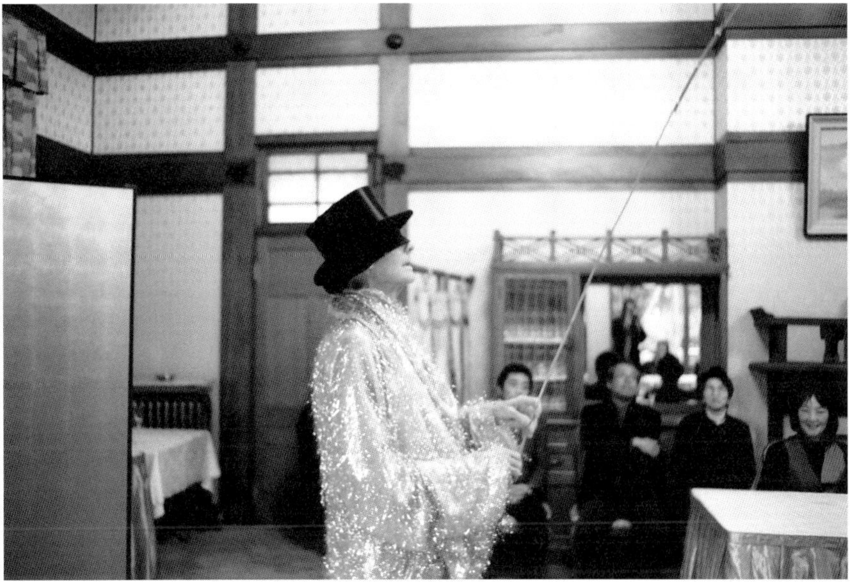

92 Byars in performance at the Nara Hotel, December 15, 1996 (photo by Aoki Masahiro)

event per day, and the Chrysanthemum Room was already booked for that day. But the hotel, which was at a loss for how to deal with Byars, hoped that letting him hold his performance there would satisfy him and make it easier to persuade him to leave. So they let him use the room—yet in the end, he didn't leave.

Byars said almost nothing about the performance beforehand, though I think he spoke with Stephan, who served as the "opening act." Byars and I spent an hour or two in the room before the performance began. I remember carrying out a number of tasks at his behest. It was beastly hot. Byars was sitting still in a chair the whole time so the room's temperature might have been comfortable for him, but I worked myself into a sweat just moving around.

Byars said it was the second time he had seen Aoki and Stephan in their ninja outfits. The first time was when he visited the Toyota Museum. As he walked from the parking lot to the museum they would suddenly emerge in front of him, then disappear, he said.

When he got angry, Byars had a habit of stomping his feet on the floor. It happened whenever something upset him. He stomped quite loudly, it didn't matter where—in a room or anywhere. When he did it in the coffee shop of the Three-M Hotel some days later, I recall the astonished looks on the faces of the other customers.

Byars had us turn down the lighting as far as possible, so the room was quite dark.

On the works Byars produced in Nara:

Byars bought a large number of deer pelts at a Nara souvenir shop and had plans to make a huge circular carpet out of them. He said he wanted to do a performance wrapped up in the carpet. But the pelts never got sewn together, and I still have them.

He made one work by cutting washi in a crescent-moon shape, crumpling it up, then stretching it out again. There's no signature on it.

Byars said that Maria Gilissen, the wife of Marcel Broodthaers, bought a work, incorporating a brush and an inkstone lid, that he made while staying at the Nara Hotel, but I don't know if he got paid for it. If he did, he would have wanted to keep the money for himself so he certainly wouldn't have told me. It was a rather large piece. I still have the inkstone because he gave it to me, saying it wouldn't work as part of the artwork.

Byars was fixated on spheres and on the number five. He dyed toothpicks in sumi ink, wrapped bundles of several hundred each in black silk cloth, and arranged five of these bundles in a row. He took five pairs of sunglasses of the sort worn by marathon runners, arranged them in a pentagon, and called it an artwork. Frequently he would wet bits of bread with saliva, roll them into tiny pellets with the grime from his hands, and lay five of these in a row.

Byars would mold single grains of boiled rice with his fingers into little round pellets that he called "One Grain Rice Buddhas." Inspired, he said, by the Shinto teaching that a god resides in every grain of rice, he presented one such pellet in a frame at his performance on December 15, explaining that it was created in the image of a tiny Buddha to be placed inside the body of the Great Buddha at Todaiji temple, next door to the Nara Hotel. [Built in 752, the Great Buddha is 15 meters tall, and it is possible to walk inside it.]

He told me to insert a sheet of black paper in a round frame and place a pellet in the center. When pressed the pellet broke and we had to make another one. We made two sets, with five works to a set, but only the paper is left now.

The things he made in Nara and declared to be "works" were all like that. In a word, they were junk, and none were in a form that would last long. Then he would say [to Michael Werner], "I've left a large number of works with Nishida." I suppose he said that so I wouldn't worry about getting paid.

He painted a great many black circles on Japanese-style writing paper, but only one or two remain. He took the rest of them with him.

He arranged five small *shijimi* clam shells in a row. He said they had served him miso soup with *shijimi* as part of an in-flight meal.

He had with him a lot of red and black silk cloths, and used the black ones to wrap his artworks. He had me do the wrapping, telling me to do it this way or that way. Byars dyed the toothpicks himself, in the sink. The maid was shocked at how stained the sink was.

He placed a single rose on a stem in a wine bottle and called that a "work" too.

He came to my gallery many times, looked at the space and made plans for an exhibition.

He often posed questions and answers involving the number five: the five elements—earth, water, fire, wind, space—or the five points of the body—arms, legs, and head.

He'd say, "We have to get prices set [for these works]" and send photos to Werner, but no response ever came.

I was contacted by Watari-um [The Watari Museum of Contemporary Art] in Tokyo about a show in 2001. They wanted to exhibit his works and asked to see some. In the end they only exhibited twenty or so Nara Hotel coasters on the back of which he had written down his ideas.

After Nara he went to Egypt, but he frequently phoned from there too. He had asked a stonemason's shop in Nara to make something for him and wanted to know how the work was progressing. His calls would usually come in the middle of the day, so he must have been calling in the morning Egypt time. In the end I didn't place an order for the work. The plan had been to do a show at my gallery when it was completed.

On the financing for Byars's days in Nara:

I paid all of Byars's expenses. Werner later reimbursed me for all invoiced items via Mr. Shiraishi. I received over ¥3 million back. Byars spent over ¥4 million during his two and a half months in Nara, and probably a total

> of ¥5 to 6 million while in Japan. I would guess that he spent about that much, or even more, in Egypt. Of the ¥3,293,345 I had receipts for, he spent ¥752,709 on phone calls, ¥1,071,025 on hotels, and ¥670,584 on meals. I was struck by how high his phone bills were.

Byars moved from the Nara Hotel to the Nara Three-M Hotel on December 26, 1996. Nishida recalls:

> Byars had to move out of the Nara Hotel, so I explained the situation to the owner of the Three-M Hotel, with whom I was on good terms. I told them he was a foreigner with no money and not much time left to live. I booked a single room for him. I figured that if the room was small and uncomfortable he might feel like leaving Japan. But the staff put him in a twin room out of consideration for his condition. The upshot was that he settled right in.
>
> I believe that Byars was prepared to spend his last days in Japan.
>
> He went to visit a Nihonga artist in Asuka named Utou Sei. He had seen a book of Utou's works and said he wanted to visit him, so some of the hotel staff took him there. I didn't hear his impressions of the visit. He also took a trip by taxi to the Byodoin temple in Uji.

Oyama Yoneko, who worked at the front desk of the Three-M Hotel when Byars was there, shared these recollections:

> We got calls from his room all the time. The hotel didn't offer room service, but we provided for him as best we could. Most of his calls were about meals. I don't think he spoke much Japanese, but he could say a few simple words.
>
> He would want to go to the doctor or some other place. The entire staff pitched in to look after him. We'd check our schedules and say, "I have tomorrow off, so I'll take him to the hospital." One reason we were so kind to him was that he was a friend of Mr. Nishida. This is a family-style hotel.
>
> He was bald on top, so he always wore a silk hat or a woolen cap of some sort. He'd wear a gold silk hat even when he was in his room. He was never seen without a hat on. If you knocked and he wasn't wearing one, he'd slap one on his head before showing his face. He didn't want anyone to see him bare-headed.
>
> He would dye his hair pink or gold. I think he dyed it himself. I re-

member an employee saying the sink was filthy. [While at the Nara Hotel, Byars had his hair dyed at a barber shop.]

His room was a mess, but he appeared to be cleaning it to his satisfaction. Sometimes he'd let a maid come in, sometimes not. He might say today was no good because the things on the floor shouldn't be thrown out, and so forth.

He also kept a lot of things on his bed. He had several dozen copies of the Heart Sutra alone. The Heart Sutra is about the concept of emptiness. He liked philosophy. He had several volumes of haiku too.

Nishida on Byars's marriage:

Byars told me his wife was the daughter of a famous American doctor. That's why he said they would toss him into a hospital and stick him with tubes if he returned home.

He had two stepchildren from his wife's previous marriage. He constantly spoke harshly of his wife, said she was a spendthrift and spoiled her kids rotten. Several times I overheard his phone conversations with her. She was asking for a divorce and wanted him to give her ninety percent of his property. Ridiculous, fifty percent is normal, and so on. He sounded extremely angry.

One day, after shouting back and forth with his wife on the phone, Byars calmed down a bit and asked me about my family. When I told him I had two sons, age four and two, he asked to see a photo of them. When I handed him a photo a few days later, he said they looked really sweet and stared at it for a while. I wonder what happened to that photo. Byars told me that he was sterile.

On Byars's diet:

Byars liked cheese, crackers, and wine. He would take sips from one small glass of wine all day. Other than that, he would order all kinds of things but couldn't eat them. He could only eat a bite at a time.

Sometimes he would eat Japanese cuisine, and sometimes Chinese prepared by the restaurant run by the hotel. They would take the Chinese meals to his room for him. One time he ordered Peking duck, but when it arrived he couldn't eat it. He wanted to, but when he put some in his mouth his body rejected it.

He knew a lot about expensive gourmet foods. He had enjoyed nothing but good food all those years, so his desire to eat was intense. He would order champagne too.

He couldn't eat MSG. I don't know if he was allergic, or just disliked it as a gourmet. Occasionally he would get into big arguments at restaurants over whether they had put any in their food or not.

On the death of Byars's mother:

Byars's mother died in mid-January. He told me she was ninety-five. He woke me up with a phone call in the middle of the night and asked me to come to the hotel. When I got there he told me his mother had died and asked me what he should do. I said he should fly home immediately.

When I visited him the next day, I told him that if he was going home he needed to get an air ticket, and asked him what he wanted to do. He said "I'm not going home. I thought about it overnight." He said if he went home his mother wouldn't be there anyway. So he didn't leave.

About Egypt:

Byars was extremely sensitive to the cold and kept saying he wanted to go someplace warm. Apparently his plan was to travel from Japan to Egypt, then Greece, then Venice, and then come back to Japan to do the exhibition at the Toyama Museum.

He booked his room at the Mena House from Japan. He had a specific room in mind and declared that if he couldn't get that room, he wouldn't go. You could see the pyramids from that room, he said. Shiraishi made the reservation for him.

When I asked him what he planned to do in Egypt, he told me that some time ago he had asked some Bedouins to procure him a black-haired goat pelt, but that it had been difficult to track them down, since they were nomads. That was why he was going back to Egypt, he said. [*The Palace of Perfect* and other catalogues state that Byars made several trips to Egypt in the 1980s.]

He wanted to book the room at the Mena House from around December 20, but it was occupied through the New Year. He was able to get the room in January, however, so we made a plane reservation for him, but Byars insisted on cancelling it. He canceled his flight plans two or three times. All he had was a return ticket to Germany. I think that he purchased a ticket to Egypt after flying to Frankfurt. The round-trip ticket between Frankfurt and Tokyo that Toyama got for him was in first class.

Nishida reminisces further:

> Byars often engaged me in Zen koan-like exchanges. He'd tell me to give him ten answers. He liked the number ten, too. "List ten things about beauty," that sort of thing. He phoned every day. If I didn't go to his room, I'd get a phone call right away. So I wound up seeing him almost daily. And yet he didn't have any particular business, nor did he speak at length. Looking back, it seems like most of our time together was spent in silence.
>
> One day he was looking out the window of his room when he suddenly exclaimed, "Look at that, Nishida. It's beautiful." But I couldn't tell what he was looking at or what it was he found so beautiful. The view was just the same one he saw every day. He would make similar comments while was riding in the car. He'd see a lawn in a park and cry out, "Nishida, that's beautiful." But I never knew what he was talking about. The light? The wind? I'm sure something had caught his fancy in that instant, something that spurred him to cry out in admiration. But no one else could tell what that was—only he could see it.
>
> Pretty much every day he'd tell me to come visit; I would go, we'd chat briefly about something or other, and that would be it for an hour or so. Silence. He would be rolling up and cutting sheets of paper with a pair of long, gold-colored scissors. I wouldn't say anything either. Then I'd leave. That was the usual pattern.
>
> If I hadn't met Koyama Tomio in Seoul on my way back from the 1992 *Documenta*, Byars would not have come to Nara. It just happened that Murakami Takashi was doing a show in Korea, and I adjusted my travel plans to see it. That's how it all started. For better or worse, Byars was a force of nature, and that's why he's so memorable. In my memory, I find myself missing him. It was hard; it was unpleasant. But looking back, I can say those were interesting times.

February 1997: Farewell to Japan

On February 4, 1997, Byars moved from Nara to Kyoto. Toyama Koichi's assistant Hirano Kazuyasu picked him up in Nara and accompanied him to Kyoto. The plan was to take Byars from there to Itami Airport, where he would take a plane to Tokyo's Narita Airport and transfer there to a direct flight for Frankfurt. But once again Byars cancelled, saying he wanted to take the Shinkansen to Tokyo and fly from there. In the end, Aoki Masahiro of the Toyota Museum and Stephan Kohler put Byars on the Shinkansen in Kyoto, and Toyama picked him up in Tokyo and put him on the plane out of Narita. Byars left Japan for the last time on February 12, 1997.

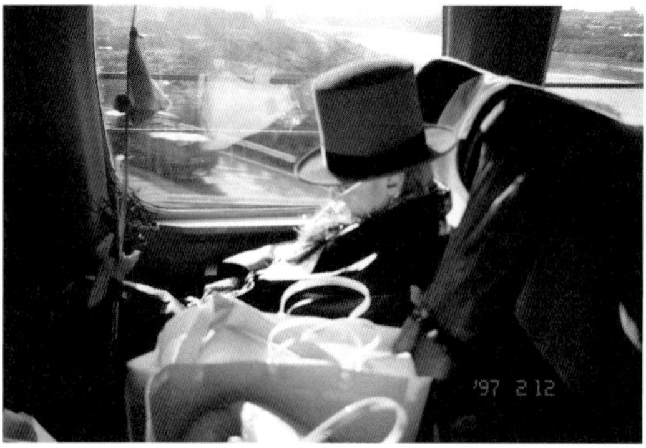

93 Byars on the Shinkansen (photo by Aoki Masahiro)

Aoki set down his recollections of this period in an article published in the *Chunichi shinbun* newspaper later that year, after Byars's death:

> James Lee Byars arrived in Japan on November 21, 1996, and visited the Toyota Municipal Museum of Art on the evening of the 26th. During his two nights and three days in Toyota, he toured the exhibits at the museum as well as the Toyota City Folk Craft Museum, where he was captivated by the Buddhist sculptures by Enku. On the evening of the 28th he headed for Nara via Ise and Kyoto in a car driven by Stephan Kohler. Over the course of the next two and a half months, until Byars left Japan on February 12, 1997, Kohler and I visited his room every time he moved to a different hotel. We saw him at the Nara Hotel, where he performed on December 15, 1996; at the Nara Three-M Hotel, where he moved at year's end; and at the Miyako Hotel in Kyoto. He was already suffering from abdominal cancer, and his belly protruded noticeably from his thin frame. Whether he was telling a joke or reminiscing about Joseph Beuys, he was nearly always lying in bed. In that condition, how did he manage to acquire so much stuff? Every one of his hotel rooms was filled to overflowing with things he'd collected and with the colors he loved—gold, red, black.

One of the twin beds was always covered with pretty objects. Byars subsequently flew to Frankfurt, then to Egypt, where he died in Cairo on May 23. In hindsight I believe that his sojourns in Japan and Egypt were nothing less than a final pilgrimage to places of spiritual sustenance to him at a time when he sensed the approach of death. [Translated from *Chunichi shinbun*, evening edition, June 8, 1997]

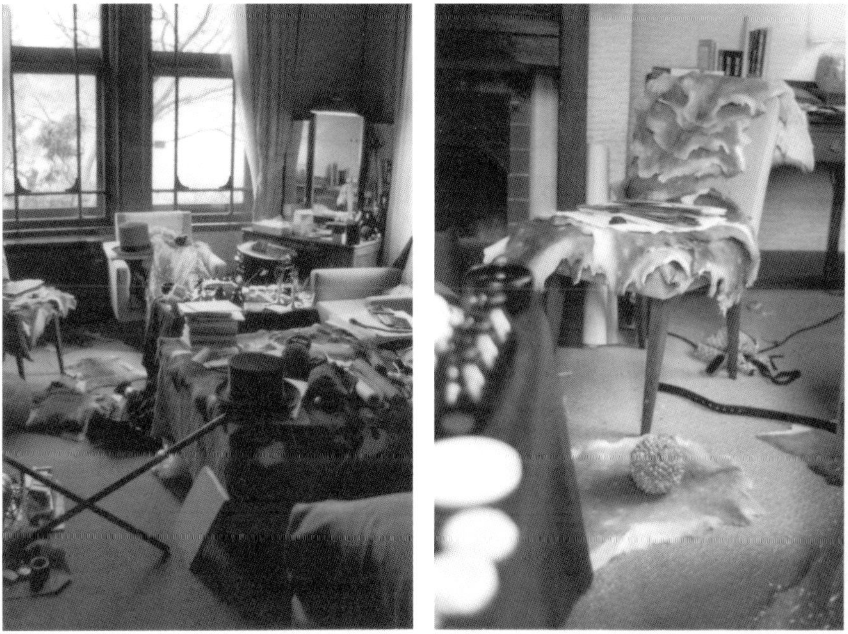

94, 95 Byars's room at the Nara Hotel (photo by Stephan Kohler)

16 Death in Egypt

Byars departed Japan on February 12, 1997, aboard a plane bound for Frankfurt. From there he flew directly to Egypt, where he checked into Room 1204, known for its unparalleled view of the Great Pyramid of Giza, at the Mena House Oberoi.

He was in the terminal stages of cancer, yet his mind continued to generate ideas for upcoming exhibitions. From his hotels in Nara and Giza, Byars sent over twenty faxes about plans for an exhibition, titled *The Palace of Perfect*, that the Serralves Foundation (Fundação de Serralves) in Porto, Portugal eventually held from October 9 to December 7, 1997, opening several months after his death. Every fax is in Byars's distinctive handwriting, the text festooned with pentagrams. The five-sided star, in which the sides form the golden ratio with one another, was an "identity mark" of sorts for Byars. In the faxes he proposed one grandiose idea after another, none of them feasible from an art museum's standpoint. These documents testify to the fact that his intense desire to make such visions a reality burned unabated right up until his death.

During his remaining days in Egypt, even as he lay in bed, his body wasted by the cancer, Byars continued to fax his friends. The last one he sent to Aoki Masahiro, one of his few friends in Japan, contained a desperate plea for money.

What thoughts passed through his mind as he approached death?

While in Kyoto, Byars had taken a group of his English students to a pond at Higashi Honganji temple to see the lotuses. He had heard that when lotuses bloom at dawn, the opening petals made a popping sound. He wanted to see if this was true.

In a note to Kawai Sumie, the young woman he met in Kurashiki on his first trip to Japan, Byars wrote, "Always be like the Egypt flower, white, JLB." By "Egypt flower" Byars was referring to the lotus or water lily. Byars inscribed his message to Kawai in a copy of Paul Gauguin's book *Noa Noa*. Perhaps his encounter with Japanese culture affected the young Byars much as Tahiti had affected Gauguin. *Where Do We Come From? What Are We? Where Are We Going?*—these are the words Gauguin famously inscribed on a painting around the time he attempted suicide. Their allu-

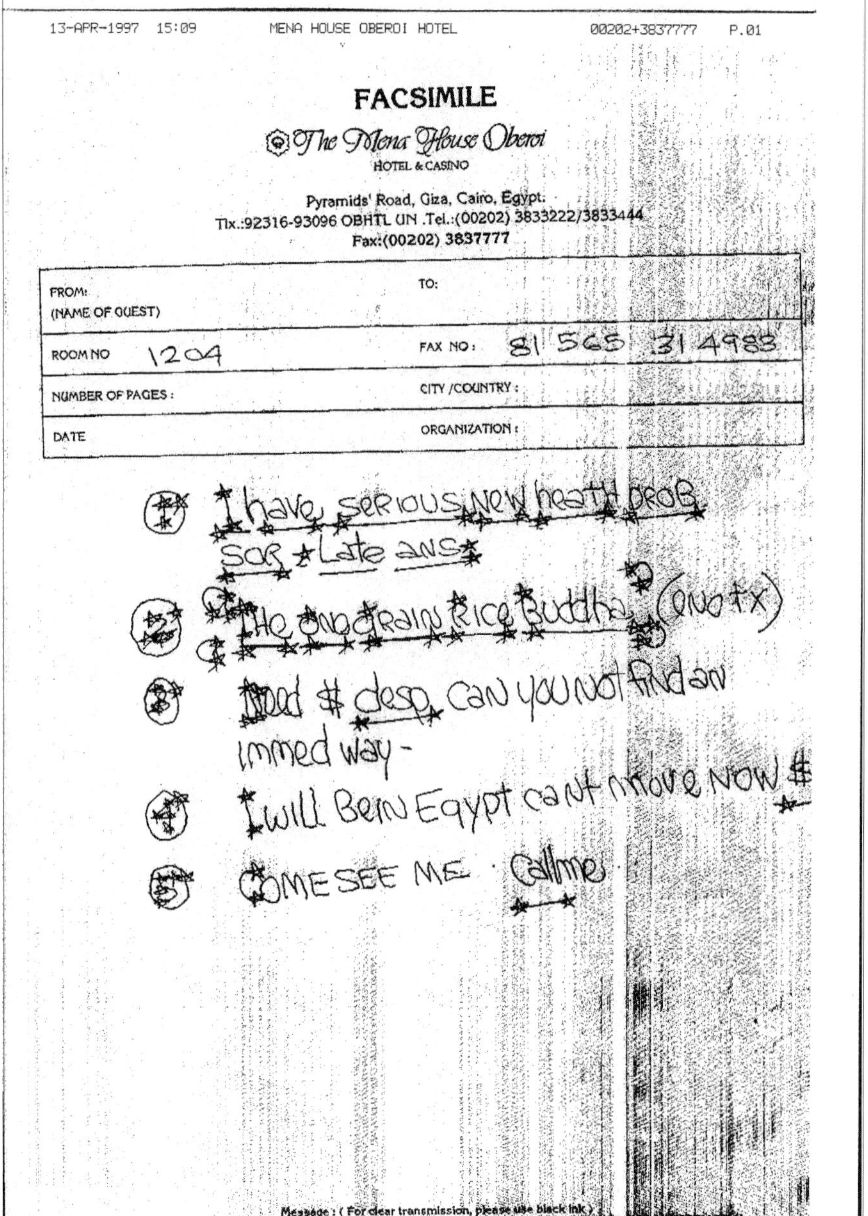

13-APR-1997 15:09 MENA HOUSE OBEROI HOTEL 00202+3837777 P.01

FACSIMILE

The Mena House Oberoi
HOTEL & CASINO

Pyramids' Road, Giza, Cairo, Egypt.
Tlx.:92316-93096 OBHTL UN .Tel.:(00202) 3833222/3833444
Fax:(00202) 3837777

FROM: (NAME OF GUEST)	TO:
ROOM NO 1204	FAX NO: 81 565 31 4983
NUMBER OF PAGES:	CITY /COUNTRY:
DATE	ORGANIZATION:

1 I have serious new heath prob sor late ans

2 The one grain rice Buddha (no fx)

3 need $ desp, can you not find an immed way -

4 I will Be in Egypt cant move now $

5 COME SEE ME · Callme

Message: (For clear transmission, please use black ink)
IF YOU DO NOT RECEIVE ALL PAGES PLEASE TELEPHONE: 3833222 /3833448/ EXT [illegible] IMMEDIATELY

96 A fax sent by Byars to Aoki Masahiro at the Toyota Municipal Museum of Art, dated April 13, 1997

sion to the ephemerality of life resonates with Byars's philosophical aversion to notions of permanence and certainty, and with the Buddhist concept of impermanence. All things are in constant flux, cycling eternally through birth, death, and rebirth. A symbol of Buddhist thought, the lotus emits a scent as lovely and fleeting as the sound of its petals opening at dawn. As Byars himself put it: "Moment by moment. A beautiful thing is just that."

Two friends who knew Byars for many years have this to say:

"As someone who gave more thought to the spiritual realm than the physical, Byars may have believed in the eternal in the same sense that the ancient Egyptians did." —Kawai Sumie

"Even in life he was already someone who had transcended life and death. He embodied the feeling that there is no such thing as an 'end' to anything." —Iida Yoko

At the Mena House, everything in room 1204—the bed, the furniture, the old photograph of the pyramids on the wall, even the bathroom—remains exactly the way it was when Byars died on May 23, 1997.

Epilogue: Final Days in Egypt

An aesthetic heretic who was one of the twentieth century's most innovative and controversial artists, James Lee Byars inspires talk of episodes from his life that today, two decades after his death, have the quality of urban legends. Endowed with a larger-than-life personality and prone to embellishing or outright inventing parts of his own history, Byars himself—as well as the stranger-than-fiction events that did occur throughout his life and in the wake of his death—seem to have encouraged some of his chroniclers to take liberties with the facts, or at the least to fail to ascertain them—admittedly an arduous and often impossible task.

No period of Byars's life has been subject to more speculation, and more contradictory information, than his last days in Egypt. In the course of my investigation into the circumstances of his death, I discovered many discrepancies in the best-known accounts of those events—particularly the writings of the art critic Thomas McEvilley (1939–2013), among them "Johnny Wakes," an article in the September 1997 issue of *Artforum*, and "James Lee Byars: A Study of Posterity," an article in the November 2008 issue of *Art in America*. McEvilley's narrative has generally been accepted as fact by subsequent writers.

It is not my intention here to point out the errors in that narrative one by one. My purpose, rather, is to provide a factual account, based on the testimony of numerous witnesses, that will serve as a historical record through which we can see how Byars, despite his suffering, was able to live his life to completion on his own terms. His final days have something to teach us about how an artist pursues his personal vision of aesthetics, and of life itself, to the very end.

The American Cemetery where Byars rests today occupies a corner of the cemetery for foreigners in the quarter of the Egyptian capital known as Old Cairo. It sits on the edge of a neighborhood where local people sell fruits and vegetables in an open-air market. Closed off by a high wall, the cemetery faces a street that is nearly deserted. The American Embassy in Cairo provided a tombstone inscribed "JAMES LEE BYARS 1932–1997"—a standard service for U.S. citizens who die overseas. What were Byars's circumstances in the weeks leading up to his burial here? What places did he visit, and whom did he meet? Through written records and people's reminiscences, I have tried to reconstruct his life during this final period.

Interviews at the Mena House

The Mena House is one of Egypt's finest and most historic hotels, a five-star establishment built in 1869 whose guests have included such celebrities as Richard Nixon, Agatha Christie, Arthur Conan Doyle, Frank Sinatra, and Charlie Chaplin. In 1943 it was the site of the Cairo Conference, attended by the three Allied leaders Chiang Kai-shek, Franklin D. Roosevelt, and Winston Churchill. The hotel consists of a main building, the Palace wing, and a new building, the Garden wing. Most guests stay in the latter. The Palace is truly fit to accommodate a royal family, and the price is accordingly high. Room 1204, where Byars spent the last three months of his life—from February 15 to May 22, 1997—is in the Palace. Several employees of the Mena House generously consented to be interviewed at length about their memories of Byars.

Hamed El Nabawi (bell captain)
In 1997 I was working as a bellboy. Mr. Byars was a regular guest who always requested the same room, 1204. He really loved the historic hotel, and treated it as if it were his home. His room was full of a variety of things—colorful fabrics in red, black, yellow, pink, orange, perhaps made of silk, and on the floor, something like pictures he was drawing with colored sand. I remember that he had luxurious bedding. He also seemed to be collecting antique urns and the like. But he wouldn't let anyone else touch them. I knew at the time that he was an artist, but to be honest, I didn't realize he was world-famous. I remember him as someone who did not talk a lot, but was kind and gentle. He always wore a gold-colored scarf around his neck. I also recall that he sometimes used a wheelchair. Mohamed Amr Ali Nasr, the housekeeper in charge of the twelfth floor, where the room was, helped him in and out of the bath, for example. He seemed to enjoy relaxing in the bath, and would sometimes spend an hour to an hour and a half there. He couldn't eat a lot of food, but sometimes he would go out and buy yogurt, honey, and fruit. I think he also visited tourist spots, like Khan El Khalili, the Hussein Mosque, and the El Azhar Mosque, that were full of shops selling Egyptian souvenirs and antiques. Sometimes he returned late at night. Of course he also visited the pyramids, and would bring back what appeared to be pieces of cut stone or sand. He employed a taxi driver named Magdy, whom he treated just like a son.

Afaf A Raouf (waitress)

Back then I was working as I am now at the Khan El Khalili Coffee Shop, located inside the hotel. I remember that Mr. Byars sometimes came to the café with two women who appeared to be mother and daughter. He always wore large baggy trousers and a long jacket that nearly reached the floor. He exuded charisma. He would often pick up the bread plate and draw a picture or something on it. He did this to entertain women at the other tables. The woman receiving the gift would take leave of her husband, move to Mr. Byars's table, sit down right next to him and chat. He was particularly fond of Matilda, the senior captain. Matilda would place cold towels on his forehead, bring him ice, and generally look after him.

Mahmoud Helmy (waiter)

I have been employed as a waiter at the Mena House since 1991. In 1997 I was working in a restaurant called the Greenery that was in the hotel garden at the time—though now it has been changed into a spa—and in the Khan El Khalili Coffee Shop. The Greenery was a huge restaurant where as many as four hundred guests would gather in the morning for breakfast. Mr. Byars liked to sit on the terrace, where he could gaze across the garden at the pyramids while having his breakfast. His order always consisted of an omelet with cheese and the round, flat salted bread called shami. He came every day. He liked to bring his camera and take pictures of the pyramids or the crows pecking at the feed scattered around the garden. He was partial to Matilda, who worked in the coffee shop, and was always looking for her and calling out, "Matilda, Matilda, where are you?" He often joked with the staff. He spoke just a little bit of Arabic. Of course he knew only a few words, the simple remarks typically used by foreigners.

Zakria Hamza (bellboy)

I went to work at the Mena House in 1983, when I was eighteen. I was a bellboy then and still am now. Mr. Byars set out for town nearly every day in the company of the taxi driver Magdy, who was like his own personal driver and a favorite of his. He was always gone for five or six hours. I think he frequently visited Islamic temples and enjoyed taking pictures. He was a very kind, wonderful person. He often tipped with American dollars. I would go to his room nearly every day, because as a bellboy I was called anytime something came up. The room was marvelous. It was full of antiques and all kinds of things. I think he stayed there for three or four months. He left here three or four days before he died. I remember that it was some time later that someone visited here from the embassy. I expect that he is still at rest in Egypt even now.

Hany Aziz (rooms division manager)
In those days I was working an irregular shift that started at 3 pm, so unfortunately I don't remember Mr. Byars, but I have made a number of inquiries about him.

Mr. Byars apparently removed all the rugs from Room 1204 so that the floor was completely exposed. Today, except for the carpeting and the television, all the furnishings in the room are the same as when he died. Because the room is small, he may have moved the coffee table and chair that were by the window outside. Of all the rooms in this hotel, Room 1204 has the best view. It's at the highest spot in the building as well as the closest to the pyramids. He obviously liked the view and asked for Room 1204 every time he came here. The bed is placed parallel to the window so that if you lie in bed and look sideways, the Great Pyramid appears right before you. The twelfth floor is at the same height as the land the pyramids are built on. In other words, you can see the pyramid rising all the way up from the ground. I do not believe Mr. Byars came here to die. When you see that amazing, beautiful view from the window, you can actually feel a mysterious energy welling up in you.

Incidentally, it is the policy of this hotel that if a foreign guest falls ill, they are first taken to the Anglo-American Hospital. The same thing is done if someone dies. Also, when a hotel guest passes away, the door of the room is double-locked so that no one can enter, and we can only hand the room keys over to a family member. That is required by Egyptian law.

Interview with Magdy Hafez

When I first met James I was holding down two jobs, as a taxi driver and as a policeman. It is not unusual in Egypt to have a dual career. I worked from 8 in the morning to 3 in the afternoon as a taxi driver, then as a policeman inside a government building from 3 until 10 pm. One day, when I was waiting for customers at the Mena House, I met an elderly man at the entrance. He was dressed all in black and had a cane. That was James. "I want to visit neighborhoods where local people live, and the agricultural area, but it's dangerous if I go alone, so I'd like you to go with me," he said. The first place I went with him was the green district along the road heading toward Cairo University and crossing the bridge near the Anglo-American Hospital, where he later died. Today the area is lined with buildings. He told me at that time that he had two big cancers in his belly. He said he had come to Egypt for treatment. When I touched them, the tumors were hard and larger than a clenched fist. From that day on, I began my daily routine by massaging James's body with warm water and towels in his room.

James was like a father to me. He taught me many things. He showed me a new world. He gave me a new name, Blue Moon. I think he named me that because back then I always wore a blue *galabeya*. I remember crawling around on the ground with James in an open space near the hospital, searching for round pebbles. When onlookers saw James, who could no longer walk, crawling around for all he was worth, they thought he was crazy.

On April 6, my birthday, James gave me a book. It was spherical, like a ball. He liked round things, and had filled this book with drawings of circles. I also remember that he was always writing something in his unique pentagram-studded script. He had in his possession several hundred tiny gold-colored spheres, about the size of sesame seeds. He would arrange those tiny spheres in a circle, then make a slightly larger circle around that. . . . It was his dream to keep creating more and more circles, making the outer circle larger and larger. Sadly he was not able to fulfill his dream. Oh, and he hated plastic.

We were always having problems due to lack of money. One day, an art dealer who was an old friend of James came to visit, so I sold her the spherical book James had given to me as a gift, without him knowing it. We desperately needed the money, which came to 2,000 American dollars. I can't forget that time, because the same evening I took the gallery owner to the airport and returned to the hotel, James's condition took a sudden turn for the worse. This gallery owner had come here many times before. Her name was Maria Gilissen and she was from Belgium. I think she came here three or four times with her daughter, Marie-Puck. One day, Maria said to me, "Magdy, we do business with you." So we started doing business. She would say, "Look in the wastebasket. Even his trash is worth money." They bought his trash for 500 American dollars a bag. I think they bought three or four bags. They also bought his golden suit. James had sewn it himself. But he refused to sell his artworks, saying they all belonged to Michael Werner.

During this period, James was getting money sent to him by Werner, who was a gallery owner. He was in Germany and never came to Egypt, but I remember James speaking to him on the phone several times. James always begged him for money. Hotel charges, hospital costs . . . James was a spendthrift who never had enough money. Yet one day he borrowed 500 Egyptian pounds—about 70 American dollars—from the hotel reception desk for my sake. It was my birthday. When I asked him, "Why are you borrowing money for me?" he replied, "Because you are my son, Magdy."

James suffered from terminal stomach cancer and could hardly eat any food. But I'll never forget this. One day he said, "Magdy, what would you like to eat?" I answered, "I'd like to eat pigeon," so he took me to Andrea's Restaurant, a famous restaurant by the canal, and treated me to a meal.

At the time James was making a golden sphere for the Fondation Cartier in France. One day, a Frenchman named François Quintin arrived here from Cartier. He stayed at the Mena House for four or five days. I still have his business card. The golden sphere was needed for an exhibition to be held at Cartier in the near future, but unfortunately James couldn't give it to him at the time, because it had lost its shape. When it was finished, James said to me, "Magdy, François is supposed to come pick up this golden sphere later on. Please keep it at your house until then, but don't let my wife get her hands on it." I believe that James spent nearly all of his final months working on the production of a variety of spheres. He was always asking the craftsman to make a hundred-percent perfectly round sphere.

Yet despite constantly suffering from lack of money, the moment he came into any, he would immediately spend it. It was a real problem. One day he paid a farm girl 1,000 Egyptian pounds (150 American dollars) for some "bull shit balls." These were bits of cow manure rolled into balls by dung beetles. Hard to believe, isn't it. The first ones the girl brought were not all that round. By paying more money, James was able to get truly spherical bull shit balls.

I remember him making a huge carpet, over 10 meters in diameter. It was woven of black goat hair, and he directed the craftsmen to use nothing but black hair. If he found even a little bit of any other color he would immediately cut it off with scissors. It was hard to find black goat hair in such large quantities. After searching throughout Egypt, we finally found some in Faiyum, near my hometown of Beni Suef. We visited Faiyum together for several days to obtain it.

A month after James died, his widow came here, just once. Her family owned Abercrombie & Kent, the world's largest travel agency. James had considerable problems with her. Before he died he was always saying to me, "Magdy, if you are reincarnated, what would you like to be reborn as? If God answers my prayers, I would like to be a dog or a horse in my next life, because she loves dogs and horses more than she loves me." When she arrived there was a great commotion. She accused me of being a thief and called the police—"Give me back the black carpet immediately!" James was always saying he didn't want to leave her a dime. But in the end, a month after his death she made them open the room and took everything with her. The black carpet had not yet been paid for, so it was still at the shop. I was suspected of stealing from James's room while he was still alive and was questioned by the police. In fact the only thing I had taken out was that golden sphere for Cartier, at James's request. It had been very difficult to make. When François came for it, the sphere had flattened into the shape of an egg, and we couldn't give it to him. In the end I gave it to them after James had died. I gave it to Hervé Chandes of Cartier. He took a photograph of me holding the golden sphere while dressed in a blue *galabeya*.

One day a friend of James named Orr came from America. He was a Jewish artist who made artworks with fire. He said he had known James for around twenty-five years. James and Orr were making works with paper together. The name Orr is Hebrew—in other words, he was Jewish. I knew that because I have many Jewish friends, so I asked him and learned it was true. James was put out and asked Orr why he hadn't told him that until now, despite their long acquaintance.

Another time a friend from Ireland arrived. According to James he was a lawyer and a friend of Maria Gilissen. James said I should talk to him if any problems arose after his death. I also recall that an American woman frequently telephoned James, and often sent him money in the form of Thomas Cook traveler's cheques.

James also taught my daughter how to draw pictures. She now teaches graphic design to students at October 6 University. Actually, James didn't like graphic design much. My daughter's name is Nagwan, which means "Two Love One Heart."

Did you go to the studio of Sayed Amin Fayed? That was one of the places where James commissioned his artworks. It's in Mina Village, right near the hotel. James already knew Sayed. He said he was introduced by some German artist or critic. François and Maria also went there with us. Sayed was not a craftsman, but a talented artist who made sculptures and paintings. He was especially good at carving stone into abstract shapes. James had him make many of his spherical objects. He died five years ago, but I've heard that he's famous in northern Europe, in places like Berlin, Oslo, and Denmark.

One day James said to me: "Magdy, this is just a dream, but someday let's go to Greece, to the Greek islands, to look for pure white limestone." James loved the colors gold and black. He said these two colors were gifts from God.

When he died, James wanted his corpse to be mummified like the pharaohs of ancient Egypt. He said that if his body was soaked in honey, then placed in a casket full of honey for preservation—that was the method handed down in my hometown of Beni Suef—he would become like a pharaoh.

I was working for James from morning to evening every day during this period. I had no days off. I went home only to shower and sleep. I was with James nearly the whole time. I lived in 6th of October City, near Giza, so it was not a long commute and the traffic was not bad. But I really didn't get a single day off. Finally I could stand it no longer and I told him I wanted to quit, I was tired, I didn't want to work with him any more. He reacted by asking me, "Are you leaving your father? Can you leave your father?" and began to cry. I cried too. I wound up staying by James's side till the very end after all. The view of the pyramid from the room at the Mena House was lovely, and he often talked about the pyramids. Sometimes his speech was dream-like. He knew about myths passed down from ancient Greece, about how there was a huge lake under the pyramids, things like that. He urged Maria to buy a house and land with a view of the pyramids.

My life has actually changed a lot since his death. Currently I run a real estate business in 6th of October City. We do big projects like moving and constructing buildings. Our latest job came from the American Embassy. It's major work.

James was fond of Islamic prayers, and we went together every morning to the Sayeda Nafisa Mosque in Old Cairo. While I was praying he would sit outside in a chair and wait. We also frequently visited the Imam Shafee Mosque. He would drink milk tea and eat round bread at the Oriental Café near the mosque. He also liked sweet potatoes, but he couldn't eat them because of his stomach cancer. He would just look at them and say, "Magdy, you eat for me." We also went to the Islamic cemetery from which you can see the pyramids. And we often visited the Necropolis, the City of the Dead near the Citadel. Cairo's Necropolis is not only a cemetery where the dead are buried, but also a place where the living make their homes. It stretches for several kilometers in all directions. More than a graveyard, it's a densely populated residential area, with streets crisscrossing it in a grid and cars and buses passing through. The tombs are just like houses, so people live in them and hang out their wash. There are even stores to shop at. I think it was about two months before he died when I began visiting the Necropolis with James. "That's really life," is what he said.

Letters from François Quintin

August 6, 2014

While [he was] in hospital in Santa Fe, I was in close contact with James Lee at that time because we were preparing his last show at the Fondation Cartier. But he was soon not able to talk. He was drugged full time. One day, he decided he would no longer take his medication, under the advice of Maria Gilissen. That you may already know.

So he decided to die away (as he said). He went to Europe, to Cologne, to ask for help and financial support from Michael Werner. He did a performance there, at the Ludwig, the "666" for Reiner Speck, that I saw. We had him coming to Paris for a while, where he did this beautiful performance in the garden, offering champagne to his friends, and leave.

Then James decided to travel, and he organized his travel plans according to materials, so that he could order the production of new pieces wherever he'd go. He wanted to go to Japan for paper, to Egypt for gold, to Greece for marble, and finish his life in Venice, that he loved so much.

In Cairo, with the help of Magdy he could produce a number of pieces, including "The Most Beautiful Jewel In The World," that we commissioned him for a show about "Love" at the Fondation Cartier.

When I arrived in Cairo, it was 2 a.m. He was waiting for me in front of the Mena House Hotel. He was all dressed, beautiful. I spent a little less than a week with him. After the second day, he could no longer walk. He spent most of his days in his bed, naked, making phone calls to his friends, including Vicente Todolí (whom he called "Machine Gun," because of his fast speaking), with whom he was preparing an exhibition.

Magdy, the driver, was a great help. He took him every day to the hospital. He took care of him for everything. Magdy considered James as his father, even though he knew him for a few weeks only. He gave his word to the merchants (which is very important for a Bedouin) so that James could order materials and craftsmen works without having any money. Among other things, James produced his "Monument to the End of Race," a 10 x 10 m black goat wool carpet to be presented in a football stadium.

I could write forever about James.

I have no info about his burial. Hervé might know a bit more, because he went to Cairo after James's death, and I remember he told me about his tomb, which Magdy had showed him.

Not long after I left Cairo, Thomas McEvilley arrived. He was the last who saw James alive. He wrote a beautiful text in *Artforum* about it, that you may know, in which he mentions this small sphere that we commissioned.

I don't think James had in mind that he would die in Cairo. He wanted to finish his life in Venice. But Cairo had something magical about death that he was very sensitive to. For instance, in his hotel room, he read a book on how to embalm dead animals, and he mummified a little dead cockroach he found in his room. I brought it back with me. It must be still in the Fondation Cartier collection, with other stuff that was in his hotel room, that he gave to the Fondation as the "Egyptian Package." When I had to go get my plane to return to Paris, he insisted to come, though he could hardly walk. He asked Magdy to go through the Necropolis, the city of the dead. It was about midnight, with a full moon, a sand storm was about to blow. These are moments I would never forget.

August 9, 2014

Thank you for your mail, and the photos. It's very moving for me to see this room. I can still see him on his bed.

Indeed the view was the reason [he chose that room].

When I arrived, at 2 a.m., I had reserved a lower class hotel room. James told me right away that they made a mistake, putting me in a shitty room, that he had arranged everything so that I could be close to his room.

We had a long discussion with glasses of champagne, then when we went to sleep, he took me to my room. He insisted that I move the bed in the room. As you can see in the photographs, it is a pretty heavy bed, particularly at 4 a.m. He wanted me to place it in a precise direction in front of the window. He insisted that I keep the window wide open, then he went to his room. When I woke up in the morning, I could see in one line my feet, the legs of the bed, and the great pyramid, as if it was an installation, just made for me.

His room was a pandemonium, as you can guess. I suppose you have seen many images of James's hotel rooms. It was full of stuff, materials that Magdy would bring back to him, papyruses, snake skins, hemp ropes, mirrors, different kinds of spheres, including bull shit spheres that he regularly asked to do from a girl in a kind of farm on the way back from the hospital. He always went back from the hospital through what he called "the green." It is the closest route to the Nile that leads to Guiseh, and indeed much greener. On the table, he had photos, and documentation, faxes, books about Egypt, and mummies . . . It was a mess. I think I took a few photographs of it, that might be in Cartier's files. I remember that we published one or two in Cartier Foundation's collection catalogue, that was released the same year.

I have no idea who made the artworks there. One evening, I went with him and Magdy to a kind of shop, where James was received like a king. They immediately brought a throne to him. Magdy was dealing with the merchants, and translating to James. The place was full of furniture, gold jars, carpets around, it was Ali Baba's cave. Then they took James's carpet out to show it to me. They brought a big black roll in the main space of the shop. They didn't unroll it, but opened it enough so that I could see the amazing texture of black goat wool. I have no idea where that was.

For the small golden sphere, "The Most Beautiful Jewel In The World," Magdy found a craftsman who I saw was polishing the sphere. Magdy was a Bedouin, and James liked to think that Bedouins could blow gold like glass. For him the jewel is all the more beautiful that it is made of the breath of a Bedouin. I doubt the sphere had been made that way, but like the Italians say, "Se no e vero e ben trovato."

Thursday, May 22, 1997

As remembered by Magdy Hafez

James's condition took a sudden turn for the worse on the night of May 22. By then James and I were visiting the Anglo-American Hospital every two days. We always went in my taxi. But that night, he was not in any shape to travel by taxi. An ambulance took him straight from the hotel to the hospital. Two doctors provided him with emergency care, Sharif Doss and Sherif Awad Abrahim. He had already been taken once before by ambulance to the intensive care unit, then discharged after receiving an intravenous drip. But the night of May 22 was different; he was in critical condition. I wasn't allowed into the room. Tonight was the critical point, I was told, so I spent the night at the hospital. In the morning, I had just gotten home to shower and change my clothes when the hospital phoned to tell me that James had died. It was Friday morning. James was alone when he died. I was the only person who had been with him.

On the day he was taken to the hospital for the last time, Maria Gilissen had been at the hotel. It was a Thursday. I took her to the airport in the evening, and it was that same night that James took a turn for the worse. That was when Maria bought the spherical book for 2,000 American dollars and took it with her. She told me not to tell James she had bought it for that price, because he would be offended if he knew . . . No one visited the hotel after Maria. I was the only one who came to the hospital. According to the doctor, James died at 6 am. It was 7 am when I got the phone call. He was already dead when I rushed there. I returned to the hotel, then went to the American Embassy with James's passport and reported that an American named James Lee Byars had died. Then I phoned Maria to tell her he had died, and I think she told various acquaintances. James had always told me, "Magdy, you must not sell any of my works before I die." When I asked why, he said, "Because people do not appreciate art until after the artist dies." Maria's husband was a very famous artist, but while he was alive they were very poor. After her husband died, though, Maria became rich. She understood how the value of art can change.

Recollections of Rita Burmester

On May 22, two people were dispatched to Cairo by the Serralves Foundation in Portugal. One was the art critic Kevin Power, the other the photographer Rita Burmester. They were sent by Vicente Todolí, who was in the midst of planning an exhibition of Byars's work for the foundation. Todolí asked Power and Burmester to go to Cairo to interview Byars for the exhibition catalogue, scheduled for publication at the end of 1997. Working with Byars on what Todolí believed would "turn out to be his last exhibition while he was still alive," he later wrote:

> I was aware of his terminal illness and always insisted on having two plans:
> 1) You are still alive and can develop the exhibition as it goes.
> 2) You are on permanent vacation and we need a plan.
> Unfortunately he went on permanent vacation six months before the exhibition, so I had to invent that part.

Rita and Kevin met at the Barcelona Airport; it was their first meeting. Rita had never met Byars before. Kevin was an old friend of Byars who had not seen him in a long time and was eagerly looking forward to their reunion. Arriving at Cairo Airport on the night of May 22, they went to their hotel and began preparing for the next day's interview. They had no way of knowing, of course, that Byars had been taken to the intensive care unit. Kevin had been expecting Byars to meet them at the airport, and Rita says she can still remember the look of disappointment on his face when Byars did not turn up.

Friday, May 23, 1997

When Rita and Kevin arrived at the Mena House the next morning, Friday, May 23, Byars's room was already closed off. It was the hotel's rule that when a guest died, they would first contact the embassy of the guest's country, then notify the police. The same procedure applied even if the guest died at a hospital, as in Byars's case. Until the body was removed, the door to the room would be double-locked and no one would be allowed inside. Only a family member could receive the key; according to Egyptian law, only immediate family members had the right to inherit the deceased's property. On top of that, the Mena House, being a five-star hotel, said it would not charge for the room until Byars's widow arrived, which did not happen for another month.

Having learned of Byars's death, Rita and Kevin spent the day visiting places associated with Byars, guided by Magdy in his taxi. They went to the vast Islamic cemetery close by the pyramids, where Byars had hoped to be buried; the Sayeda Nafisa Mosque that he visited every morning; the atelier of Sayed Amin Fayed, in Mina Village, where Byars had so many of his objects made (a tiny room the size of a car, it was painted gold from floor to ceiling; Byars had planned to hold a performance there). At the shop where Byars's huge black goat-wool carpet was kept, they had it spread out on the rooftop for viewing. They also accompanied Magdy to the shops where Byars had not yet completed his payments, and made notes of how much was owed. They thought of this as an act of thanks and obligation to Magdy, who had shown such devotion in caring for Byars.

At the Anglo-American Hospital, they spent only ten minutes there while Kevin viewed the body. Rita says she waited at the entrance.

She does not remember when they met Thomas McEvilley, but it was in the lobby of the Mena House, and he told them that he, too, was unable to enter Byars's room. He was with his girlfriend, and the two groups went their separate ways until the funeral.

Saturday, May 24, 1997

When Hervé Chandes, the director of the Fondation Cartier, heard the news of Byars's death from François Quintin, he dropped everything and rushed to Cairo. He had to pick up the golden sphere as quickly as possible. When François had gone there at the beginning of May it had not been ready. Cartier had commissioned it, so it could not be allowed to fall into other hands.

Hervé met Magdy at the Mena House and learned that the sphere was being kept at Magdy's home. He had Magdy bring it to him that same day, and through Magdy paid off the sum owed to the craftsman. He left that evening on a flight for Paris.

Sunday, May 25, 1997

Magdy says that the funeral for Byars took place four days after his death. However, since Rita and Kevin left on May 27, it seems likelier that the funeral was on Sunday, May 25.

The American Embassy handled everything from the hospital charges to Byars's burial in the American Cemetery in Old Cairo, including the hiring of a priest and the placement of the tombstone. In cases where a family member could not get there soon after someone's death, it was standard procedure for the embassy to cover all costs and bill the family later.

It is Islamic custom to bury the body right away, ideally within twelve hours, but in practice twenty-four hours—in other words, within the same day—appears to be the norm. Magdy conveyed to the American Embassy staff what he knew of Byars's wishes: his interest in Islam, his frequent visits to mosques, and finally, his stated desire to be buried in the Islamic Cemetery. However, the embassy seemed reluctant to take this information at face value. So far as it could tell, Magdy and Byars were complete strangers. There were plenty of people who knew of the bond between them, such as the hospital staff who saw Magdy bring Byars to the hospital every other day. On the other hand, they could be viewed as just a taxi driver and his passenger. What with the need to contact Byars's family about his death, establish the cause of death, obtain permission for the burial, and so on, several days passed before the funeral could be held.

Attending the funeral were Magdy Hafez, Rita Burmester, Kevin Power, Thomas McEvilley, Joyce Burstein (McEvilley's girlfriend), some American Embassy officials, and Priest Huw Thomas.

Byars's body was being kept at the Anglo-American Hospital. Located close by the Cairo Tower on an island in the Nile, the hospital was said to have the most reliable doctors in Egypt. When foreign hotel guests fell ill or died, they were nearly always taken here. The morgue was a concrete-block building in back of the hospital. On this day Byars's body was placed in a casket and taken to the American Cemetery.

May is a time of fresh greenery and pleasant weather—a "blessed season" in Cairo. Perhaps the heat and humidity on the day of the funeral was an anomaly. McEvilley's girlfriend suffered heatstroke and had to lie down during the funeral, cradling her head. In a photo taken by Rita, she can be seen sitting down and looking quite unwell. McEvilley is standing by the casket, holding a thick book in one hand and praying with the elderly white-haired priest. Rita says that McEvilley asked her to take the picture. The American Cemetery appears to have been suffering from neglect, because it looks much like a jungle in this photo. In Egypt gravedigging is a hereditary profession, with members of one family inheriting the job from generation to generation at each cemetery. Byars's burial was no exception. The cemetery's gravediggers dug a hole, a local priest hired by the American Embassy said some prayers, the gravediggers covered the casket, flowers were arranged in the shape of cross, and that was that.

What Is "Perfect"?

Several months after Byars's death, from October 9 to December 7, 1997, the Serralves Foundation in Porto held an exhibition titled *James Lee Byars: The Palace of Perfect*. In his introduction to the exhibition catalogue, Vicente Todolí wrote:

> When James Lee Byars visited Serralves, we knew that he was very ill. For this reason we suggested that he work upon two possibilities simultaneously: on the one hand, as he liked to say, to take the hypothesis to the limit, with a project in continuous mutation, which also included new works

> and whose final definition would be given by his participation in the setting of the exhibition. One the other hand, if he were no longer with us—as unfortunately happened—we would have to work with a pre-established plan, with pieces that could function without their definition being given by an installation carried out by the artist. Byars accepted the plan proposed to him, taking his aim to be that of fusing his own art with the spirit of the house, in order to transform it into "The Palace of Perfect." For this reason, in this catalogue we are publishing pictures of the house from previous times, when it was inhabited, as well as the correspondence which Byars maintained with us during the preparation of the exhibition.

Byars made frequent calls from Egypt to Todolí in Portugal—about plans for the exhibition, expenses for new works, requests for money. He sent over twenty faxes from the Mena House as well as the Three-M Hotel in Nara. Several times he writes, "Call Me, Machine Gun." In an email dated March 10, 2015, Todolí reminisces:

> When he was in Porto his project was to get Michael Jackson singing "I am a white man" in the Art Deco Villa in Serralves. But he said to hurry up before his only black part, the nose, would turn also white and then he would crumble to pieces. He was also obsessed with getting black underwear for himself. He thought he was dying after lunch in the teahouse in Serralves park with Joao Fernandes, deputy director of the museum. He collapsed but after a short time he walked around the park with Joao, asking him to look for the perfect pebble or stone. At dinner in Alvaro Siza's Teahouse by the sea he explained to the Portuguese waiters how port wine should be served. On the way to the hotel he asked the taxi driver to drive faster . . . faster . . . faster . . . in a country where people drive too fast, including that taxi driver. I was very scared. While in Egypt we sent each other faxes and spoke sometimes on the phone. He was often asking for moneygrams in order to buy beautiful objects he had seen. We couldn't send any. Once he said about his compulsive buying: I wish my Father would have been called Sellers (or Sellars, I don't remember well) instead of Byars!

A universe of roundness . . . spheres carved from stone or marble, round mirrors, balls of wood, circular objects of wool, spherical books. . . . The photos taken by Rita Burmester show a myriad of such objects. All of them were commissioned by Byars in Egypt. They include a number of works made for the Serralves exhibition—all of them spheres. Several urns are also pictured. We see a room with a gorgeous chandelier hanging from the ceiling, a shop selling colorful carpets, a stone quarry, craftsmen at work, the mosque that Byars visited every morning, the Islamic Cemetery with its view of the pyramids, the Anglo-American Hospital, the American Cemetery, and the gravediggers at work. . . . One picture is particularly shocking: the deceased Byars, with McEvilley sitting by his side. It was taken in a room at the hospital before the body was placed in a casket. Rita recalls that when she hesitated, McEvilley took her by the arm, led her to the room and asked her to take the photo. It was Rita's first view of Byars, whom she had never met while he was alive. He lies there with his mouth and both eyes open wide.

According to Rita, "Kevin told me that McEvilley had spent some time alone with James Lee Byars when he was already dead."

In Zen, a circle painted with a single sweep of the brush may be viewed as a complete work of art and a window into the soul of the painter. That circle, said to represent absolute truth, is often described as the shape of enlightenment, a symbol of all creation. But its interpretation is left to the eye of the beholder.

I would like to conclude by revisiting the words of Rand Castile, the curator and critic who knew Byars so well: "If I were not convinced he is a genius, I would think he is a madman."

Byars's days, his way of living, were, in themselves, his art.

Afterword

On November 21, 2015 I met Vicente Todolí, who was visiting Japan. Nicknamed "Machine Gun" because of his rapid manner of speaking, he had served for seven years as director of the Tate Modern and was what one might call a pillar of the art world. I wondered whether I would be able to greet him properly in English or understand his rapid-fire speech. I arrived twenty minutes early at the hotel lobby where we were to meet and was a bundle of nerves by the time he arrived. But the moment I met him my nervousness vanished. His all-embracing aura and friendly smile made me feel as if I were meeting a long-revered benefactor for the first time. It was indeed our first encounter, but I felt completely at ease. Actually, this scenario was repeated often in the course of my research on James Lee Byars. I think I understand why, but let us save that for later.

Todolí informed me that all the faxes and other correspondence he had exchanged with Byars were still preserved at the Serralves Foundation in Portugal, where he had organized a Byars exhibition very shortly after the artist's death. Saying that I was welcome to see them, he thereupon arranged to have all of those records emailed to me. The correspondence is almost entirely about the upcoming exhibition, with Byars tossing out one idea after another off the top of his head, followed by discussions of how much it will cost and what size, shape, material, and arrangement will be required to give concrete form to each of his visions. Even two decades after his death, the energy in Byars's dispatches was bracing and made me want to know more, hear more. No doubt it was a similar impression that spurred Todolí to send the art critic Kevin Power, who was assisting him with the show, to Egypt with the photographer Rita Burmester. Sadly, they were unable to book an immediate flight to Cairo and were forced to wait for cancellations. On May 19—five days before Byars's death—Todolí sent him a fax announcing that Power and Burmester would be on a flight arriving the night of the 22nd. It was to be his final communication with Byars. When the two got to Cairo, Byars had already been hospitalized for the last time and would be dead by dawn.

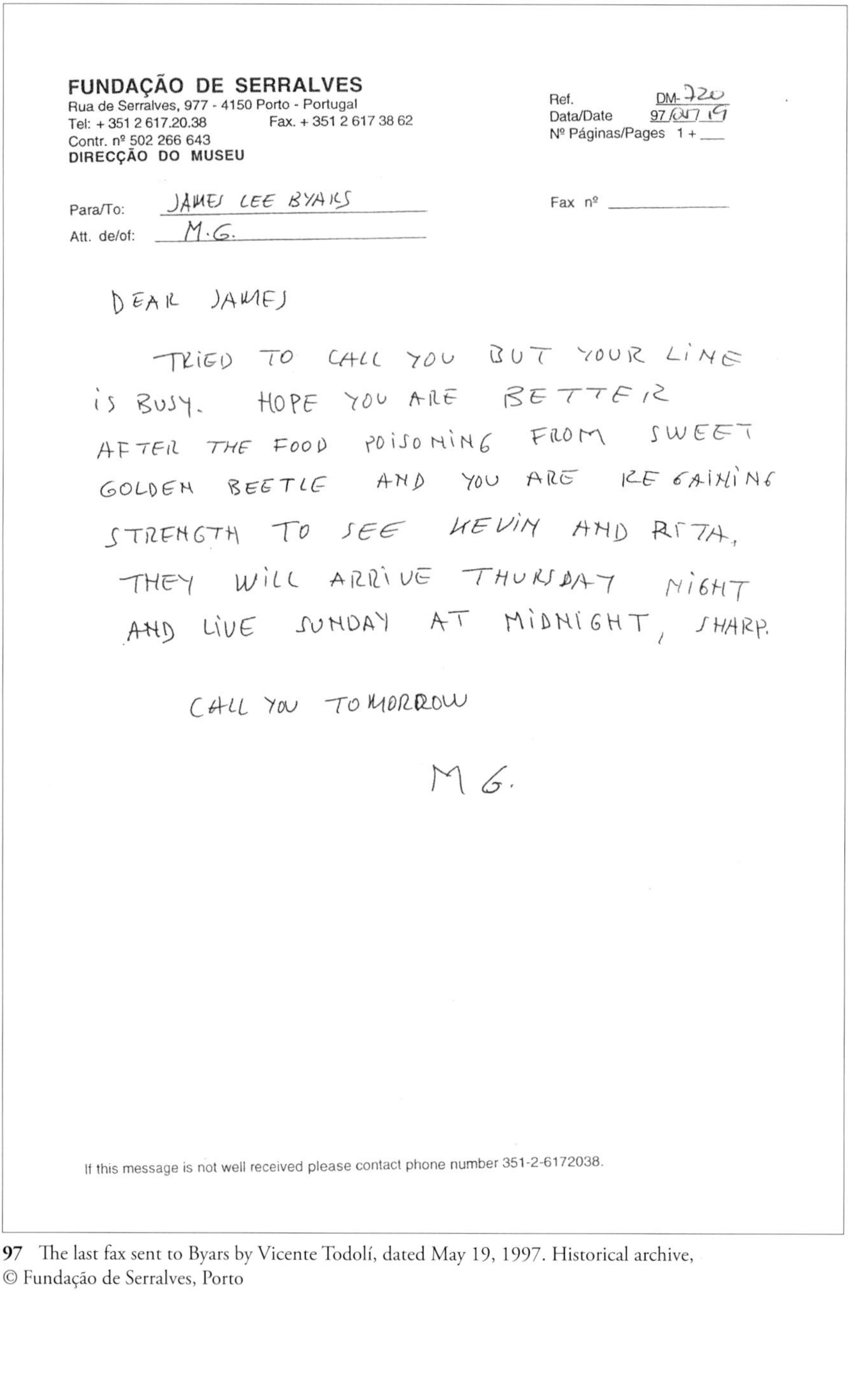

FUNDAÇÃO DE SERRALVES
Rua de Serralves, 977 - 4150 Porto - Portugal
Tel: + 351 2 617.20.38 Fax. + 351 2 617 38 62
Contr. nº 502 266 643
DIRECÇÃO DO MUSEU

Ref. DM-720
Data/Date 97/05/19
Nº Páginas/Pages 1 + ___

Para/To: JAMES LEE BYARS
Att. de/of: M.G.

Fax nº ___

DEAR JAMES

TRIED TO CALL YOU BUT YOUR LINE IS BUSY. HOPE YOU ARE BETTER AFTER THE FOOD POISONING FROM SWEET GOLDEN BEETLE AND YOU ARE REGAINING STRENGTH TO SEE KEVIN AND RITA, THEY WILL ARRIVE THURSDAY NIGHT AND LIVE SUNDAY AT MIDNIGHT, SHARP.

CALL YOU TOMORROW

M G.

If this message is not well received please contact phone number 351-2-6172038.

97 The last fax sent to Byars by Vicente Todolí, dated May 19, 1997. Historical archive, © Fundação de Serralves, Porto

What, I wondered, was the meaning of "FOOD POISONING FROM SWEET GOLDEN BEETLE" in Vicente Todolí's final fax? Is "golden beetle" eaten in Egypt? Even if it were, and even given Byars's fondness for all things golden, would he really have eaten dung beetle (*koganemushi*, literally "gold bug" in Japanese)?

Also known as the golden beetle and the scarab, the dung beetle stands on its front legs and uses its hind legs to roll tiny balls of cow dung. Associated in ancient Egypt with the rolling of the sun god Ra across the sky, the beetle became a symbol of the cycle of life and reincarnation. Perhaps inspired by this myth, Byars himself had done performances in which he walked along rolling a sphere. One of the items on Byars's list of works planned for the Serralves exhibition was "bull shit balls," as he called the spheres made by the dung beetle. Byars was clearly fascinated by the little creature, so perhaps that was why he brought it up in this context, I thought. Could he have been referring to his own life as an artist when he spoke of "poisoning by the golden beetle"?

Confounded by this puzzle, I did some reading about the golden beetle itself and learned that it infests sweet potatoes as a parasite. Then it all became clear. Though I omitted some of the details from the interview that appears in the Egypt epilogue, here is a summary of what Byars's friend Magdy Hafez told me:

1. Byars loved sweet potatoes, but couldn't digest them due to the cancer.
2. Byars was taken to the intensive care unit of the hospital twice. The first time he was discharged after getting his stomach pumped. Immediately afterward he began crawling around in an empty lot next to the hospital, searching for round pebbles. The doctors at the hospital thought he was "crazy." On Thursday, May 22, the day he left the hospital, Maria Gilissen visited him in his hotel room, and Magdy drove her to the airport that evening. That night Byars once again took a turn for the worse and was taken to the hospital again. He died early the next morning, on Friday, May 23, 1997.

Gordon VeneKlasen, director of Michael Werner Gallery, which paid Byars's hospital bill, says that the direct cause of his death was not cancer but "food." Thus it seems reasonable to surmise that Byars tried to eat sweet potatoes in spite of his stomach cancer and was accidentally poisoned by dung beetles infesting the potato. Though he initially seemed to recover and was able to leave the hospital after getting his stomach pumped on his first visit, the stress was too great for his cancer-ravaged body, and he died after being hospitalized the second time. Of course, this is no more than speculation on my part.

One anecdote has it that Byars breathed his last while climbing a pyramid. It would have been a final act of madness, but nothing out of the ordinary for Byars. Indeed, we might wish that were how he had died; it would have been so fittingly Byars to expire in pursuit of one last pure, simple desire. Childish, perhaps, but then, so is death by potato, and so is the character of a man who at age sixty-five was crawling around on all fours looking for perfectly round pebbles. That was how Byars lived his life. To the very end, he never grew up. An eternal child, he was always looking for the perfectly round sphere of perfectly pure gold. He craved the primitive, the undeveloped, the simple, seeking to reduce the complex to its most basic form. That is why his works, in their simplicity, are philosophical, even spiritual in essence, as well as aesthetically faultless. They serve as the point of origin for an infinite expansion of thought, and their appeal aims straight at the heart of the viewer.

Taki Sachiko, Byars's companion during his Kyoto days, muses: "It's often said that there is only a fine line between genius and madness. He was probably a little bit of both. But because those close to him did not dismiss him as a madman, the things that shone so brightly within him were able to thrive. That was possible because people who met him could sense that radiance and were moved by it."

An adult must live within all manner of constraints that do not exist for us when we are children. We can no longer do exactly as we please. We have to give careful thought to our every action—and in so doing, we abandon the dreams we cherished and lose the child within. Perhaps we see, in the innocent behavior of children, a radiance that we ourselves have lost.

The acquaintances of Byars whom I met revealed their memories of him to me like someone offering a glimpse of a precious jewel they have long kept hidden. Then, responding to my own intense desire to learn more about him, they opened their hearts to me and generously assisted me in my search. It may be that the image of Byars that lives on in their memories reminds them of the lingering radiance in their own hearts.

This book is imbued with the light in the hearts of everyone who was touched by Byars's words and deeds. That light may have already faded, or it may lie hidden deep out of sight. My hope has been to make a book that is like a tapestry woven from all those beautiful strands of mutually resonating light.

Acknowledgements

This book is a greatly expanded version of *James Lee Byars: Days in Kyoto*, a series of ten articles I wrote for the Japanese-language art monthly *Aida*, which published them in issues 197 (October 20, 2012) through 209 (November 20, 2013). Fukuzumi Haruo, the editor in chief of *Aida*, has been one of Japan's leading art journalists since his legendary work in the early 1970s as editor of *Bijutsu techo*, the country's flagship journal of contemporary art. He is also a well-known translator under the pen name Takashima Heigo. In 1993 he translated an essay by the art critic Robert Fleck for the catalogue of the *James Lee Byars* exhibition held that year at the Tokyo gallery SCAI The Bathhouse. The designer of that catalogue was Oishi Kazuyoshi, who designed this book. From the outset of my own research and writing on Byars, who is still virtually unknown in Japan, the only publication I ever envisioned for my writings was *Aida*, the journal edited by Mr. Fukuzumi, whose knowledge and understanding of Byars's work is unrivalled.

Excerpts from my *Aida* articles were translated into English for publication in the catalogue for *James Lee Byars: 1/2 an Autobiography*, an exhibition held at MoMA PS1, New York, from June 15 to September 7, 2014. Organized by curator Peter Eleey and curatorial assistant Jocelyn Miller, this was the first major exhibition anywhere to examine Byars's days in Japan, and was a great source of inspiration for me. The MoMA translation of my *Aida* articles was handled by Takako Oishi-Marks, Shimpei Shirafuji, Saori Kashio, and Natalie Hegert of the Art-Ka translation company. After my extensive revisions and additions to that text, including an epilogue about Byars's days in Egypt, Alan Gleason produced the final translation of the book.

Mr. Gleason was introduced to me by the New York-based poet and translator Sato Hiroaki, a friend of Byars in his Kyoto days. Mr. Sato provided me with invaluable advice on the translation and publication of this book, and his reminiscences about Byars are a significant contribution to it.

Stephanie Cannizzo, curator at the University of California, Berkeley Art Museum and Pacific Film Archive, was also tremendously helpful in giving me access to materials on Byars from the collection of the late curator James Elliott.

This book contains around 100 photographs. Seven of these, taken by Anzai Shigeo at the 1993 SCAI The Bathhouse exhibition, movingly chronicle Byars's emotions as he visited Japan for the first time in twenty-seven years, so I have allotted several pages to them.

Publication of this book was made possible by a generous grant from the Pola Art Foundation. I would also like to thank art critic Aoki Masahiro, who wrote the letter of recommendation to the Pola Art Foundation, for his tireless support of this project.

Finally, I wish to thank Meg Taylor for editing the English translation of this book, and Ray Furse of Floating World Editions for publishing it.

About the Author

Sakagami Shinobu is an art historian and museum curator. Born in Tokyo, she earned a master's degree at Kyoto City University of Arts. Since 2009 she has worked as a curator at the Yamazaki Mazak Museum of Art in Nagoya. As a historian she specializes in the prewar and postwar history of the avant-garde art movement in Kyoto, and has published several Japanese-language books on the subject, among them *Hikosaka Naoyoshi: Three Events in Kyoto, 1972*; *Shiko-kai: Birth of the Ceramic Avant-garde in Kyoto, 1947-1956*; and *Kyoto Post-modernism in the Eighties*. Her ten-article series *James Lee Byars: Days in Kyoto* ran in the art monthly *Aida* in 2012 and 2013, and an abridged translation appears in the catalogue for the exhibition *James Lee Byars: 1/2 an Autobiography*, held at MoMA PS1, New York in 2014. She also edited *50 years of galerie 16*, a history of the avant garde Kyoto art gallery by that name.